Jerusalem, May 79

To Richard
with best wishes
J. aylor

IZHAK ENGLARD

RELIGIOUS LAW IN THE ISRAEL LEGAL SYSTEM

כי צו לצו, צו לצו
קו לקו, קו לקו
זעיר שם, זעיר שם   ישעיה כ"ח י'

For it is precept by precept, precept by precept
Line by line, line by line
Here a little, there a little   Isaiah 28:10

RELIGIOUS LAW
IN THE
ISRAEL LEGAL SYSTEM

by
IZHAK ENGLARD

HEBREW UNIVERSITY OF JERUSALEM • FACULTY OF LAW
HARRY SACHER INSTITUTE FOR LEGISLATIVE RESEARCH
AND COMPARATIVE LAW
1975

©
All Rights Reserved to the Author
Printed in Israel, 1975
at Alpha Press, Jerusalem

in profound esteem of
Professor G. Tedeschi
Scholar and Mentor

ACKNOWLEDGEMENTS

This book originated in a number of articles in Hebrew which appeared in *Mishpatim*, the Law Review of the Hebrew University of Jerusalem. The Hebrew text was translated by Mrs. M. Losowick and Mr. P. Elman. The latter also revised the entire translation and helped to prepare the text for publication. The tables of statutes and cases and the bibliography were prepared by Mrs. A. Levine. To all of them I am deeply indebted.

I must also express my gratitude to the Ford Foundation, through the good offices of the Israel Foundations Trustees, for the research grant which enabled the writing of the first two Parts.

CONTENTS

Abbreviations 11

Introduction 13

PART ONE — RELIGIOUS LAW AND THE LAW OF THE STATE

Chapter I The Legal Nature and Actual Validity of Religious Law 19

Chapter II Unity and Plurality of System—General Relationship between State and Religious Law 33

PART TWO — RECEPTION OF RELIGIOUS LAW

Chapter I Introduction 49

Chapter II Direct Reception 53

Chapter III Reception by Reference 56

PART THREE — THE APPLICATION OF RELIGIOUS LAW

Chapter I Introduction 81

Chapter II Ascertainment of Religious Law 88

Chapter III Adjudication of Religious Law by the Courts 103
1. The Judicial Process 103
2. The Relationship between Secular and Religious Judgments 109
3. Decisions on Religious Law by the Supreme Court and the Doctrine of *Stare Decisis* 126

CHAPTER IV Limitations on the Application of Religious Law — 136
1. Defining the Problem — 136
2. Public Policy — 139
   A. General — 139
   B. The Negative Function of Public Policy: Rejection of Religious Law by Reasons of its Content — 142
   C. The Positive Function of Public Policy: Direct Application of Secular Norms — 152
   D. Mixed Function of Public Policy: The Principles of Natural Justice — 161
   E. The Public Policy of Religious Law — 168
3. Substantive Law and Procedure — 177
   A. Introduction — 177
   B. Formal Grounds for the Distinction — 177
   C. Material Grounds for the Distinction — 180
   D. The Proposed Solution: Direct Application of Civil Procedure for Reasons of Efficacy and Public Policy — 183
   E. Substance and Procedure in Case Law — 184
      Competence of Witnesses and Modes of Proof — 185
      Burden of Proof, Presumptions and Weight of Evidence — 190
      Quantum of Maintenance — 195

CHAPTER V The Grafting of Religious Law upon Secular Law and the Process of Adaptation — 199

ADDENDUM — 209

BIBLIOGRAPHY — 213

TABLE OF LEGISLATION — 225

TABLE OF CASES — 229

INDEX — 236

NOTE

All titles of books and articles published in Hebrew are given in translation. The three Hebrew language law journals appearing in Israel are: *HaPraklit*—published by the Israel Bar; *Iyune Mishpat*—Tel Aviv University Law Review; *Mishpatim*—Hebrew University of Jerusalem Law Review. Hebrew book titles given in translation are accompanied with the indication "(Hebrew)". The laws of the State of Israel are cited in their authorised English translation, in the series of the *Laws of the State of Israel*, published by the Ministry of Justice. General literature on Israel Law and further material on the subjects treated in the book may be found in Wegner, *A Bibliography of Israel Law in English and Other European Languages* (Jerusalem 1972).

ABBREVIATIONS

A.G.	— Attorney General
C.A.	— Civil Appeal
C.E.O.	— Chief Execution Officer
Cr.A.	— Criminal Appeal
H.C.J.	— High Court of Justice
F.H.	— Further Hearing
Is.L.R.	— Israel Law Review
Mo.	— Motion
P.D.	— Piskei Din (Judgments)—Law reports of the Supreme Court published by the Ministry of Justice (1948–) (Hebrew)
P.L.R.	— Palestine Law Reports, (1920–1947) (English)
P.M.	— Pesakim Mehosiim (District Decisions)—Law reports of the District Courts, published by the Israel Bar Association (1949–) (Hebrew)
R.	— Collection of Judgments, edited by Rotenberg (1919–1936) (English)
S.C.J.	— Annotated Supreme Court Judgments (1937–1942) (English)
S.J.D.C.	— Selected Judgments of the Supreme Court of Israel (1948–) (English)
S.J.S.C.	— Selected Judgments of the District Court (1943–1947) (English)
S.T.	— Special Tribunal

INTRODUCTION

The expression "religious law" may convey the misleading impression that a single normative system is the subject of the present study. In reality, a number of systems of religious law each having very little in common with the others apply today in Israel. The reasons are largely historical. The present order has its roots in the Ottoman Empire. Taken over by the British Mandatory regime, it came in turn to be accepted in the State of Israel.

Under the Ottoman Empire recognition of religious laws was a concomitant of the status given to its religious communities in what was known as the *Millet System* under which considerable autonomy was accorded to non-Islamic religious groups treated as "nations". This autonomy included the maintenance of an independent legal system with prescribed jurisdiction for each of the recognized religious communities.[1] The British Mandatory regime, in undertaking to preserve the status quo, made no fundamental change in the autonomy of the recognized religious communities. The strong centralizing tendencies of the Mandatory regime led, however, to systematic integration of religious law into the general legal system. Although the application of religious law was not directly restricted, concurrent jurisdiction in the civil courts began to develop and the entire religious system came under over-riding supervision of the High Court of Justice.

The establishment of the State of Israel marked a fundamental change as regards Jews now no longer a minority religious community, but preservation of the status quo became a matter of concern for the other religious communities. The status of Jewish religious law acquired wholly different significance. On it centred the ideological conflict over the very nature of the State and the proper relation between state and religion, involving debate on religious coercion and freedom from religion and the

---

[1] Young, *Corps de droit ottoman* (Oxford 1905) Vol. II, pp. 12–165; S. Sidarouss, *Des Patriarcats* (Paris 1907) pp. 265 et seq.

INTRODUCTION

striving for an independent national legal system. The ideological debate considerably affected the legal debate.

The value of the confrontation of ideas in this crucial area clearly cannot be denied but the ideological debate seems to have overshadowed the purely legal aspects of the problem. The truth is that we lack the legal tools with which to analyse the status of religious law in the State's legal system. Nor is this surprising since such tools are not to be found either in Jewish legal tradition or in the Anglo-American legal system and even in most civil law systems.[2] Yet the tools—legal concepts and legal institutions—are as vital in this as in every other area. That does not mean that court decisions generally are the result of logical deduction from clear-cut presuppositions and that one may not rely on meta-legal value systems. On the contrary, such value systems lie behind many court decisions but it is the task of the judge to cast his ideology into a legal mould so as to give his decisions an essential measure of certainty and permanence if the law is to avoid being arbitrary.

A legal-conceptual approach is possible and necessary even in legal questions touching on the relationship between religion and state. It enables problems and solutions to be judged from a systematic frame of reference. Solutions are not to be tested solely by conformity with a particular scale of values but rather by dogmatic consistency in the framework of the entire system. In this sense the question of the status of Jewish law has aspects which it shares with all religious systems. Since, however, the question of its status arises more frequently and more sharply in Israel because of the peculiar ideological background and since any comprehensive discussion in depth of the other religious systems requires an intimate knowledge of all these systems, which the author regretfully cannot claim, our main attention must be confined to Jewish law.

This study is concerned with two main problems, the general status of religious law in the legal system of the state and the application of religious law by the secular courts.

Its ambit is therefore limited. Questions of the jurisdiction of the religious courts and interpersonal and interreligious law are only touched upon where relevant to the discussion.

The problem of the application of religious law by the secular courts

---

[2] The problem has only been dealt with extensively in Italian law which is outstanding for its theoretical approach and the primary status it accords to legal theory. See the sources referred to below in this study.

has many parallels in the application of foreign law under private international law. One of the aims of this study is to clarify the intermediate position of religious law (in itself an autonomous system) as compared to the law of the State on the one hand and to foreign law on the other.

The work comprises three parts. Parts I and II treat of the theoretical foundations, namely, the general relationship between State Law and religious law seen as two independent normative orders and of the different modes of reception of religious law.

Part III examines the problems which arise from the practical application of religious law by the secular courts.

PART ONE

RELIGIOUS LAW AND THE LAW OF THE STATE

CHAPTER I

THE LEGAL NATURE AND ACTUAL VALIDITY OF RELIGIOUS LAW

The status of religious law in the Israeli legal system is basically a question of the *relationship* between two normative systems. In order, however, to determine this relationship we must first know the character of the two systems. Are they identical in nature?

This question has troubled the students of jurisprudence not a little with regard to the status of Canon Law. It has been claimed that Canon Law does not constitute a normative system of a legal nature. Prominent among those who deny any legal character to religious law are members of the Positivist School who postulate that the only body capable of creating law is the State; outside the State therefore no *legal* order can exist.[1] A similar idea is expressed by those who maintain that the law of the State is the only law having a positive character since it is the expression of sovereign command.[2]

These positivists, known primarily for their denial of natural and international law, have also influenced the debate on the status of Canon Law, a debate which was one of the focal points of the *Kulturkampf* which stirred a number of West European countries in the last century. In denying legal character to Canon Law, a dogmatic basis was found for the general conception of the supremacy of the State over the Church,

---

[1] Von Jhering, *Der Zweck im Recht*, 1. Band (2. Aufl., Leipzig 1884), p. 320 et seq., Lasson, *System der Rechtsphilosophie* (Berlin 1882), pp. 37, 335 et seq. 412; Somló, *Juristische Grundlehre* (Leipzig 1917), p. 330. For additional sources, see Ago, "Positive Law and International Law" 51 (1957) *A.J.I.L.*, 691, 699, n. 20; Id., *Scienza giuridica e diritto internazionale* (Milano 1950), pp. 32 et seq.; Lechleitner, *Der Mensch zwischen Staat und Kirche*, (Zürich 1957), Nos. 16, 18, 42; De Luca, *Diritto ecclesiastico ed esperienza giuridica*, (Milano 1969), pp. 57 et seq.

[2] Austin, *Lectures on Jurisprudence* (5th ed., London 1885), Lecture VI, p. 330: "Every positive law (or every law simply and strictly so called) is set, directly or circuitously, by a sovereign individual or body, to a member or members of the independent political society wherein its author is supreme." Cf. Paton, *Jurisprudence* (4th ed., Oxford 1972), pp. 74 et seq.

which reinforced the *political* ideology that demanded the Church's complete subjection to State authority.[3]

The Positivist approach has been criticized by the best legal thinkers the world over and we can only join in their conclusion that the law of the State is not the sole possible legal system,[4] for all that it is the most comprehensive in the range of matters it regulates. This conclusion may accord with the view of the Normativist school, represented by Kelsen, that the law and the State are identical,[5] because the equation of the two has the different purpose of negating the generally accepted duality of the state and the law as separate entities. Kelsen maintains that the state is none other than the legal order. But the contrary proposition is not true; according to Kelsen himself, not every legal order can be treated as a state.[6] That depends upon the measure of centralization of power. The state, in this sense, is a legal system with a developed structure, in contrast, for example, to international law.[7] This, it may be suggested, is the sense in which Kelsen's assertion about the Catholic Church—"If the church is legal order, then it is State."[8]—is to be understood. What he appears to be saying is that the strong hierarchical struc-

---

[3] Lasson *op. cit.*, pp. 335 et seq., 590; cf. De Luca, *op. cit.*, pp. 59 et seq. For Italy, see F. Scaduto, *Diritto ecclesiastico vigente in Italia* (2a ed., Torino 1892, 1894), Vol. I, p. 2; Vol. II, pp. 734 et seq.; D. Schiappoli, *Manuale di diritto ecclesiastico* (Napoli 1913), p. 32; cf. *generaliter* De Luca, *Il concetto del diritto ecclesiastico nel suo sviluppo storico* (Padova 1946) *passim;* Id., *Rilevanza dell'ordinamento canonico nel diritto italiano* (Padova 1943), pp. 19 et seq.; cf. Paton, *op. cit.*, p. 76.

[4] From among the extensive material we may mention the important work of an Italian scholar who is less well known outside Italy: Santi Romano, *L'ordinamento giuridico* (Pisa 1918), spec. Cap. II, La pluralità degli ordinamenti giuridici e le loro relazioni, pp. 94 et seq.; cf. J. Stone, "Two Theories of 'The Institution'," *Essays in Jurisprudence in Honour of Roscoe Pound* (1962), pp. 296, 316 et seq., 336 et seq.

[5] Kelsen, *Pure Theory of Law* (Berkeley, 1970), pp. 286 et seq.

[6] *Ibid.*, "As a political organization, the State is a legal order. But not every order is a State." Hauser, *Norm, Recht und Staat* (Wien 1968), p. 109.

[7] Cf. Paton, *op. cit.*, p. 77 n. 2. As regards international law, there is no need to express here any opinion about its legal character. In this connection see: Levontin, *The Myth of International Security* (Jerusalem 1958) who denies the legal character of international law according to the criteria of Kelsen himself.

[8] *Allgemeine Staatslehre*, in *Enzyklopädie der Rechts und Staatswissenschaft*, Abt. Rechtswissenschaft, XXIII, (Berlin 1925), p. 133: "Ist die Kirche Rechtsordnung, dann ist sie Staat."

ture of the Catholic Church justifies its being considered as an actual state, according to the organizational criterion adopted by him.[9]

Denial of the legal nature of religious law was not, however, based solely on the extreme positivist conception of the state as a perfect social entity; it also followed from the content and aims of religious law. In a view publicized throughout the Christian World, Sohm declared, on grounds of Protestant theology, that so fundamental and irreconcilable an opposition exists between the spiritual essence of the church and the worldly essence of the law that the law of the church must be denied existence.[10] Sohm's religious outlook is highly consistent with his positivist perception of the state as the sole source of law.[11] His views were clearly unacceptable to Catholic thinkers[12] and were even rejected by well-known Protestant theologians.[13] Yet his theory had considerable influence, historically, in

---

[9] Indeed, Kelsen concludes the sentence in which he states that the church is a state with these words: "...zumal wenn die kirchliche Ordnung arbeitsteilig funktionierende Organe zur Realisierung der von ihr normierten Zwangsakte einsetzt." But all this is only correct in principle and confining our attention to a single normative system. In view of the central importance which Kelsen attaches to physical coercion as a vital element of every legal order, no religious law can in practice be regarded as positive law. Since in reality the state has a monopoly in the exercise of physical force, religious law manifests itself either as a moral order (without physical coercion) or as part of state law (enforcement by the state). Thus it seems that Kelsen's view approaches that of such Positivists as Jhering, who also attach central importance to the element of physical force. We incline to the view that the concept of sanction should be somewhat broadened: see note 47 below. But see, Hauser, *Norm, Recht und Staat*, p. 126–127; the author's assertion that the lack of physical sanctions is of no theoretical importance seems to us incompatible with Kelsen's view. Kelsen's idea of monism will be dealt with below.

[10] Rudolph Sohm, *Kirchenrecht*, I (Leipzig 1892), pp. 1 et seq.: "Das Wesen der Kirche ist geistlich, das Wesen des Rechts weltlich... Das Wesen des Rechts ist dem idealen Wesen der Kirche entgegengesetzt." Cf. Carnelutti, *Teoria generale del diritto* (Roma 1940), p. 172; De Luca, *Diritto ecclesiastico, op. cit.*, pp. 73 et seq.

[11] Cf. O. Friedrich, *Einführung in das Kirchenrecht* (Göttingen 1961), pp. 30 et seq.; Eichmann, Mörsdorf, *Lehrbuch des Kirchenrechts*, 1. Band (11. Auflage, Paderborn 1964), pp. 23 et seq.; De Luca, *ibid.*; Forchielli, "La giuridicità del diritto canonico al vaglio della dottrina contemporanea," *Studi in onore di V. Del Giudice*, vol. 2 (Milano 1953), p. 471, 485 et seq.

[12] Eichmann, Mörsdorf, *ibid.*; Lesage, *La nature du droit canonique* (Ottawa 1960), pp. 24 et seq., 41 et seq.; Fedele, in *Enciclopedia del diritto*, Vol. XII, p. 871; D'Avack, *Corso di Diritto canonico*, Vol. I, *Introduzione sistematica al diritto della Chiesa* (Milano 1956), pp. 94 et seq., 97 et seq.

[13] K. Barth, *Die Ordnung der Gemeinde* (München 1955), pp. 16 et seq.; Erik

those Protestant countries where the organization of religious institutions rested on state law.[14]

In truth, however, the debate is ideological. It does not go to the *nature* of a given normative reality but rather to evaluating it according to a scale of values. The dispute is not about the legal character of religious law, but whether it is proper and desirable to uphold such law in light of certain religious and moral principles. For this reason it lies beyond the scope of the present study.

Another argument raised against the legal character of Canon Law touches its very essence. The argument assumes that as a *social ordering* the law is intended for the settlement of differences between individuals with conflicting interests and that it is the essential purpose of law to coordinate human activities, both as between individuals and as between the individual and the social body generally. The law thus possesses an "external" quality not consummated in the individual but projected beyond him and operating at an "interpersonal" level (*Intersubbiettività*).[15] Thus Canon Law cannot be considered a normative system of a legal character since by its nature it is not directed to ordering any human social relationships but to determining the relationship between man and his Creator, a relation which exists at an "internal" level (*Intrasubbiettività*).[16] Religious law contemplating man's inward self is similar to morality. Central to it, is not social justice but the eternal salvation of the soul (*salus aeterna animarum*).

This critique of the legal character of Canon Law has exercised many Catholic writers.[17] Some, while accepting the idea that Canon Law differs from secular law in fundamental purpose, have not rejected its legal char-

---

Wolf, *Ordnung der Kirche* (Frankfurt a/M 1961), pp. 493 et seq.; cf. Friedrich, *op. cit.,* pp. 32 n. 37; Bäumlin, "Staatslehre und Kirchenrechtslehre, über gemeinsame Fragen ihrer Grundproblematik," in *Staatsverfassung und Kirchenordnung, Festgabe für Rudolf Smend* (Tübingen 1962), pp. 3, 5 et seq.; Ernst Wolf, "Sinn und Grenze der Anwendung der Zwei-Reiche-Lehre auf das Kirchenrecht," in *Staatsverfassung und Kirchenordnung,* cit., p. 443.

[14] Cf. V. V. Schrey, *Die Generation der Entscheidung* (München 1955), p. 154.

[15] Cf. Lesage, *op. cit.,* p. 79; Del Vecchio, "A propos de la conception étatique du droit," *Justice-Droit-Etat* (Paris 1938), pp. 282, 287–288 (Translated in [1937], *Journal of Comp. Legisl. and Int. Law*).

[16] D'Avack, *op. cit.,* pp. 91 et seq.; Fedele, *op. et loc. cit.;* Id., *Discorsi sul diritto canonico* (Roma 1973), pp. 1 et seq.

[17] See especially the bibliography given by the two writers cited in the previous footnote.

acter. It is unnecessary, they have urged, for a legal system always to be directed to reconciling opposing interests; its aim may be to achieve the common interest of all members of a given society. Unlike the state, the church is not a social body embracing opposing interests but a body based from its inception on community of interests. This "shared" purpose, notwithstanding its transcendent nature, serves as a basis for a true legal system.[18]

Without entering into a discussion on the essence of the Catholic Church, we also incline toward the view that the idea of law should not be restricted to the purpose of settling interpersonal disputes.[19]

Nonetheless, the question which concerns us here requires a different approach. The legal character of a given norm is to be found in the manner of its enforcement. If the threat of a societal sanction[20] supports a rule of behaviour, that demonstrates that the society creating the rule has a direct interest in obedience to the norm. In this respect it is perhaps possible to speak of a conflict of interests: the individual's personal interest in freedom of action and the public interest as represented by the enforcing organ. However that may be, the factor determinative of the legal character of a norm is that society is prepared to enforce compliance upon the individual. The legal character is not in the least diminished if the norm subsumes a transcendent concept. It follows, in our opinion, that all such religious norms as are attended by a societal sanction constitute together a legal system.[21] At the same time there can be little doubt that the unique

---

[18] Cf. Fedele, *ibid.*
[19] Cf. F. Zanchini, *La Chiesa come ordinamento sacramentale* (Milano 1968), pp. 58 et seq.; Forchielli, *op. cit.*, p. 509.
[20] As opposed to a *purely* transcendent sanction. On the distinction between the two types of sanctions, see Kelsen, *Pure Theory of Law*, pp. 28 et seq. There is no doubt that in the sphere of religious law sanctions are often mixed. We are inclined to the view that every sanction should be regarded as social, which is executed by a human factor, even if its only significance is transcendent, such as the denial of the sacrament to a Catholic. A non-social punishment would be one exclusively in the hands of a superhuman authority.
[21] D'Avack (*op. cit.*, pp. 91 et seq., 108 et seq.) differentiates between norms which lend themselves to the coercive authority of the church (*potestas fori externi*) and those which the church leaves solely to the conscience of the individual (*potestas fori interni*). In his view, the first are of a legal nature while the latter have a purely moral character. But see the contrary view of Fedele, *op. et loc cit.; Id., Lo Spirito del diritto canonico* (Padova 1962), pp. 148 et seq.; Lesage, *op. cit.*, pp. 174 et seq. On the general nature of a legal sanction see also below n. 47.

character conferred on religious law by the transcendent religious concept differentiates it from the law of the state.[22]

This conclusion may also serve in solving a somewhat similar problem but with a completely different background: the legal nature of Moslem law. Here also it has been argued that Moslem law does not constitute a legal system, by reason of the special characteristics of the *fiqh*.[23] But as we have said, the legal quality of every religious norm is to be ascertained by its sanction.[24]

If we turn now to Jewish law, the outstanding fact is that the question of its legal character has never disturbed those concerned with it. This is no matter for surprise since for the observant Jew the supra-human and universal validity of Jewish law cannot be called into question. Any doubts he might have actually concern the binding effect of the law of the state in which he lives. Clearly, the idea that the state is the sole source of the legal system could not flourish in the historical experience of the Jewish people.

Jewish law, however, also differs in its nature from ecclesiastical law. Historically, the centre of gravity of Judaism lies in the Jewish religious law—the *Halakha*—which aspires to a total shaping of human life in all its manifestations. Since the *Halakha* makes no functional distinction between wordly matters, given over almost exclusively to the political authority, and matters touching the well-being of the soul, coming within the jurisdiction of religious organs, no problem concerning the interpersonal nature of Jewish law could arise. Human affairs are an integral concern of the *Halakha,* in precisely the same manner as matters between man and the Divinity. Beyond that, the *Halakha* often conceives of the latter in terms of legal categories. Thus in discussing the legal nature of Talmudic law, Justice Silberg makes the following perceptive remarks:[25] "Jewish law, unlike practically all other legal systems, does not limit itself to the sphere of 'between man and man.' It also places the relations

---

[22] Zanchini, *op. cit., passim;* Lesage, *op. cit., passim;* Fedele, *op. et loc. cit.*

[23] Bousquet, *Précis de Droit musulman* (3e éd., Alger), p. 50; C. Snouck Hurgronje, "De la nature du 'droit' musulman," *Oeuvres choisis* (Leiden 1957), p. 256.

[24] See, in particular, the sharp criticism of the view which denies the legal character: A. Colomer, "A propos du lien entre le droit et le religion dans les systèmes juridiques orientaux, le droit musulman existe-il?", *Etudes de droit contemporain (nouvelle série),* (Paris 1966), p. 67; Y. Linant de Bellefonds, (1964) *Rev. int. dr. comp.,* 644; Milliot, *Introduction à l'étude du droit musulman* (Paris 1952), nos. 172–174.

[25] Silberg, *Talmudic Law and the Modern State* (New York 1973), p. 1.

between man and God in juridical categories, it speaks of them in juridical terms, and it approaches them with a juridical conception. The Holy One... is deemed as a kind of legal person, enjoying rights, being subject to obligations, heeding His own precepts and entering as a subject of civil jurisdiction, as it were, in the complex of relations between Himself and His creatures." And he goes on to demonstrate how an array of legal terms and concepts has come to be applied to all areas of the *Halakha*.[26]

Another instance typical of this approach is found in the following passage from the Talmud:[27]

"The rabbis have taught that it is forbidden for man to enjoy anything of this world without a benediction, and if anyone should do so, it is as if he committed sacrilege.... R. Hanina ben Papa said: [He] is like one who steals from the Holy One and the community of Israel."[28]

These ideas, as they come to expression in the *Aggada*, are far reaching in their implications, but extreme legal conclusions are not to be drawn from them. Even if they are ultimately expressive of a characteristic normative tendency, God is so exalted in the Jewish understanding that His nature cannot be perceived, even in legal categories.[29]

In the Talmud, therefore, the legal nature of the *Halakha* is accepted without question. Equally upon the establishment of the Jewish State with a legal system of its own, the question was not raised. The reason for that is manifold. Israeli law, influenced as it is by the Anglo-American system, tends to avoid abstract theoretical questions which have no immediate practical bearing. Again, the legal practice of referring back to religious laws stems principally from the Ottoman tradition which recognized the

---

[26] See his conclusion, "The relationship between a man and God, which practically speaking is the relationship between a man and himself, between man and his own deepest moral and religious sentiments is caught up in the network of juridical relationships... that were created by the Lawgiver." (p. 8).

[27] Babylonian Talmud, *Berachot*, 35a, 35b.

[28] For the idea that obligations are placed, as it were, on the Creator, see the legendary story (*Hullin*, 60b; *Shevuot* 9a): "Rabbi Shimon ben Lakish said, 'What distinguishes the sacrificial goat of the New Moon of which it is said that it is 'to the Lord'? It is as if the Creator said, "This goat is my atonement for diminishing the moon'." Cf. the interpretation given to this legend by Rabbi Joseph Soloveichik, "The Man of Halakha," (1944) *Talpioth*, at p. 65 (Hebrew).

[29] In this connection, see the interesting comments of Prof. Levontin in his book review of Prof. Silberg's book, (1962) *HaPraklit* 182 n. 3. Prof. Levontin criticizes the thesis that the Talmud expands the idea of the rule of law beyond the sphere of the relations between man and man. In his view this is a *theological* thesis which is not drawn from immediate observation or from a direct examination.

autonomy of the religious communities. As a result, the legislature did not conceive of religious law as being essentially different from any other national law. Even for the Mandatory lawmaker, the concept of "personal law" included both national and religious law.[30] The use of the single term "personal law" to denote both foreign law and religious law indicates clearly that the extreme positivist conception mentioned above was alien to the spirit of the local system.[31]

If all religious systems recognized in Israel are governed by this attitude, Jewish law possesses still another aspect in being regarded as the national law of the Jews, the practical significance of which can be seen at the legislative level. The Israeli legislator has striven to introduce a legal system of an independent national character based on the Jewish legal tradition. In this endeavour to change the existing system, the legal character of the *Halakha* and its inspiration for the shaping of a future Israeli legal system with a national character, have been stressed. The perception of Jewish law as a *national law* is one more reason why even those who are not considered religiously observant Jews approach the religious order as if it were a *legal system*.

In a well-known *obiter dictum*, Justice Agranat relied on this national approach in drawing a practical conclusion in current law. In *Skornik* v. *Skornik*,[32] dealing with recognition of a marriage between Jews celebrated outside Israel in accordance with Jewish law alone, but in a place where such law is not recognized, Justice Agranat observed that he did not attach a great deal of importance to the question of the validity of Jewish law, as part of the municipal law of foreign states, as regards their Jewish inhabitants. "I do [not do so], since the very moment that we admit—as we are obliged to admit—the continued existence of the Jews, in all the generations and all the lands of their dispersion, as a separate people, we must test the nature of Jewish law by the *historic* relationship of the Jewish people to this law. We shall then conclude—against our will—that the Jewish people really treated Jewish law, throughout their existence and dispersion, as their special property, as part of the treasure of their culture. It follows that this law served in the past as the national law of the Jews,

---

[30] See Article 47 of the Palestine Order in Council, 1922, and also Article 64. See C.A. 26/51, *Kotik* v. *Wolfson*, 5 P.D. 1341, 1345.

[31] On the other hand, we would not rely on the fact that religious laws are included in the term "law" under the Interpretation Ordinance. There it is indeed expressly provided, "Religious laws ... as in force in Palestine before the establishment of the State or as in force in the State."

[32] C.A. 191/51, 8 P.D. 141; English translation in 2 S.J.S.C. 327.

and even today possesses this national character in respect of Jews wherever they may be."[33]

In fact Justice Agranat proposed widening the meaning of the expression "law of his nationality", which appears in Article 64 (2) of the Palestine Order in Council, so as to include Jewish law when Jewish citizens of a foreign country are married abroad in accordance with that law alone. "It is proper to prefer here, over and above the foreign national law (*lex patriae*) which governed the parties at the time of their marriage and which only recognizes marriages celebrated in particular civil form ... Jewish law."[34]

This viewpoint—and this is not the occasion to enlarge on its substantive correctness[35]—reveals the influence of the national approach on the understanding of the legal nature of Jewish law. Another phenomenon, no less characteristic, is the frequent reliance found in Supreme Court decisions on Jewish law sources with regard to questions which are fully regulated by the provisions of the civil law. Such reliance does not arise out of the necessity to find a substantive solution for the point involved but out of a desire to demonstrate the approach of Jewish legal tradition. A consequence of the researches of several justices expert in *Halakha*,[36] it is due to causes which are fundamentally national or religious.[37] The

---

[33] *Ibid.* at 177–178, (2 S.J.S.C. 371–76); see also C.A. 65/67 *Kurz v. Kirshen,* 21 P.D. 20, 25, 27.

[34] Compare the view of Justice Olshan, *ibid.* at 1610 (2 S.J.S.C. 337).

[35] With respect to the emphasis on the national—as apposed to the religious—character of Jewish law, see the criticism of Feinberg, " 'Obiter Dictum' which calls for interpretation (People and Nation, Religious Law and National Law)," (1954) *HaPraklit* 289, and the reply thereto by Dykan, *Law of Marriage and Divorce* (Tel Aviv 1957), pp. 16 et seq. (Hebrew). See also the present writer, "The Problem of Jewish Law in a Jewish State," 3 (1968) *Isr. L. Rev.* 259. On the question of the application of religious law as the *national law* outside the boundaries of the State, see Silberg, *Personal Status in Israel* (Jerusalem 1957), pp. 237 et seq. (Hebrew). On the general question of the application of the religious law retroactively by the religious courts outside the boundaries of the State, see Tedeschi, "Transition from Secular to Religious Matrimonial Status, and the Retroactive Application of the Latter," *Studies in Israel Private Law* (Jerusalem 1966), p. 212. It should be noted that the Israeli legislator expressly recognizes the existence of religious marriage performed outside Israel, for the purpose of bigamy, see sec. 4 of the Penal Law Amendment (Bigamy) Law, 5719—1959 from which it may be inferred that the legislator regards religious law as a legal system comparable to the law of any other state.

[36] In particular, Justices Silberg, Cohn and Kister of the Supreme Court.

[37] In this context, cf. the remarks of President Zmoira at the opening of the Supreme Court (reprinted in [1969] *HaPraklit,* 145, 146): "However, despite

truth is that the heterogeneous character of the law of the State, to a great extent the result of historical accident (the Ottoman and the British Mandatory regimes) induces a feeling of strangeness towards many legal rules which were evolved in entirely different social circumstances. There is understandably a desire for a legal order with its own tradition, which in turn accounts for the sympathetic approach to Jewish law.

It follows from the foregoing that Jewish law is of a juridical nature by reason both of its essence and of the recognition it has received in Israeli law. Yet the question of its juristic nature is not settled by the recognition that in principle a normative religious system may bear a legal character. There is the further problem whether a given religious legal system constitutes an actual valid system judged by its effectiveness. Let it be said at once that it is not the intention here to analyse the concept of "Positive Law (*ius positivum*)," which according to some writers is identical with the concept of effective law.[38] Our concern is with empirical reality, the actual enforcement of a normative system without endeavouring finally to resolve the conceptual question. It should, however, be observed that theoretically, notwithstanding its lack of efficacy, a normative system remains fundamentally "law,"[39] and there is nothing to prevent the legal system of a state from establishing some relationship with it.[40] On the other hand, in all other respects, decisive importance attaches to whether we are dealing with a living system in actual operation, or a system which is simply of theoretical interest.

Empirically it is impossible to establish precisely the extent to which a normative system finds realization without engaging in inductive researches. But our aim here is the far more modest one of determining

---

the limitations placed upon the judge in relation to the existing law, I am sure that our courts also can make a contribution to the renaissance of Jewish law even before we have our own new laws. They can do so by giving an original Hebrew form to their judgments and in some cases by a comparative citation of the rules of Jewish law even when they cannot rule in accordance with that law." See generally. M. Elon, "Jewish Law in the Law of State," *HaPraklit* (1969) p. 27.

[38] Cf. Ago, *Positive Law, cit.*, pp. 700 et seq.

[39] Cf. Tedeschi, "On the Inductive Study of Law," *Studies in Israel Law* (Jerusalem 1960) pp. 1, 3.

[40] On the connection between normative systems, such as reference and reception, see in the sequel. In truth, the law of the State can create a connection with any normative system, even if it does not have a legal character; for example, reference to the principles of morality by a State law, such as that found in section 30 of the Law of Contracts (General Part), 5733–1973.

whether a particular religious system has in a *general way* been put into effect. It appears that at least as regards Jewish and Canon law it is possible for this purpose broadly to rely on general knowledge of the situation.

The base of any legal system is always human society, and in the case of religious law a religious society.[41] Accordingly the effectuation of a religious system in actuality involves the existence of an autonomous religious society. There is a crucial link between the independent organization of a religious society and the vitality of its basic normative system.

Does an organized religious Jewish society in fact exist, a society which is regulated by the binding order of the *Halakha*? Framed in such general terms the question, to our thinking, admits only of a negative answer. The Jewish religious community, viewed as a whole, does not constitute an *organized* society with independent organs concerned to enforce the law of the Torah by the sanctions provided in that law. But in saying all this, we have not yet exhausted the subject. The picture must be completed by reference to the characteristic features of Judaism. The absence of central organs having authoritative power, is not a phenomenon new to Judaism. For many generations it has lacked a unitary organization to justify its being viewed as a single ordered society. In fact, within a single historical period a variety of Jewish societies have existed, which whilst maintaining more or less strong ties with one another did not attain to any social organizational consolidation. There have indeed been not a few individuals who, by reason of their greatness in Torah scholarship, achieved wide spiritual authority, but this authority did not rest on a unified fixed political-organizational structure. This is the situation today as well; the Jewish religious community throughout the world is composed of separate units, mostly of a local character. Moreover, even for those religious bodies which in principle accept the discipline of the Torah and its commandments, considerable portions of the *Halakha* are no longer an actuality, and this is true not only of those *mitzvot* which according to the *Halakha* itself relate to Messianic times, but also of those which are presently binding, such as laws relating to economic matters.

A vast rift between the applicable scope of the *Halakha* from the internal dogmatic aspect and actual compliance with it, exists both on the personal level (whilst the entire Jewish people is commanded to live according to

---

[41] On the concept of the religious society and its relation to the political society, see Jemolo, *Premesse ai rapporti tra Chiesa e Stato,* (Milano 1965), pp. 1 et seq.; *Id., Lezioni di diritto ecclesiastico* (2a ed., Milano 1957), pp. 1 et seq.

religious rule, in reality only a small proportion accepts "the yoke of the Kingdom of Heaven"), and on the substantive level (the main area in which the *Halakha* still prevails in any real sense is in matters of religious prohibitions and permissions, as distinguished from civil law matters). There are indeed groups in Israel and abroad which can be thought of as independent organized religious societies, such as the Hassidic "courts" with their strongly centralized and independent leadership. Generally, however, there is no *worldwide* Jewish religious society of a unified order. The situation in Israel itself is characterized by the continuing desire to organize the religious community by means of the State. Reliance on the State, beginning in the Ottoman period under the *Millet* System [42] and continuing during the Mandatory period when the Chief Rabbinate and Knesset Yisrael were established,[43] has been further strengthened since the founding of the State. The process obviously cannot be considered as the expression of a single and continuous trend; the ideological background was radically different in each of these periods, but this is not a matter for extended discussion here.[44]

In examining the real authority of the religious system, it is necessary to disregard the coercive power of the State's "secular arm." This combination of the two systems does not give a true picture of religious law, as the living normative system of a religious society. On the contrary, in many cases the dependence of the religious system on the State is indicative of the weakness of the former. Were we therefore to examine the reality of organized religious society from the viewpoint of its independence, the conclusion must be that there is no such general *organized* religious society in Israel. That is not, however, to deny that there exist certain groups of limited scope sufficiently coherent to be considered autonomous religious bodies (for example, the ultra-orthodox group) as distinct from a single entity representing the entire religious population.[45] It follows that the

---

[42] See the constitution of the institutions of the Jewish community of 1864 which were approved by the Sultan, in Young, *Corps de droit ottoman* (Oxford 1905), vol. II, pp. 3–9, 143 et seq.

[43] It should be noted that historically the religious community structure served as a basis for organizing the Jewish Yishuv (Settlement) in order to advance national and not necessarily religious interests. Cf. E. Goldman, *Religious Issues in Israel's Political Life* (Jerusalem 1964), pp. 18 et seq. On the statutory sources of these institutions, see England, "Status of the Chief Rabbinical Council and the Power of Review of the High Court of Justice," (1966) *HaPraklit* 68.

[44] See generally England, "The Relationship between Religion and State in Israel," *Scripta Hierosolymitana*, (Jerusalem 1965), vol. 16, pp. 254, 265.

[45] The religious public in Israel functions in part within the framework of religious

religious order does not manifest itself as a legal system, since breach of a religious norm does not entail any socially organized sanction. A comparison of the ideal as mirrored by the specific content of the religious order with the present reality of religious society shows the independent coercive power of religious organs to be conspicuously absent. Judging religious norms by their actual efficacy, we must conclude that they have effect among the general religious public not as legal but rather, in the accepted terminology, as moral norms.[46]

As will become clear in the sequel, the absence of real efficacy as a legal system, has considerably affected the status of Jewish religious law in the framework of the law of the State. For the same reason the true status of the religious organs set up with the help of the State and enjoying its coercive power is problematic.

As for Canon Law, it can be said that it is maintained by an organized religious society with strong and independent organs. The Catholic Church is a body having a hierarchical structure, headed by a supreme authority. It has central organs which carry out legislative, executive and judicial functions and it possesses real power to impose societal sanctions[47] on those who contravene religious rule. Even today the Canon Law constitutes

---

political parties, the status of which is not unambiguous, and which are not to be viewed in themselves as autonomous *religious* bodies.

[46] "Moral" here in a purely formal sense, the manner in which the norms are enforced. They lack socially organized coercive acts; the sanction is either a non-organized social one or a transcendent one. Cf. Kelsen, *op. cit.*, pp. 62 et seq.

[47] Cf. Gény, *Science et technique en droit privé positif*, vol. 1, p. 60: "De fait, le droit positif de l'Eglise existe, comme existe un pouvoir capable de l'édicter et de le sanctionner. Et, si la sanction en reste aujourd'hui d'ordre purement spirituel, ce n'en est pas moins une sanction éminemmment sociale, qui peut aller jusqu'à exclure du groupe les fidèles obstinément rebelles à l'autorité (excommunication)." According to Kelsen the decisive criterion of law as a coercive order is the element of *physical* force. This element seems to be lacking in the actual enforcement of religious norms by religious institutions, in view of the fact that the modern State claims a monopoly of force. But the sanctions imposed by the Church are more than a mere "approval of the norm-conforming and the disapproval of the norm-opposing behaviour" (Kelsen, *ibid.*), they can effectively deprive a person of certain benefits by excommunication without recourse to physical force. These sanctions imposed by organised judicial institutions of the Church may therefore be considered as coercive acts characterizing a legal order. On the general problem of legal sanctions see also Paton, *Jurisprudence, cit.*, p. 78 et seq.; Bobbio, in *Novissimo Digesto Italiano*, vol. 16 pp. 530 et seq., and see above note 9.

a legal order of effective force.[48] The Catholic Church does not require aid from a secular state power for the purpose of its internal organization. In Israel as well, the Latin Patriarchate and the other recognized Catholic communities maintain their internal organization without help from the state. Each of them, however, calls for separate study, and we therefore refrain from expressing any view about the actual efficacy of its religious law.

---

[48] D'Avack, *op. cit.*, pp. 87 et seq.; Lesage, *op. cit.*, p. 198. Lechleitner, *Der Mensch zwischen Staat und Kirche*, cit., pp. 45 et seq.; Germann, *Grundlagen der Rechtswissenschaft* (Bern 1950), pp. 196 et seq.; Fleiner, "Geistliches Weltrecht und weltliches Staatsrecht," *Ausgewählte Schriften und Reden* (Zürich 1941).

Chapter II

UNITY AND PLURALITY OF SYSTEM
GENERAL RELATIONSHIP BETWEEN STATE
AND RELIGIOUS LAW

The concept of "system" or "order" presupposes a complex of rationally related norms forming a unitary whole. Indeed, the requirement of unity is in the very nature of every normative system whose purpose is to regulate human conduct. The idea of order reflects the principle that a single standard must exist for the deontic evaluation of human activities. If we wish to regulate human behaviour, those things which are permitted or forbidden must be definable in unambiguous terms, otherwise an untenable situation is created in which a person will be required both to act and to refrain from acting.[1] But the avoidance of contradiction is only one aspect of the concept of unity, going to the content of the norms, the nature of the obligation imposed on the individual. A legal system possesses essentially—according to Kelsen—a dynamic character; its validity is based not on *any particular qualitative content* of the norms of which it is constituted but mainly on the *way* in which these norms are created.[2] It follows that whilst internal consistency is essential for the effective application of a normative system and the achievement of the objective for which it exists, the regulating of human behaviour, it is not the existential basis of the normative system as such, since it necessarily operates within an *existing* system,[3] concerned with its internal unity[4] and

---

[1] This situation is unsatisfactory from the point of view of the purpose of the law. That, however, does not mean that the inconsistency constitutes a *logical contradiction*. Two norms of contrary content may both be valid, and the result will be that both the act and the failure to act will entail a certain sanction. This situation is not desirable, but it is *possible*, from a logical point of view. See particularly Kelsen, *Pure Theory of Law,* pp. 25 et seq., 205 et seq.; Gavazzi, *Delle Antinomie* (1959), *passim;* cf. Stone, *Legal System and Lawyer's Reasoning* (Stanford 1964), pp. 26 et seq.

[2] Kelsen, *op. cit.,* pp. 198 et seq.; *sed* cf. Stone, *op. cit.,* pp. 105 et seq.; cf. Batiffol, *Aspects philosophiques du droit international privé* (Paris 1956), pp. 48 et seq.

[3] N. Bobbio, *Novissimo Digesto Italiano,* Vol. I, p. 667: "Si dice che ha luogo un'antinomia quando due norme appartenenti ad uno stesso ordinamento giuridico sono incompatibili."

[4] The concept of the unity of a normative system has various meanings. See

not determinative of the limits of the system. The latter is resolved by the concept of normative validity. The system is composed of valid norms since the concept of validity is of the essence of the norm.[5]

Logically it is impossible to assert that a given norm is at once valid and invalid.[6] The criterion must be the same for all norms, if a system is to be unitary and if the norms belonging to it are to be identified. A normative system is thus the totality of all those norms having validity according to the same criterion.[7]

Opinion varies about the nature of the criterion. The difference is at times the consequence of differing methodological assumptions. The positivist-dogmatic school,[8] for instance, begins with the social reality in order to derive *from* it the foundations and concepts of the system. The normativist school[9] seeks to discern the essence of the law by *a priori* tests applied *to* the reality. For the present purpose, it is interesting to note that both these schools conclude that the test of validity of a given legal rule rests on what they call the basic or primary norm which is the reason for the validity of the whole system.[10] It is true that some critics

---

generally Engisch, *Die Einheit der Rechtsordnung*, (Heidelberg 1935); *Id.*, *Einführung in das juristische Denken* (5. Aufl., Stuttgart 1971), pp. 156 et seq.; cf. Larenz, *Methodenlehre der Rechtswissenschaft* (2. Aufl. Berlin 1969), pp. 159 et seq.

[5] Kelsen, *op. cit.*, p. 10: "By the word 'validity' we designate the specific existence of a norm."

[6] As distinct from a contradiction in the content of a norm, see note 1 above. Here the conflict is a logical contradiction in the strict sense; the assertion, "norm A is valid" logically excludes the contrary.

[7] Perassi, "Teoria dommatica delle fonti di norme giuridiche in diritto internazionale," 6 (1971) *Riv. dir. int.*, 195, 200 et seq.; Hart, *The Concept of Law* (Oxford 1961), p. 100: "To say that a given rule is valid is to recognize it as passing all the tests provided by the rule of recognition and so as a rule of the system."

[8] Perassi, *op. et loc. cit.*, *passim*; cf. Bellini, "Per una sistemazione canonistica delle relazioni fra diritto della Chiesa e diritto dello Stato," in 30 (1954) *Annuario di diritto comparato et di studi legislativi*, *passim*; De Luca, *Rilevanza dell'ordinamento canonico nel diritto italiano* (Padova 1943), pp. 77 et seq.; Larenz, *op. cit.*, p. 70; and generally E. Paresce, *Enciclopedia del diritto*, vol. 13, pp. 699 et seq.

[9] Kelsen, *op. cit.*, *passim*; Larenz, *ibid.*; Bellini, *op. et loc. cit.*

[10] Perassi, *op. et loc. cit.*, p. 204; "Il postulato per la dommatica è la giuridicità della suprema norma sulla produzione giuridica"; Kelsen, *op. cit.*, p. 205: "Since the basic norm is the reason for the validity of all norms belonging to the same legal order, the basic norm constitutes the unity of the multiplicity of these norms." *Id.*, *General Theory of Law and State* (New York 1961), p. 124. Cf. spec. De Luca, *op. et loc. cit.*, pp. 90 et seq.

have observed that in arriving at their conclusion about the basic norm, both have strayed from their particular methodological assumptions.[11] But there is no need here to decide this question, nor whether the basic norm is an integral part of the system, as many think, or a hypothesis external to it, as Kelsen argues.[12] Ultimately we can agree in principle even with those who contest the abstract nature of the "basic norm" and for that reason adopt some other criterion resting exclusively on reality, such as, the realization of the norms in the courts or other rules of recognition.[13] What matters to us is the assumption common to all that every normative system rests on a single validity criterion which gives it unity. Unity is used here in a formal sense, since the relationship of the norms comprehended in a system is formal.[14]

Thus far we have emphasized the positive side of the validity criterion, namely, the identification of normative system by the identity of its norms. But the same principle of identification (*principium individuationis*) embodied in a single validity criterion also operates negatively by excluding every norm which does not accord with it. Thus externally the unity of the system presents another feature, which is no more than the logical consequence of its very being, its *exclusiveness*,[15] since only those norms are valid within its structure which satisfy the single criterion.[16] Using

---

[11] Bellini, *op. et loc. cit., passim.*

[12] Engisch, *Die Einheit der Rechtsordnung*, pp. 11 et seq.; Stone, *op. cit.*, p. 104; Kelsen, *Reine Rechtslehre* (2. Aufl., Wien 1960) p. 206 n. 2.

[13] Hart, *The Concept of Law*, pp. 97 et seq.; Stone, *op. cit*, pp. 131 et seq.; Raz, *The Concept of Legal System* (Oxford 1970), *passim*.

[14] Cf. Latham, *The Law and the Commonwealth* (London 1949), pp. 522 et seq. On the various meanings of the concept of unity, compare Engisch, *Einheit der Rechtsordnung, passim;* Wengler, "Betrachtungen über den Zusammenhang der Rechtsnormen in der Rechtsordnung und die Verschiedenheit der Rechtsordnungen," *Festschrift Laun* (Hamburg 1953), pp. 719–743.

[15] C. Ghirardini, "La comunità internazionale e il suo diritto," 13 (1919) *Riv. dir. intern.* 9; Ago, *Teoria del diritto internazionale privato* (Padova 1934), pp. 106 et seq.; Id., "Règles générales des conflits de lois", 58 (1936) *Recueil des Cours*, IV, pp. 247, 302; Anzilotti, *Corso di diritto internazionale* (Roma 1925), pp. 57 et seq.; De Luca, *op. cit.* cap. 3; Perassi, *Lezioni di diritto internazionale*, vol. II (Padova 1952), pp. 45 et seq.: "Ogni ordinamento giuridico, in quanto è originario ed indipendente, è per conseguenza esclusivo"; Kelsen, *Das Problem der Souveränität und die Theorie des Völkerrechts* (Tübingen 1920), pp. 105 et seq.

[16] Cf. etiam Batiffol, *Droit international privé* (5e éd. Paris 1970) tome 1, no. 327; Id., *Aspects philosophiques du droit international privé* (Paris 1956), pp. 119 et seq.; Bernardini, *Produzione di norme giuridiche mediante rinvio*

the concept of the basic norm to express the idea of exclusiveness, we can say that a given rule of behaviour is legally binding if it is related to the basic norm and draws its validity from it;[17] every norm which is not connected to the basic norm is devoid of legal validity.[18]

This last postulate gives rise to another question touching directly on our present theme. Assuming that unity and exclusiveness are essential features of every legal system, what is the nature of the relationship between different legal systems? This question, too, is but part of a broader question—the relationship between different *normative* systems not necessarily of a legal character.

This question has been discussed in a number of connections: the relationship between municipal law and international law;[19] the relationship between the legal system of one state and those of other states (especially in private international law);[20] the relationship between law and morality,[21] between state law and ecclesiastical law,[22] between state law and private contracts[23] and so on. Much of the ensuing debate stems from differences in methodological approach. But every difference of opinion which does not clearly define the methodological assumptions of the parties is sterile, since many of the arguments of the one party seem, of necessity, irrelevant to the other.[24]

(Milano 1966), pp. 2 et seq.; Cammarata, *Il concetto del diritto e la pluralità degli ordinamenti giuridici* (Catania 1926), p. 32.

[17] Kelsen, *Pure Theory of Law*, pp. 221–222. Cf. De Luca, *op. cit.*, pp. 90 et seq.

[18] We understand the concept of exclusiveness in the sense that a foreign norm is without validity in the particular system and not as denying its internal normative validity in another system. This problem is discussed hereafter.

[19] Cf. Oppenheim, Lauterpacht, *International Law* (8th ed., London 1955), pp. 35 et seq.; Kelsen, Tucker, *Principles of International Law* (2nd ed., New York 1967), pp. 551 et seq.

[20] Cf. Batiffol, *op. et loc. cit.;* C. David, *La loi étrangère devant le juge du fond* (Paris 1965), *passim;* Bernardini, *op. cit., passim;* Goldschmidt, "Jacques Maury et les aspects philosophiques du droit international privé," *Mélanges Maury*, t.1. pp. 153, 157 et seq. And see the bibliography given by the foregoing authors.

[21] Cf. Kelsen, *Pure Theory of Law*, pp. 329 et seq.; *Id., General Theory of Law and State*, pp. 374 et seq.

[22] See the sources cited in the sequel and above. For a list of sources of Italian thinking, see also F. Margiotta Broglio, "La qualificazione giuridica delle relazioni fra lo Stato Italiano e la Chiesa cattolica," 165 (1963) *Archivio Giuridico*, 53; Lechleitner, *Der Mensch zwischen Staat und Kirche, op. cit.*

[23] Cf. G. Tedeschi, "Volontà privata autonoma," (1929) *Riv. int. di filosofia del diritto*, fasc. VI; W.C. Sforza, "Il diritto dei privati," (1929) *Riv. it. per le scienze giuridiche*, fasc. I-II.

[24] Cf. *spec.* P. Bellini, "Per una sistemazione canonistica," *op. cit.*, pp. 338 et seq.;

The problem, as we see it, emerges from the opposition between the *normative level*, where the system appears unitary and exclusive, and the *factual level*, where we encounter a plurality of normative systems. We therefore have two different points of departure, each offering its own way of looking at the relationship between different systems.[25]

For the *normativist school* the only legal-scientific approach is to view the situation from the standpoint of the "ought to be" (*sollen*) rather than the "is" (*sein*).[26] Whilst obviously this does not impugn the opposite approach, it contends that the latter deviates from the true science of law.[27] We withhold judgment on the methodological debate, following upon the contentions of the "Pure Theory of Law" school.[28] It does, however, appear that this school does well to depict the possible relationships among different normative systems *from the pure normative viewpoint*. According to Kelsen[29] three kinds of relationships are possible between two normative orders: subordination, supremacy, and co-ordination.[30] These alone can produce a harmonious system normatively, and thus *a priori* no other relationship between different normative orders is possible. Thus system X may receive validity from another, higher system; system X, the lower, constitutes part of the higher system which is determinative of its scope and the limits of its organs' authority. The

---

370 et seq.; *Id.*, "Osservazioni sulla completezza dell'ordinamento giuridico canonico," (1957) *Il diritto ecclesiastico*, pp. 121, 170 et seq. This writer emphasizes particularly the difference between the *a priori* and the *a posteriori* approaches in legal science.

[25] Cf. Hart, *The Concept of Law*, p. 118.

[26] Kelsen, *Hauptprobleme der Staatsrechtslehre* (2. Aufl. Tübingen 1923), pp. 7 et seq. But see the criticism of this distinction in Larenz, *Methodenlehre der Rechtswissenschaft*, pp. 77 et seq.; E. Kaufmann, "Kritik der neukantianischen Rechtsphilosophie," *Gesammelte Schriften*, vol. 3 (Göttingen 1960), pp. 193 et seq.

[27] Kelsen, *Pure Theory of Law*, pp. 1, 101 et seq.; *Id.*, *General Theory of Law and State*, pp. 162 et seq.

[28] Larenz, however, expresses doubt about the relation between the theory of pure law and dogmatic legal science, *ibid.*, p. 70: "Die 'Reine Rechtslehre' befasst sich ... nicht mit den Inhalten, sondern nur mit der logischen Struktur der Rechtsnormen.... Indessen gibt sie sich selbst als Rechtswissenschaft und es ist zum mindesten nicht deutlich, wieweit Kelsen daneben noch eine 'dogmatische' Rechtswissenschaft als Wissenschaft anerkennt, die sich nicht mit der Form, sondern mit dem besonderen Inhalt eines bestimmten positiven Rechts befasst."

[29] *Das Problem der Souveränität*, pp. 102 et seq.; *Pure Theory of Law*, pp. 332 et seq.; *General Theory of Law and State*, pp. 373 et seq., 407 et seq.

[30] Cf. Conte, *Novissimo Digesto Italiano*, Vol. 12, p. 53.

basic norm of the subordinate system is relative since its ultimate validity is found in the superior system. The latter is an inclusive system since its basic norm is the final reason for the validity of all norms, including those of the subordinate system.[31] The second possibility is the same relationship but from the viewpoint of the superior system, and thus requires no further explanation. A relationship of co-ordination, presupposes the existence of a third, higher system which includes the two others which draw their validity from it. The supreme system determines the mutual relationship between its two subordinates by defining the sphere of validity of each of them. Here also, as in the simple subordinate-superior relationship, all the systems together constitute one system. The basic norm of the superior system is the single reason for validity; the subordinate and co-ordinated systems are parts of the total supreme system.[32]

The normativist conception postulates legal monism; the coexistence of separate *valid* normative systems is inconceivable. Scientific cognition demands a unitary viewpoint.[33] And if the starting point is the norm's validity, the "ought to be," then logically only *one* system and *one* criterion of validity is possible.[34] Normative unity is thus an epistemological postulate.[35] According to this approach the only possible relationship between two different norm systems is the creation of a single system. A clash of norms between two separate systems cannot be envisaged since that would assume the simultaneous validity of two independent systems, a

---

[31] "Two sets of norms can be parts of one normative system because one, being an inferior order, derives its validity from the other, a superior order. The inferior order has its relative basic norm, and that means, the basic determination of its creation, in the superior order." *General Theory of Law and State*, ibid.

[32] *Ibid.*: "The basic norm of the superior order is the ultimate reason of validity of all the norms, including those of the inferior orders"; *Pure Theory of Law*, ibid.; Hauser, *Norm, Recht und Staat*, pp. 128 et seq.

[33] Kelsen, *Das Problem der Souveränität*, p. 105: "Denn das Postulat der *Einheit der Erkenntnis* gilt unbeschränkt auch für die normative Ebene und findet hier seinen Ausdruck in der Einheit und Ausschliesslichkeit des als gültig vorausgesetzten Normensystemes, was gleichbedeutend mit der notwendigen Einheit des Betrachtungs-, Bewertungs- oder Deutungsstandpunktes ist"; *Pure Theory of Law*, p. 328.

[34] Kelsen, *Das Problem der Souveränität*, p. 111: "Das Ergebnis jeder normativen Betrachtung, die gültige Sollsätze erkennen will, kann immer nur ein logisch geschlossenes einheitliches Normensystem sein."

[35] Cf. *Id.*, *Principles of International Law*, p. 569: "The unity of national and international law is an epistemological postulate"; cf. De Luca, *op. et loc. cit.*

situation which not only contradicts the basic postulate but is also insoluble because of the absence of a unitary point of reference.[36]

If we accept the methodological assumptions of the normativist school, we cannot escape legal monism, the existence of a single valid normative system. But the normativist is only one of the possible views. The world of reality is another. There we encounter a plurality of normative systems, the relationship of which is likely to take on entirely different features because of the different perspectives.

We will not engage in the debate whether only such a method as the unity of the object of study (a single legal system) or whether equally a broader examination of the concept of law (a reality of various legal systems) can legitimately be termed the science of law.[37] The debate seems to a great extent a semantic one.[38] The main thing is to bear in mind the theory's point of departure, the normative world or reality. The distinction between them is important, but we only obtain a complete picture of the phenomenon of law by viewing things in both perspectives.

Reality tells us that in human society, both within a given state and outside it, many legal and ethical normative systems determine human behaviour. This plurality is productive of real clashes between conflicting rules of conduct. Even if from a pure normative view no conflict exists, factually the conflict often manifests itself sharply in respect of an individual who sees himself personally subject to two different normative systems.[39] There is, however, no logical inconsistency between unity of system dogmatically and plurality of systems factually. Each is correct

---

[36] *Ibid.*, pp. 108 et seq; *Id., Principles of Law and State*, pp. 374 et seq.; *Id., Principles of International Law*, pp. 570 et seq.; De Luca, *op. et loc. cit.*

[37] See, especially, De Luca, *op. cit.*, ch. III.

[38] Obviously, the methodological question itself is most material. The debate about the term *science of law* seems to us semantic. If the area of interest of the jurist is not limited to logical-formal categories but also extends, in one way or another, to the world of reality — as we contend — there is no special significance in the name of the study. The principle of the method is important, not its name. As to the question of method, see in general Larenz, *Methodenlehre der Rechtswissenschaft.*

[39] Kelsen himself does not ignore this possibility, but he emphasizes its psychological-factual nature. See *Das Problem der Souveränität*, p. 110; *Id., Principles of International Law*, pp. 571 et seq.: "The concept of a so-called conflict of norms or collision of duties means the psychological fact of an individual's being under the influence of two ideas which motivate him in opposite directions; it does not mean the simultaneous validity of two norms which contradict one another." cf. Hauser, *op. cit.*, p. 127.

at its own level, and neither confutes the other.[40] Thus we see no reason to impute to the normativist school the view that unity of system involves denying the quality of law to every other autonomous system.[41]

Determination of the legal quality of a particular normative system is a question of fact and not of normative validity. Legal quality is determined by known tests operative in the given normative reality; and the determination as such is not concerned with the system's objective validity. We can, for example, determine that the normative system of a certain tribe possesses a legal character, without taking up any position on its normative relationship to another system.

Yet many writers dispute monistic construction, seeing a discrepancy between the postulate that normatively only *one valid* system exists and the reality in which *many valid* systems are found, particularly the different state systems.[42] The argument goes that in reality it is very possible for one legal system to recognize others without considering them all as part

---

[40] Cf. Hart, *op. cit.*, p. 118. We are not completely convinced of the correctness of the author's claim (in the note on page 248) that a *factual* assertion about the validity of another system is not possible in Kelsen's view. We do not think that Kelsen rejects outright factual statements of this type. See in particular, *Das Problem der Souveränität*, pp. 110–111; *Principles of International Law*, p. 572. On the other hand, it is true that Kelsen sees these assertions as belonging principally to the area of sociology and psychology and not to that of legal theory. On this point we accept the opinion of Hart, as well as particularly the well-taken criticism of G. Balladore Pallieri, "Le dottrine di Hans Kelsen e il problema dei rapporti fra diritto interno e diritto internazionale," 14 (1935) *Riv. dir. intern.*, 24, 48: "Il vero è che la teoria svolta dal Kelsen è in non piccola parte una teoria dualistica. Si osservi infatti che, se si vuole riferire l'ipotesi fondamentale solo a sistemi giuridici positivi, vi è, per il giurista, possibilità di scelta tra due o più ipotesi fondamentali *solo in quanto vi siano due o più ordinamenti positivi*. Il giurista è libero di assumere l'uno o l'altro ordinamento come unico ed esclusivo solo, evidentemente, ove più ordinamenti esistano che possano essere trattati secondo i criteri giuridici, e che siano suscettibili di ricevere, attraverso l'ipotesi razionale, la qualificazione di ordinamenti giuridici positivi." This does not derogate, as the writer expressly emphasizes, from the basic correctness of Kelsen's teaching (*ibid.*, p. 47).

[41] Cf. E. Betti, *Problematica del diritto internazionale* (Milano 1956), pp. 128 et seq.; *Id.*, "Grundprobleme des internationalen Privatrechts," *Jus et Lex, Festschrift Max Gutzwiller* (Basel 1959), pp. 233, 238 et seq. This writer charges those who profess the principle of exclusiveness with solipsism. In this connection Kelsen's comments on the supremacy of international law are interesting; *Principles of International Law*, pp. 585 et seq.

[42] E. Betti, *op. et loc. cit.*; P. H. Neuhaus, *Die Grundbegriffe des internationalen Privatrechts* (Tübingen 1962), pp. 222 et seq.

of itself. For example: a state may recognize in its private international law the normative validity of legal systems of other states, without regarding the latter as part of its internal law.[43] Another view holds that the denial by one system of normative validity to every other system is a possible position but not logically compelling,[44] and so the normative relationship between different systems is not to be determined *a priori* but after looking at the normative reality.[45] In our view these arguments are incorrect, since they overlook the distinction between the normative and the factual levels.

What do unity and exclusiveness of system mean? These concepts express the idea that every norm in a given system must pass a uniform validity test. Without entering on a detailed discussion of the status of foreign law in private international law (to be considered later), we find that it is correct to assume here as well that foreign law has no validity in the domestic system unless it has passed its validity test.[46] In this regard there can be no dispute that the foreign and the domestic systems are one. The unity is purely formal and does not tell us anything about the actual formation of the relationship between the two systems (interpretation etc.).[47] Accordingly a finding that a domestic system recognizes a foreign system as independent, is ambiguous. Formally from a normative view-

---

[43] Cf. Maury, "Règles des conflits de lois," (1936) III *Recueil des Cours*, 329, 380 et seq.

[44] Cf. Santi Romano, *L'ordinamento giuridico* (2a ed., 1945) p. 119 n: "Il principio che ogni ordinamento originario è sempre esclusivo deve intendersi nel senso che esso *può*, non che *debba necessariamente* negare il valore giuridico di ogni altro."; Betti, *Problematica*, p. 129; cf. Bellini, "Osservazioni sulla completezza, *etc.*," p. 174 n. 50.

[45] Cf. spec. Bellini, *op. et loc. ult. cit.*, pp. 170 et seq.

[46] In this spirit see also, Batiffol, *Aspects philosophiques etc.*, pp. 120 et seq.; *Id.*, *Droit international privé*, tome 1, p. 393; cf. H. Dölle, "De l'application du droit étranger par le juge interne," 44 (1955), *Rev. crit. dr. int. pr.*, 233, 238: Cf. Kelsen, *General Theory of Law and State*, pp. 243 et seq. These scholars are not at one in their understanding of the legal system and the nature of the validity test. For example, Batiffol distinguishes between a rational and an imperative element in law. For this distinction, see the criticism of Maury in 46 (1957) *Rev. crit. du dr. int. privé*, 229, 238 et seq.; Goldschmidt, "Jacques Maury et les aspects philosophiques du droit international privé," *Mélanges Maury*, t. 1, pp. 152, 157 et seq.

[47] For this reason, in our view, the criticism of some writers misses the mark. They have relied largely on the ground that foreign law preserves its independent character when it is being applied by the referring judge and is therefore not to be considered a part of the internal law. Cf. Bernardini, *op. cit., passim*. The argument is not convincing. To hold that foreign law derives its normative

point, such a finding is meaningless, since the source of the foreign law's validity *within the internal system* is that system itself[48] (ignoring the theoretical possibilty of mutual co-ordination effected by international law as a superior order). On the other hand, it has considerable meaning on the substantive-factual level; recognition of another system as independent means that (in the sphere of its recognized validity) the substantive solutions are left fully or almost fully to the autonomy of the other system.

Summing up the discussion of unity and plurality, we reach the following conclusions. There are two points of departure, the normative and the factual. The *first*, which proceeds from the "ought to be", assumes a single system, everything being judged by the internal rules of the unitary system. So to look at the matter, which according to the normativist school is alone the science of law, is called by others "dogmatic".[49] In this view every legal system is of unitary and exclusive character and there can be no relationship with any other system which does not constitute part of a single comprehensive system. The *second* point of departure proceeds from a reality in which a multiplicity of systems exists. Viewing the relationship of the various systems from an external standpoint, it is called "pre-dogmatic" or "extra-dogmatic".[50] This approach observes the conflicts between the competing systems, as well as the situation of the individual who sees himself subject to two different systems. It also examines the dogmatic position of one system vis-à-vis the other systems, and vice versa. It is interested as well in the actual formation of the relationship between various systems and the practical implications of opposing dogmatic positions. One approach does not exclude the other, and although we must distinguish between them, they complement each other for the purpose of comprehending the entire phenomenon.

If we turn now to the question of the general relationship between state

---

validity *in* the internal system *from* the internal system, does not tell us anything about the manner of its reception and its treatment in the latter system. The lawmaker in referring to the foreign law can freely set up its status in internal law in respect of proving it, its interpretation and so on.

[48] This conclusion is compelling either on the *a priori* or the *a posteriori* approaches to law. Even if a given system recognizes another law as autonomous, the normative validity will flow either from the first or from a superior system. We therefore disassociate ourselves on this point from the position of Bellini, *op. et loc. cit.*

[49] But see note 28 above. Cf. also De Luca, *op. cit.*, pp. 105 et seq.

[50] De Luca, *ibid.*; cf. Morelli, *Nozioni di diritto internazionale* (5a ed., Padova 1958), p. 73; cf. Hart, *The Concept of Law*, p. 118.

law and religious law, the principles we have been discussing must also apply here.

From the *dogmatic* viewpoint, the law of the state is a unitary and exclusive system. Thus religious law has no normative validity unless and to the extent that it is recognized by state law.[51] This conclusion was stated explicitly by Justice Witkon in *Skornik* v. *Skornik*:[52] "And if it be argued that Jewish law is universal, the reply is that every religious law, in its application in this country, flows from an act of the secular legislator... —from the point of view of the basic norm according to the theory of Kelsen—and derives its force therefrom."[53]

But this observation itself suggests that the religious system itself proceeds on a different dogmatic assumption. And indeed, from the internal viewpoint of the religious system, it also sets up claims of unity and exclusiveness. Thus, from the perspective of religious law, state law has no normative validity beyond that which it recognizes. The extra-dogmatic approach regards both systems together, noting that respective unity and exclusiveness are an important *fact* which compels a further conclusion: the *relativity* of every normative system.[54] In truth, the relativity derives from the essential unity of the one system from a dogmatic viewpoint, as well as from the existence of another system. The very meaning of unity and exclusiveness is that a normative statement of a system can have no validity except within the system itself. The perception of only one valid legal order negates the possibility of any of its norms penetrating any other system which, from its viewpoint, does not even exist. The idea was well described by De Luca,[55] that the relativity of a system is merely the reflection on the extra-dogmatic level of the concept of dogmatic unity.[56]

---

[51] For the various types of recognition, see below. And for a general view of the relationship between state and church, see Kelsen, *Allgemeine Staatslehre*, pp. 134 et seq.; Hauser, *op. cit.*, pp. 126 et seq.

[52] C.A. 191/51, 8 P.D. 141, 179–80 (2 S.J.S.C. 327, 378); cf. also M. Sternberg, "The Basic Norm of the Law in Israel," 9 (1953) *HaPraklit*, 129, 140–141.

[53] For the status of Canon Law in Italian law, see D'Avack, *Lezioni di diritto ecclesiastico italiano*, I (Milano 1963), pp. 84–109; De Luca, *op. cit.*, passim and the bibliography there. Generally see also, Fleiner/Giacometti, *Schweizerisches Bundesstaatsrecht* (Zürich 1949), pp. 326 et seq.

[54] Cf. Morelli, *op. cit.*, p. 72; De Luca, *op. cit.*, p. 98 n. 72; cf. V. Crisafulli, *Enciclopedia del diritto*, vol. 17 (1968), pp. 930–33 (*Fonti del diritto*).

[55] *Op. cit.*, pp. 106 et seq.

[56] "... Il principio della relatività dei valori giuridici non sia altro che il riflesso— in sede extra-dommatica—del principio dommatico dell'esclusività dell'ordinamento giuridico che si considera" (p. 107).

This discussion is not simply theoretical, witness the differences between Supreme Court Justices in *Balaban* v. *Balaban*.[57] The question was whether the abolition of the husband's rights in his wife's (*melug*) property as a result of the Women's Equal Rights Law, 5711–1951, affected the wife's right to maintenance. The President of the Supreme Court, Justice Olshan, found "no authority for the statement that the secular legislator cannot abolish a norm of religious law. In the absence of a constitution, the secular legislator is omni-competent."[58] This assertion is not correct, since it ignores the relativity of each legal system. The lawmaker may perhaps be omni-competent in his own system but his authority cannot extend beyond its borders. The better approach is that of Justice Silberg: "the secular legislator cannot abolish a norm of religious law since he is not the source of religious legislation. What he can do—by virtue of the sovereignty of the State—is to order the courts, including the religious courts, not to give judgment in accordance with that norm."[59] Justice Silberg's conclusion accords with the relativity concept. But the latter is better formulated in terms of normative validity, rather than in those of direction of the civil and religious courts.

Clearly, the fundamental conclusion of the dogmatic approach cannot affect social reality in which, alongside state law, other normative systems make appearance, having *actual* validity and sometimes operating as systems of a legal character. The various dogmatic approaches may, however, have decisive influence, as a factual matter, on the actual scope of conflicts between the different systems, particularly state law and religious law. This important point requires clarification. As we have said, no conflict between different systems is possible dogmatically since each system is unitary and exclusive. Conflict is primarily the psychological reaction of an individual needing to resolve the conflicting demands made upon him, according to a subjective scale of values.[60] The decision to reject one norm in favour of another clearly does not affect in the slightest the internal normative validity of the first norm. But the individual considers himself "bound" only by the norm to which he gives preference in his value judgment.[61] From his viewpoint it can be said that he creates by his personal decision an independent system of norms of personal morality.

---

[57] C.A. 313/59, 14 P.D. 285.
[58] *Ibid.*, at 291; the dictum was quoted with approval by Justice Etzioni in C.A. 61/71 *Cohen* v. *Cohen*, 25 (2) P.D. 327, 333.
[59] *Ibid.*, at 287.
[60] See the sources in note 39 above.
[61] Cf. Lechleitner, *Der Mensch zwischen Staat und Kirche*, pp. 70 et seq., 135

The personal acceptance of the "binding force" of certain norms is of great significance at the social-factual level when it is shared by many. The significance may be positive or negative; if, for example, many people deny the "binding force" of certain norms of state law and in practice prefer religious norms, the state will hardly be able to ignore the situation for long.

Thus far of the possibility of real conflict between state and religious law in the consciousness of the individual. But the scope of the conflict is directly affected by the mutual dogmatic relationship between the two systems. The clash can be avoided in one of three basic ways. (1) The two systems may operate, from a substantive viewpoint, in completely different fields, without contact.[62] (2) The state system may recognize dogmatically the superiority of religious law in a situation of conflicting norms. (3) Religious law may recognize the superiority of state law in such a situation.

To delimit the actual conflict is of decisive importance when both systems concern a single subject matter. The extent of the actual conflict between state law and religious law can therefore not be determined without a thoroughgoing examination of the three points mentioned above. Examination of the dogmatic positions of religious law with regard to state law lies outside this study, but the problem has been considered at length in respect of Canon Law, which has a long tradition in the matter of church-state relations.[63] In Jewish *Halakha* as well there are certain rules of co-ordination with secular law (the rule: "The Law of the State is Law"[64]) but these were never systematically developed. Furthermore the *halakhic* rules relate principally to the status of the law of a gentile state. The question of the relationship between the law of a Jewish state and Jewish religious law is a special one. In any event, there is in reality

---

et seq. The writer sees in the coexistence of a state authority and a religious authority, both of which are independent, a guarantee of individual freedom.

[62] Cf. Kelsen, *Das Problem der Souveränität*, p. 107.

[63] Bellini, "Per una sistemazione canonistica delle relazioni tra diritto della Chiesa e diritto dello Stato," *op. cit.;* Ciprotti, *Contributo alla teoria della canonizzazione delle leggi civili* (Roma 1941); D'Avack, *Corso di diritto canonico*, I (Milano 1956), pp. 245 et seq.; Del Giudice, *Nozioni di diritto canonico* (11a ed. Milano 1962), pp. 395 et seq.; Eichmann, Mörsdorf, *Kirchenrecht*, pp. 35 et seq.

[64] See Englard, "The Relationship between Religion and State in Israel," *op. cit.*, pp. 258 et seq.; see now the comprehensive study of S. Shilo, *Dina De-Malkhuta Dina, The Law of the State is Law* (Jerusalem 1974) (Hebrew).

a broad area of conflict between state law and religious law, witness frequent political struggles in this regard.[65]

The acuteness of a conflict over a given matter depends obviously on many varied social factors which cannot be evaluated in the abstract.

We may conclude this chapter with two additional comments of a factual and psychological bearing. Great importance may be ascribed to the difference in dogmatic position over those religious organs operating in the state. For example the state regards the religious courts as acting under authority granted by it and subject to its laws. The religious judges see their role in a different light; for them the applicability of religious law is not conditioned upon the secular lawmaker's will. They look upon their courts as autonomous bodies which derive their authority primarily from a separate, independent normative system. A similar disagreement in dogmatic conceptions exists over other organs of the religious communities,[66] but is particularly marked in the case of Jewish religious organs[67] whose internal organization is greatly dependent on the state. In the sequel we shall deal in greater detail with the ambivalent position of these organs and the practical implications thereof.

The final comment concerns the socio-psychological background of the non-Jewish minority. This minority has largely an Arab-nationalist consciousness. Consequently the problem of conflict between the religious society and the political society is not merely an expression of a parallel phenomenon which exists in many states. For this minority, the State of Israel, as a *Jewish* state, presents the further problem of political identity. Whereas in other countries a religious community for the most part identifies with the political structure, even as it struggles to shape its values, (this applies also to the Jewish majority in Israel), in the State of Israel this identification poses a serious problem. Thus the question of the relationship between religion and state assumes a unique form in Israel.

---

[65] Englard, *ibid.*

[66] In this connection compare Jemolo's incisive note on the different conception of the status of religious organ: "La classifica dei rapporti fra Stato e Chiesa," *Pagine sparse di diritto e storiografia* (Milano 1957), pp. 69, 96.

[67] Compare Z. Wahrhaftig, *Rabbinical Jurisdiction in Israel* (Tel Aviv 1955) (in Hebrew), p. 17: "In my view the religious courts should generally be imperialist to the greatest extent possible and should not relinquish their powers. The Rabbinical Court of Appeal has in one of its judgments held that 'in effect all is within our ambit but the law has taken away some part'." Generally see E. Vitta, *Conflitti interni ed internazionali*, vol. I (Torino 1954), pp. 87, 138 et seq.

PART TWO

RECEPTION OF RELIGIOUS LAW

CHAPTER I

INTRODUCTION

Our starting point is the legal system of the state, and we consider the status of religious law primarily as it is reflected in state law. Our examination of the theoretical relationship between the two systems led us to conclude that, in a formal sense, the normative validity of religious law within the state system is conditional on recognition by the latter.[1] We have intentionally used the indefinite concept of "recognition" so as not to depart from the formal aspect which has thus far been our central interest.

In the present Part, however, we shall analyse the various ways in which one system may "recognize" the normative validity of another system. For this purpose "recognition" is not the most suitable term for describing the phenomenon as a whole, since it implies the previous independent existence of the system granted recognition.[2] The term "reception," used here in its widest possible sense, is to be preferred, although it also is not entirely apt for indicating all the situations which interest us, since reception (*receptio*) has a specific meaning in legal literature.[3] We shall use "reception" in its broadest rather than in its technical sense, to embrace all the many situations in which one legal system is "assisted" by another in shaping its content. We have thus a broad spectrum of possibilities, beginning with indirect influence (a source of inspiration) and ending with the grant of autonomy, partial or complete, to another system.

---

[1] Cf. Perassi, *Lezioni di diritto internazionale, II, Introduzione al diritto internazionale privato* (Padova 1952), pp. 50 et seq.
[2] The concept of recognition is indeed used by Gismondi, who regards the reception of the Canon Law as a unique phenomenon unlike the ordinary reception of foreign law (see below). He holds that Canon Law has an independent normative existence which the State recognizes: *Il potere di certificazione della Chiesa nel diritto italiano* (Milano 1943), pp. 28 et seq.
[3] Cf. G. Tedeschi, "On Reception and on the Legislative Policy of Israel," *Scripta Hierosolymitana,* Vol. XVI (Jerusalem 1966), pp. 11 et seq.; M. Rheinstein, "Types of Reception," 6 (1956) *Annales de la Faculté de Droit d'Istanbul* 33.

The Italian school has been outstanding in the theoretical analysis of the types of reception. On foundations laid by German scholars at the end of the last century,[4] its analysis of the problems of reception, albeit mainly in the realm of public and private international law, has exerted very considerable influence on students of ecclesiastical law in Italy, seeking to clarify the status of religious law under state law.[5]

In the light of general concepts developed in public and private international law a sharp and prolonged debate ensued among students of ecclesiastical law over the question whether these concepts are applicable to the relationship between state and religious law.[6] Many doubted the use of conceptual forms which had been developed to describe the techniques of reception in the legal systems of different states.[7] The argument was that no analogy is to be drawn from the status of one country's law within another country to the status of religious law within a single country. The two situations are fundamentally different in both background and purpose. The church itself functions within the state and addresses citizens directly; thus religious law and state law apply to the same public and give rise to a kind of competition between the two systems. In contrast, the relationship between different states is based on the idea of the mutual recognition of sovereignty and no one state seeks to infuse its rules of law into the body of another state.[8]

These differences certainly exist and great significance attaches to them at the substantive level. They affect the substantive establishment of a relationship between different normative systems. The *content* of the re-

---

[4] A. Bernardini, *Produzione di norme giuridiche mediante rinvio* (Milano 1966), *passim;* Szászy, "Interpersonal Conflicts of Laws," *Multitudo Legum—Ius Unum,* (Berlin 1973) Band 2, pp. 793, 799–800.

[5] To a certain degree the conclusions have exerted influence even on the question of the status of state law in the Canon law; see P. Bellini, "Per una sistemazione canonistica delle relazioni fra diritto della Chiesa e diritto dello Stato," 30 (1954) *Annuario di diritto comparato e di studi legislativi, passim.*

[6] See the review in F. Margiotta Broglio, "La qualificazione giuridica delle relazioni fra lo Stato e la Chiesa Cattolica," 165 (1963) *Archivio Giuridico* 51.

[7] Cf. D'Avack, "La posizione giuridica del diritto canonico nell'ordinamento italiano," (1939), *Archivio di diritto ecclesiastico,* 205; Id., *Trattato di diritto ecclesiastico italiano* (Milano 1964), pp. 155 et seq.; Jemolo, "La classifica dei rapporti fra Stato e Chiesa," *Pagine sparse di diritto e storiografia,* (Milano 1957), pp. 69, 89 et seq.; Giacchi, "L'ordinamento della Chiesa nel diritto italiano attuale," *Chiesa e Stato* (Milano 1939), vol. II. p. 345; Gismondi, *op. cit.,* pp. 23 et seq.; Id., *Lezioni di diritto ecclesiastico* (2a ed. Milano 1965), pp. 3 et seq.; Margiotta Broglio, *op. cit., passim.*

[8] Cf. Jemolo, *op. et loc. cit.;* D'Avack, *op. et loc. cit.*

sulting order varies as a result of the profound difference in the background of the problem. Yet we must distinguish between the substantive and the formal levels. We see no obstacle to resorting to general concepts developed in other areas, if they express the formal aspect of the relationship between receiving and received law, that is, to the technique of reception.[9] It would appear that the debate arises largely from a failure to distinguish between the formal and the substantive levels.[10]

But even if importance attaches to the development of legal concepts and their use—a subject discussed above—the intention here is not to stress the theoretical analysis of the various technical forms, an analysis which has so greatly occupied Italian thinking. The object is not to fashion abstract concepts of a singular and fixed nature but the much more modest one of describing the normative *reality* by means of concepts which can be used as convenient tools for understanding the phenomenon.[11] We do not believe that the conceptual forms can give clear-cut solutions to substantive questions. They may serve as one basis, at times an important one, for finding a solution, but often there is neither complete nor necessary identity between formal shape and actual solution.[12]

In point of legislative technique two principal ways of receiving another system—direct reception and reception by reference—are distinguishable: In direct reception the local system is indeed "aided" by the other in moulding the content of its provisions but it prescribes these in all their details *directly* by itself. By contrast, in the case of reception by reference, the receiving system does not directly prescribe the content of the legal rules but turns for this purpose to the other system. These two types of situations will be discussed separately. It should, however, be remembered

---

[9] Checchini, "Introduzione dommatica al diritto ecclesiastico italiano," *Scritti giuridici e storico-giuridici*, vol. III (Padova 1958), p. 11; Id., "L'ordinamento canonico nel diritto italiano," *Scritti giuridici*, p. 71; cf. Giacchi, *op. ult. cit.*, p. 366; Bernardini, *op. cit.*, pp. 320 et seq.

[10] Cf. Englard, "Il diritto ecclesiastico italiano visto da un giurista straniero," (1968) *Il diritto ecclesiastico* 22, 49 et seq.

[11] It is not our intention here to venture a clarification of the problem of the general nature of legal concepts, a complicated and difficult problem. The question has occupied many writers on church-state relationships. See, Jemolo, *op. et loc. cit.*; Id., "I concetti giuridici," *Pagine sparse*, pp. 100 et seq.; "Ancora sui concetti giuridici," pp. 117 et seq.; G. Caputo, *Il problema della qualificazione giuridica dello Stato in materia religiosa* (Milano 1967), pp. 3 et seq., spec. p. 6, n. 9.

[12] Cf. Jemolo, "La classifica" etc., p. 81; Larenz, *Methodenlehre der Rechtswissenschaft* (Berlin 1969), pp. 332–333, 412 et seq., 419.

that although a clear technical distinction exists between these two modes of reception, in practice they may merge. For example, a domestic law may repeat word by word the text of a foreign provision and this would constitute a case of direct reception. Nevertheless, exactly the same result is achieved by a general reference to the foreign provision, which is a case of reception by reference. In most instances, however, the distinction is of importance, especially in the field of religious law.

Chapter II

DIRECT RECEPTION

The characteristic feature of direct reception is that although the lawmaker relies on another system, he himself legislates fully as with any other law, not only in the formal sense (which is always necessarily an independent and complete act) but also in the substantive sense. The regulatory content is made explicit in statutory language as such.[1]

Obviously, the extent of reliance on another system is a question of degree, varying from literal reproduction to more remote influence on the form or content of a legal rule.[2] Israeli law, comprising as it does many and varied strata, is a living example of direct reception of various kinds.

The reproduction of entire sections of foreign legal codes was effected under the Ottoman regime in the previous century,[3] and traces still remain. Direct reception of complete legislative acts occurred in not a few cases even in Mandatory times, when British laws[4] or codifications of English common law which had been prepared for the colonies were introduced with only minor changes.[5] Today the independent lawmaking of the Israeli legislature is more eclectic.

In the sphere of religious law, we do not come across direct reception

---

[1] Since our interest lies in the relationship between one system and another, we do not consider here the possibility of an internal reference from one legal rule to another in the same system. Internal reference is a common technique in legislation. Moreover, the content of the regulation of a specific situation is generally not found in a single norm but in the integration of the norm in the general normative framework.

[2] Cf. Rheinstein, *op. et loc. cit.*, p. 36; Tedeschi, "On Reception," *cit.*, pp. 23 et seq.

[3] Cf. Belgesay, "La reception des lois étrangères en Turquie," (1956) *Annales de la Faculté de Droit d'Istanbul*, 93.

[4] For example, the Interpretation Ordinance, 1945; Company Ordinance, 1929; Bankruptcy Ordinance, 1936; Bills of Exchange Ordinance, 1929.

[5] For example, the Criminal Law Ordinance, 1936; Civil Wrongs Ordinance, 1944.

of entire religious legal enactments. The reason is simple. Jewish religious law, the *Halakha,* has not undergone a final process of codification and its rules lie scattered throughout the "sea of the Talmud." [6] Accordingly, even had the secular lawmaker wished to take over some Jewish religious law, he could not do so because of the absence of any legislative enactments in modern form. In Israeli law the direct reception of Jewish law is mainly of two kinds. In the area of civil law, the main reason for receiving Jewish law is national and no ideological questions of individual freedom in religious matters arise. The religious character of Jewish law is not recognizable in such reception; the lawmaker simply borrows terminology,[7] formulas,[8] legal institutions and even substantive solutions.[9] The second kind of direct reception occurs in the area of religious practices. Here reception is carried out differently since the purpose of the legislation is different. What is largely involved is the introduction of religious prohibitions in connection with the observance of the Sabbath and the dietary laws.[10] The purpose is to achieve a specific result sought by religious law, a certain kind of conduct compatible with religious prescript. The emphasis therefore is on finding effective means of achieving

[6] For a general discussion of the question of codification of the Jewish law, see M. Elon, *Jewish Law—History, Sources, Principles* (Hebrew) (Jerusalem 1973) vol. 3, pp. 938 et seq.

[7] Such as "defamation," (Lashon HaRa) (Prohibition of Defamation Law, 5725–1965), "bailee for hire," "gratuitous bailee" and "borrower" (Bailment Law, 5727–1967). In other cases, the Talmudic term is only a translation of a concept taken from English Law. On this phenomenon and the problems it raises see, Tedeschi, "On Reception," *cit.,* pp. 34 et seq.

[8] Such as "A person's agent has the same status as that person himself," sec. 2, Agency Law, 5725—1965. On this legal maxim in Jewish Law generally see N. Rakover, *The Jewish Law of Agency in Legal Proceedings* (Hebrew) (Jerusalem 1972) pp. 11 et seq.

[9] See, in greater detail, M. Elon, "Jewish Law in the Law of the State," (1969) *HaPraklit* 27, 34 et seq.; N. Rakover, "The Principles of Hebrew Law in the Gift Law, 5728—1968" (1969) 24 *HaPraklit* 496. On the question of principle involved in this form of reception, see Englard, "The Problem of Jewish Law in a Jewish State" (1968) 3 *Is.L.Rev.* 245, and the reply of Elon, *op. cit.,* pp. 45 et seq. For a general discussion of the reception of concepts, see also Triepel, *Völkerrecht und Landesrecht* (Leipzig 1899), pp. 163 et seq.; *Id.,* "Les rapports entre le droit interne et le droit international," (1923) *Recueil des Cours,* pp. 77, 96 et seq.

[10] For example, the Prohibiting of Pig Raising Law, 5723—1963; and cf. M. Elon, *Religious Legislation* (Hebrew), (1968), pp. 4–5, 24 et seq. Cf. also the problem of autopsies, Anatomy and Pathology Law, 5713—1953, and see Elon, *ibid,* pp. 24 et seq.

the result and not on the manner of drafting. This is reception of the *purpose of religious law*. The content of state law may thus be varied in order to achieve the desired result. The influence of religious law need not be felt in the language of state law.

Laws still exist in the State of Israel which are the product of direct reception of Moslem law effected during the Ottoman regime. Since Moslem law also remains uncodified, the Ottoman lawmaker was obliged to edit. The result was the Mejelle, some of the provisions of which are still in force in Israel, based on Hanafite Moslem law.[11]

Direct reception of any kind creates no basic problems concerning the relation between autonomous normative systems since the legislative technique results in the *absorption* of the foreign system into the local one and but for our knowledge of the legislative history we would not in many cases know which came first.[12] The major problems in this area relate to the possibility of referring to the sources of the received law for purposes of interpretation and supplying *lacunae*.

---

[11] Cf. Omar, "La codification d'une partie du droit musulman dans l'empire ottoman," 4 (1954) *Annales de la Faculté de droit d'Istanbul* 90. See generally Tedeschi, "One Hundred Years of the Mejelle," (1969), 25 *HaPraklit* 312. Another question is whether the Ottoman legislator should be regarded as a secular and foreign body from the point of view of Moslem religious law. It is possible that the codification and introduction of a legal code based on religious law was legitimate legislation even from the religious point of view; thus the legislator exercised his authority as the leader of the faithful. Cf. the report of the Mejelle Commission: C.A. Hooper, *The Civil Law of Palestine and Trans-Jordan* (London 1934), pp. 1 et seq.

[12] Cf. generally, Perassi, *Lezioni di diritto internazionale*, p. 59; Magni, *Teoria del diritto ecclesiastico civile*, I (2a ed., Padova 1952), pp. 83 et seq.

CHAPTER III

RECEPTION BY REFERENCE

Apart from private international law, there are many instances in Israeli law of references to other normative systems, such as the English. The most part of the reception of religious law has been carried out by this technique of reference. Any systematic type-classification, however, meets with considerable difficulties. Despite the abundant intellectual effort expended on theoretical analysis of the institution of reference, particularly by the Italians, the variety of views hinders a systematic presentation. In addition to differing points of departure, most writers are not strict in applying a single criterion. More particularly they err in confusing three fundamental elements: legislative policy and the attitude to received law; the structure of the receiving norm and the influence of reception on this structure; the status of the received norm within the receiving system. These three elements are beyond doubt of the utmost importance in any analysis of the matter, but the persistent endeavour to arrive at some synthesis in the form of a single concept (a type of reference) has led to a lack of systematic precision and ultimately a blurring of concepts. We shall concentrate on those distinctions which seem important in the reception of religious law, not forgetting that there are other aspects to make the picture complete.

As with "direct reception", there are many degrees of reliance on the foreign system,[1] but two types may be distinguished. One is specific to

[1] The extent of the reliance on a foreign system is not dependent only on the scope of the matters on which the legislator refers to the foreign system. The "depth" of the reception is most important. Sometimes a provision taken from a foreign system is closely interconnected with many other provisions of the normative system and cannot exist without them. In such case, it can only be transplanted with the other norms. On the other hand, there are provisions which are not so interrelated with other norms and can easily be isolated and introduced into another system. The latter include technical provisions such as those relating to age, time and the like; the former include basic legal institutions. This important distinction has been emphasized by Magni, *Teoria del*

the technique of reference. Whilst in direct reception the legislative will extend always to every detail of the provision prescribed, in reference reception the lawmaker is often quite unfamiliar with the substantive content of the provision to which reference is made or pays no regard thereto. Thus a greater degree of reliance occurs in point not of substantive ambit but of the confidence reposed in the received system. But the concept of reference also covers situations where a lawmaker turns to a specific piece of foreign legislation. Such reference,[2] instances of which are to be found in our system,[3] is very close in nature to direct reception of a legislative act. The difference is that in the former the lawmaker forgoes a literal reproduction of the original and is satisfied with a reference to it. In both cases, however, he has knowledge of the content, has taken heed of it and finds the specific solution which it embodies desirable.[4] In the case of religious law no reference to a specific version is to be found in our law for the same reasons that there is no direct reception of a complete enactment. We need not therefore discuss this aspect any further.

The degree of reliance on another system is not judged according only to the scope of the matters to which the reference applies; it may also be affected by the structure of the receiving norm. To clarify this point, which

---

diritto ecclesiastico civile, I (Padova 1952), pp. 87 et seq., who speaks of degrees of combination (*grado di combinabilità*) or valency (*valenza*).

[2] This kind of reference is variously described in the literature: "receiving reference," "substantive reference," etc.; Perassi, *op. cit.,* pp. 60 et seq.: *"rinvio ricettizio o materiale."* Bernardini, *op. cit., passim,* (*"rinvio redazionale"*); Balladore-Pallieri, *Diritto internazionale privato* (Milano 1946), pp. 23 et seq. (*rinvio ricettizio*).

[3] See the British laws applied in Palestine by Article 35 of the Palestine Order in Council, 1922. In the local law there is another type of reception of a complete law in an intermediate manner: a reference to a foreign law set out in an appendix to the local law. See the Carriage of Goods by Sea Ordinance, 1926, which gives force to an international treaty; the treaty provisions appear in the schedule to the Ordinance.

[4] On the nature of a reference to a specific version and clarification of the relation between such a reference and a receiving reference, see Bernardini, *op. cit.,* pp. 115 et seq.; cf. Balladore-Pallieri, *op. cit.;* De Luca, *Rilevanza dell'ordinamento canonico nel diritto italiano* (Padova 1943), pp. 146 et seq. These authors note the important fact that even in the case of a reference to a formula or specific version the process of reception effects a change in the content of the received norm. The integration of the foreign provisions into the receiving normative system involves changes resulting from the necessity of *adaptation* of the received rules to the other rules and the different factual situation. On the problem of adaptation see below pp. 199 et seq.

yields a most important distinction in the types of reference, let us look briefly at the typical structure of a legal rule.

In general it may be said that every legal norm in its simplest form comprises two elements—a *fact situation* and a *legal result*.[5] The *fact situation* is an event occurring under circumstances formulated in general abstract form.[6] Within the framework of the norm it is regarded as a hypothetical situation likely to occur in a multitude of instances. The *legal result* is the consequence which the law attaches to the fact situation,[7] that is, the creation or change or extinction of a legal situation.[8]

Three types of reference emerge from this analysis, which are actually two. First, the lawmaker may refer to the foreign law in order to complete one or other base of the fact situation, but reserve to himself the determination of the legal result. Secondly, the lawmaker may himself determine the fact situation and turn to the foreign system for the legal result. The third possibility is a combination of the first two and thus contains no

---

[5] Larenz, *Methodenlehre der Rechtswissenschaft*, (Berlin 1969), pp. 149 et seq., 187: "Seiner Form nach ist der Rechtssatz eine *hypothetische Geltungsanordnung*. Er besagt: Wenn der Tatbestand T in einem (konkreten) Sachverhalt S verwirklicht ist, dann gilt jeweils für diesen Sachverhalt die Rechtsfolge R; kürzer: für jeden Fall von T gilt R."; Engisch, *Einführung in das juristische Denken* (Stuttgart 1971), pp. 12 et seq.; Enneccerus-Nipperdey, *Allgemeiner Teil des bürgerlichen Rechts* (14. Aufl. Tübingen 1955), 136; Bernardini, *op. cit.*, pp. 8 et seq., Pescatore, *Introduction à la science du droit* (Louxembourg 1960), pp. 192 et seq.

[6] With respect to the nature of the fact situation, see the sources cited in the preceding note. One should emphasize the difference between the hypothetical fact situation indicated in the legal rule and the concrete fact situation encountered in reality. See Engisch, *op. cit.*, p. 34.

[7] For example, a legal rule may provide that if one causes harm to another by his negligence, he is liable for damages. The fact situation is the negligent causing of harm; the legal result—the liability to pay damages. Here there is also a difference between the abstract consequence and the concrete result of the liability to pay a certain sum as a result of a specific harm. On the relation between the fact situation and the legal result, see Engisch, *op. cit.*, pp. 35 et seq.; Larenz, *op. cit.*, p. 192: "Die Rechtsfolge selbst ist kein raumzeitliches, in diesem Sinne 'reales' Geschehen—sie darf nicht mit dem angestrebten *tatsächlichen* 'Erfolg' verwechselt werden —, sondern eine Veränderung in der Welt des rechtlich Geltenden, d.h. des vermöge seiner inneren Bindkraft als massgeblich Erachteten." And see the sources given in Engisch, *ibid.*, n. 22.

[8] The nature of legal consequences is in dispute. Some hold that it always goes to the legal rights and duties. In Kelsen's view, the complete legal norm includes the determination of the sanction. Kelsen, *Pure Theory of Law*, pp. 51 et seq.; cf. Larenz, *ibid.*; Engisch, *op. cit.*, pp. 19 et seq.

theoretical novelty.[9] The two main possibilities may be illustrated from Israeli law in connection with the reception of religious law.

Regulation 192 of the Civil Procedure Regulations, 5723—1963, prescribes the manner of administering an oath to a priest or member of a religious order. It provides that the oath is to be administered by the bishop or the head of the religious order. The regulation speaks of a priest, member of a religious order, bishop and head of a religious order without defining, for obvious reasons, these individuals. Here we have an example of reference to the various religious laws which determine the status of the people mentioned. But the determination of status by religious law is only part of the fact situation of the receiving norm; the legal result is entirely determined by the regulation itself—hearing of the testimony as if the witness had been sworn in court.

Again, section 1 of the Rabbinical Courts Jurisdiction (Marriage and Divorce) Law, 5713—1953, states that matters of marriage and divorce of *Jews* shall be under the jurisdiction of rabbinical courts. The term "Jew" not being defined, a reference to Jewish religious law is required for determining who is a Jew for the purposes of the Law.[10] But being Jewish is only one element of the fact situation with which the legal result,

---

[9] For the three types mentioned see also, De Luca, *op. cit.*, pp. 160 et seq.; Bellini, "Per una sistemazione canonistica delle relazioni tra diritto della Chiesa e diritto dello Stato," (1955) *Ann. di dir. comp. e di studi legislativi*, 338, para. 75; cf. Larenz, *op. cit.*, pp. 164 et seq.; Zitelmann, *Internationales Privatrecht*, I (1897) pp. 208–210; Lewald, *Règles générales des conflits de lois*, (1941), pp. 9, 78 et seq.

[10] This was the interpretation of the Supreme Court in *Rufeisen* (H.C.J. 72/62, 16 P.D. 2428, 2437, English translation S.J.S.C., Special Volume 1971, p. 10): "The Rabbinical Courts Jurisdiction (Marriage and Divorce) Law was enacted for the purpose of extending rabbinical jurisdiction. It is an 'open secret' that the extension was sought and granted in order to widen the application of Jewish religious law to Jews. Hence the further question who is a Jew for the purposes of this law must be answered according to Jewish law. If it were to be answered on the basis of other considerations, extrinsic, secular or outside the framework of Jewish law, then the law applicable would no longer be Jewish religious law." See also A. L. Globus, "Responsa Concerning Family Law and Personal Status (Who is a Jew Under Existing Law)," (1954) 10 *HaPraklit*, 225, 231 et seq.; S. Perles, "Rabbinical Courts Jurisdiction (Marriage and Divorce) Law, 5713–1953, and its Relationship to Earlier Laws" (1954) 10 *HaPraklit*, 272. See also M. Silberg, *Personal Status in Israel* (Hebrew) (Jerusalem 1957) p. 352: "Jewish law alone therefore determines whether a person is a Jew, just as Christian or Moslem religious law exclusively determines whether a person is Christian or a Moslem."

(jurisdiction of the religious court), determined by the lawmaker himself, is connected.

This type of reference, of which many more examples involving religious law may be found,[11] has already been explored by Triepel,[12] one of the first to attempt a classification of the different forms of reference. He called this type of reference of completing the fact situation, a "non-receiving blank legal rule" (*nicht-rezipierender Blankettrechtssatz*).[13] It therefore goes to the structure and function of the referring norm. Others have called it *formal* reference[14] or reference to a presupposed law since the foreign system is intended not to be applied (in the technical sense)[15] but to serve as a pre-condition to the application of domestic law.

It is noteworthy that in a great many cases we do not find *express* reference to another system or to religious law. The lawmaker's intention to refer is implied from his use of concepts taken from the other system.

---

[11] A further example is Article 54 of the Palestine Order in Council, 1922, which grants jurisdiction to the Christian religious courts. The existence of these courts and their composition are determined by various religious laws. See E. Vitta, *Conflict of Law in Matters of Personal Status in Palestine*, (Tel Aviv, 1947) pp. 115 et seq. In the State Education Law 5713–1953, "religious state education" is defined as "State education, with the distinction that its institutions are religious as their way of life, curriculum, teachers and inspectors." The Law does not define the religious way of life. For that we must turn to religious law. See also Section 18 of the Law which permits the disqualification of employees on *religious grounds*. Cf. Section 146 of the Criminal Law Ordinance, 1936 which speaks, among other things, of injury to "an object which is held sacred." See also the Palestine Order in Council (Holy Places), 1924, which restricts the jurisdiction of the courts concerning the Holy Places and religious sites, as well as the Protection of the Holy Places Law, 5727–1967. The term "Holy Place" is not defined and it must be understood in accordance with the various religious laws or traditions. See also the Protection of Holy Places (The Tomb of Rabbi Shimon Bar Yohai in Meron) Regulations, 5728–1968, which prohibits the desecration of the Sabbath or Jewish holidays in the mausoleum and its courtyard. Desecration is determined by religious law and the legal consequence (the imposition of punishment) by the Regulations.

[12] Triepel, *Völkerrecht und Landesrecht* (Leipzig 1899), pp. 156 et seq.; *Id.*, "Les rapports entre le droit interne et le droit international," (1923) *Recueil des cours*, 77 et seq., 92.

[13] *Op. cit.*, pp. 162, 226 et seq.; cf. Bernardini, *op. cit.*, pp. 73 et seq., 78 et seq.

[14] Anzilotti, *Corso di diritto internazionale*, I (Padova 1955), pp. 58 et seq. Perassi, *op. cit.*, pp. 51 et seq.; Bellini, *op. et loc. cit.* Confusion of terms must be avoided. The expressions "formal reference" and "substantive reference" appear in various meanings which are occasionally contradictory. As we shall see, note 30 employs the term "formal reference" in a different sense.

[15] Cf. Bellini, *op. et loc. cit.*; Bernardini, *op. cit.*, pp. 364 et seq.

This may create difficulties in those cases where we are not certain whether the lawmaker wished indeed to refer to another system, or whether he intended to give his own meaning to the concept employed.[16] This problem has special relevance in Israeli law, where the lawmaker often borrows terms from Jewish legal tradition in order to express his independent ideas.[17] A good example in the area of religion-state relations is provided by the *Rufeisen* case.[18] The question was how to interpret the term "Jew" in the original Law of Return, 5710—1950. The court decided unanimously—although not explicitly mentioning the technical concept of reference—that the status of "Jew" for the purposes of this Law is not to be determined by the categories of Jewish religious law but that the term is to be construed by the ordinary rules of interpretation.[19] In maintaining that the legislator intended to give the term "Jew" an independent meaning the Court denied reference to religious law for completing the

[16] Triepel, *op. cit.*, pp. 163 et seq.; W. Wengler, *Völkerrecht*, Band 1 (Berlin 1964) pp. 86 et seq.
[17] Cf. Tedeschi, *On Reception, cit.*, pp. 34 et seq.
[18] H.C.J. 72/62, 16 P.D. 2428; (English translation in S.J.S.C., Special Volume 1971, 1).
[19] *Ibid.*, at 2438 (10) (per Justice Silberg): "For all its immense historical importance this law is a secular Law, and in the absence of definitions, either in the statute itself or in the case law, we must interpret its terms according to their ordinary meaning, having regard, where departing from that, for the legislative purpose behind its provisions"; at 2445 (19) (per Justice Landau): "The fate of this petition will not be decided by religious law, but solely by the Law of Return which is a secular Law of the State of Israel. The question before us is what did the legislature intend when it used the term 'Jew' in that Law?" We are not convinced by the argument that since the Law of Return is a secular law, one should not refer to religious Jewish law in order to determine who is considered a Jew for its purpose, because every reference to religious law must be based on a law of the State. The holding of Justice Cohn (at 2440) (14) that "Religious law does not apply in Israel save in matters of marriage and divorce," is not correct, as has been shown in the examples of reference cited at note 11. In principle there is no reason to prefer the assumption that there is here no reference to Jewish law over the contrary assumption. Both possibilities exist and the choice between them should be based on the intention of the legislator. The decision of the court has led to a splitting of the term "Jew" with different significance in different Laws. The truth is that the term "Jew" in the Law of Return has not been completely cut off from the tests of religious law. The popular interpretation of the term which the Court put forward is a mixture of various tests in which religious tests play an important if not always decisive role. A similar phenomenon in the relationship between domestic and international law was noted by Wengler, *op. et loc. cit.*: "Selbstverständlich ist es auch möglich, dass das staatliche Recht unter

fact situation.[20] After it had affirmed this interpretation in *Shalit*,[21] the legislature intervened by adding a statutory definition of "Jew".[21a]

The second type, reference for determining the legal result, is also frequent in the area of religious law. The traditional and general principle in Israeli law, that questions of personal status of residents are decided according to the law of their religion may serve as an example. The principle itself is extremely broad and is not restricted to any one fact situation or any particular legal result. It embodies a complex of fact situations and of legal results prescribed by religious law. (The principle would appear to constitute basically the third possibility mentioned, ref-

Umständen dieselben *Worte* verwendet wie ein Völkerrechtssatz, dass es aber den Inhalt der mit dem Wort bezeichneten Begriffe 'autonom' bestimmt, wenn sich auch oft der autonom bestimmte Begriffsinhalt grossenteils mit dem Inhalt decken wird, den das Völkerrecht mit dem betreffenden Wort verbindet."

[20] In *Rufeisen* the court proceeded from the assumption, that, in accordance with *Halakha*, an apostate is nonetheless considered a Jew. "In accordance with its general basic principles, the Jewish religion refuses to recognize the capacity of any Jew to remove himself from all that makes up Judaism, however much he may wish to do so. This is not due to any attitude of tolerance or forbearance towards the Jew who voluntarily embraces Christianity. The reason is rather that complete disregard of the act of conversion is necessary in determining his personal status as a Jew, of one who forever remains a Jew" (at 2444). Therefore the Court argued that if the meaning of "Jew" in the Law of Return were identical with its religious meaning, it would have been necessary to grant the petition, that is to say, to recognize the legal consequence of granting the petitioner citizenship as a Jewish immigrant. This approach has been highly criticized on the grounds that according to Jewish law, an apostate would not be considered a Jew *entitled to benefit from the rights granted by the Law of Return*. If this case had been decided by a religious court it would have reached the conclusion that the petitioner should not be recognized as a Jewish immigrant in the meaning of the Law of Return as did the secular court in accordance with the secular test (See M. Elon, *Religious Legislation*, [Hebrew] pp. 52–53). This criticism is not well taken. Had the Court rejected the petition on this ground, it would have turned to religious law for the sake of determining not the factual situation but *the legal consequences;* a Jew is considered a Jewish immigrant under the Law of Return if this status is recognized under Jewish law. Such an interpretation is quite inconsistent with the terms of the secular Law which alone set out the legal consequences. The only possibility was a reference for determining the fact situation of the legal rule, and this possibility was rejected by the Court.

[21] H.C.J. 58/68 23 P.D. (2) 477 (S.J.S.C. Special Volume, 1971, 35).

[21a] Section 4B of the Law of Return (inserted by an amendment of 1970): "For the purpose of this Law, 'Jew' means a person who was born of a Jewish mother or has become converted to Judaism and who is not a member of another religion". See below n. 68.

erence for completing the fact situation combined with reference for determining legal result.)[22]

A more specific example is found in the matter of maintenance. Section 2 of the Family Law Amendment (Maintenance) Law, 5719–1959, states that "a person is liable for the maintenance of his spouse in accordance with the provisions of the personal law applying to him." The legal result here is the duty to maintain and it is determined by reference to religious law. A similar provision is found in section 3 of the same Law, dealing with the maintenance of minor children.

The distinction between a reference for completing a fact situation (hereafter called a *fact reference*) and one for determining legal result (*law reference*), already noted by Triepel,[23] has met the approval of the vast majority of writers.[24] The main difficulties arose when the attempt was made to classify the various law references and understand their nature. As we shall see, these attempts also had their effect on religious law references. Triepel's analysis can serve as a starting point since later Italian studies are based on it.

Triepel differentiates between three types of law reference:

1) The receiving reference, or the "receiving blank legal rule" (*rezipierender Blankettrechtssatz*). Here the referring norm provides for the actual reception of the content of the external norm into internal law, as when the legislator provides that a certain fact situation is to be regulated in domestic law *exactly as it would be in the other system.*[25]

2) The rules of private international law constitute another and separate type of reference. These are "rules of conflict" or "rules of application"[26] which do not result in a reception of the contents of the external

---

[22] "Personal status" is defined in Article 51 of the Palestine Order in Council 1922. It specifies, however, the framework in which the personal law will apply in a general manner only. The concrete legal consequences in matters of personal status are related to the factual situations which are also determined by the personal law. It follows that the law of State defines the boundaries of the application of the religious law whilst religious law itself determines the various elements of the fact situation to which it attaches legal consequences. Cf. De Luca, *op. cit.*, pp. 165 et seq.

[23] Above note 12; see also, Zitelmann, *Internationales Privatrecht*, I (München 1914), p. 165.

[24] Bernardini, *op. cit.*, pp. 303 et seq.; and the sources given there. *But* see the approach of Pau who tends to equate the two forms: *Caratteri del riconoscimento di situazioni giuridiche straniere nell'ordinamento italiano* (Milano 1958); cf. Bernardini, *op. cit.*, p. 365 n. 147 (*in fine*, p. 368), p. 456, n. 10.

[25] Triepel, *op. cit.*, pp. 156 et seq., 226 et seq.

[26] P. 158: "Kollisions-oder Anwendungsnormen."

law or in the latter becoming an organic part of the internal law. The significance of private international law rules lies in *limiting* the application of internal law by directing the judge to apply the foreign law to a given fact situation.

Having regard to the foreign element, the legislature wishes to leave the substantive solution to the foreign law as such. The legislature, as it were, abdicates its power to dispose the matter by its own rules.[27]

3) Reciprocal references between municipal law and international law constitute, according to Triepel, a special type of reference. There is no receiving reference (the first type) and not even a rule of conflict on the pattern of the second type. The reason is that the two systems regulate, from the outset, different subject matter and thus their respective legal results cannot be identical. This identity is an essential element in the receiving reference. Triepel sees in references between municipal and international laws an outcome of a non-receiving blank legal norm, similar to fact reference.[28]

On the basis of Triepel's analysis an extensive literature has grown up, particularly in Italy, in which the suggested classification has been evaluated and many theories evolved, mainly in the area of private international law. Considerable influence has been exerted by the division between receiving reference and the rules of private international law[29] which constitute a special type of reference, called by many writers *formal reference*.[30] A sharp debate ensued on the question of the nature of the rules of reference in private international law, and the correctness of the proposed division. The immense effort made to clarify these questions

---

[27] *Ibid.*, pp. 158–159. Triepel bases his analysis on Zitelmann's viewpoint.

[28] *Op. cit.*, pp. 228–229; *Id.*, "Les Rapports," *op. cit.*, p. 97: "On ne peut naturellement parler d'une réception du droit international par l'Etat que si le contenu de la règle étatique correspond exactement au contenu de la règle juridique internationale. Toute modification du droit exclut la notion de réception juridique. Il est impossible, bien qu'on le fasse très souvent, de désigner sous les appellations d' "acceptation," ou d' "appropriation," ou d' "incorporation," le procédé par lequel l'Etat, pour remplir des devoirs internationaux, édicte des régles correspondantes au droit international. Car le plus souvent ces règles sont des ordres addressés aux individues; elles ne sont donc pas de pures reproductions de règles internationales." It is difficult to see how this type of reference enters the category of fact-references. Compare Bernardini, *op. cit.*, pp. 78 et seq.

[29] See the sources in the comprehensive study of Bernardini, *op. cit.*, *passim*.

[30] Cf. De Luca, *op. cit.*, pp. 55 et seq.; Bernardini, *op. cit.*, pp. 16 et seq. It should be remembered that the phrase "formal reference" is used in various ways, some of them mutually contradictory. See above note 14.

may well surprise a jurist trained in a more pragmatic system who is not particularly interested in the harmonious structure of legal concepts and institutions so long as no real practical consequences follow.[31] As was stated earlier in this chapter, we do not intend to make any innovations in the theory of references, but it is proper to mention at least the main trends so as to be able to study their significance in the area of the state-religious law relationship.

The concept of formal reference has been greatly criticized for being based on the idea that foreign law applies as such where the internal legislator has limited the application of its own law. The objection was that a normative system does not apply "of itself" in a given area simply because another lawmaker "forgoes" applying his internal law. So to hold is contrary—it is argued—to the principle of the exclusiveness and relativity of every normative system.[32]

Writers, recognizing the weight of this criticism, have sought to create a concept of reference which on the one hand bases the application of foreign law on the will of the internal lawmaker alone, and on the other hand is inclined at the same time to explain the autonomous status which foreign law preserves when applied in internal law.[33] Most have agreed that the rules of private international law should be regarded as instru-

---

[31] See the criticism of the Italian school by Francescakis in 45 (1956) *Revue critique de droit international privé* 603–604; cf. E. Rabel, *The Conflict of Laws* (Ann Arbor 1958), Vol. I, pp. 67 et seq.

[32] Anzilotti, *op. cit.*, pp. 58 et seq. And see the other sources in De Luca, *op.cit.*; Bernardini, *op. cit.*, pp. 81 et seq.

[33] We disregard here the approach which ascribes to the rules of the private international law a function under public international law. In this view, which is accepted by many writers, the basis for the application of foreign law is found in the provisions of public international law. On this approach there is place for the concept of *formal reference,* but its basis is completely different, the primacy of public international law defining the boundaries of jurisdiction of the different national legal orders. See in this connection, K. H. Etter, *Vom Einfluss des Souveränitätsgedankens auf das Internationale Privatrecht* (Zürich 1959), pp. 154 et seq.: Cf. Checchini, "Introduzione dommatica al diritto ecclesiastico italiano," *Scritti giuridici e storico giuridici,* vol. III, (Padova 1958), p.35. For the present purpose there is no need to express any opinion on the relationship between private and public international law, since it is clear that in the general relationship between the law of the state and religious law there is no function for the public international law or any other normative system which stands above the two and coordinates them. Hence whatever the situation regarding the rules of private international law, criticism of the concept of formal reference mentioned above is justified in regard to the relationship between the law of the state and religious law. On the function and status of the rules

mental rather than substantive norms.[34] That is to say, the external law does not become part of the norm which refers to it, as if the latter left a place vacant to be filled by the application of the foreign law. The referring norm is an instrumental norm in the sense that it determines the manner in which the foreign norm becomes a norm with internal validity. The purpose of the rules of private international law is to regulate the manner in which rules of conduct in the internal system are created, as distinct from directly determining the substantive solution, which in turn is found in the external norms.[35]

This theorising has produced a new term: *creative reference*,[36] which attempts to express the idea that the rules of reference are norms which affect the way the law is created.[37] But opinion was again divided about the exact technique of this norm-creation. According to one approach, the purpose of the rules of reference is to grant the foreign lawmaker the authority to make binding laws in a limited and defined area for the internal system.[38] This approach is highly artificial and has attracted criticism,[39] and mention will be made only of the principal theories which

of private international law, see also W. Niederer, *Einführung in die allgemeinen Lehren des internationalen Privatrechts* (Zürich 1954), pp. 126 et seq.; Betti, *Problematica del diritto internazionale* (Milano 1956), pp. 126 et seq. and the sources cited there.

[34] On the distinction see De Luca, *op. cit.*, pp. 86 et seq. The author also explains the approach of the normative school which sees no essential distinction between the two types of norms. Cf. Kelsen, *Pure Theory of Law*, p. 235.

[35] See generally Bernardini, *op. cit., passim;* Etter, *op. cit.*, pp. 156 et seq.; Battifol, *Droit international privé* (5e éd. Paris 1970), vol. 1, pp. 389 et seq. Again, no opinion need be expressed about the correctness of this view in relation to the rules of private international law. It is incorrect in the eyes of those who see in them rules of jurisdiction and competency connected with public international law; see note 33. See also the view of Balladore-Pallieri (*op. et loc. cit.*) who actually considers the rules of private international law substantive rules.

[36] *"Rinvio di produzione giuridica."* Cf. Betti, *op. cit.*, p. 139, who criticizes the phrase, preferring *"rinvio riproducente."*

[37] Bernardini, *op. cit.*, pp. 163 et seq.; cf. Wengler, *Völkerrecht, cit.*, pp. 64 et seq., 442 et seq.; De Nova, "New Trends in Italian Private International Law," 28 (1963) *Law & Contemp. Problems,* 808, 812–13; cf. Szászy, "Interpersonal Conflict of Laws," *cit.* p. 800.

[38] Ghirardini, "La comunità internazionale e il suo diritto," (1919), *Riv. Dir. Intern.* 3; cf. Bernardini, *op. cit.*, pp. 172 et seq.; De Luca, *op. cit.*, pp. 62 et seq.

[39] Bernardini, *op. et loc. cit.;* De Luca, *op. cit.*, pp. 64, 128 et seq.; Balladore-Pallieri, *op. cit.*, pp. 26 et seq. and the sources mentioned.

offer a different explanation. One maintains that the rules of reference confer legal validity upon the foreign system by viewing the foreign law (as distinct from the foreign legislature) as legal acts or, according to a more common approach, as legal facts.[40] Another theory, also found in varying forms, understands differently the creative role of the reference norm, in holding that once the elements of the fact situation are present, the reference norm creates a new norm in the local system whose content corresponds to that of the referred foreign norm.[41] Without going into the various viewpoints, it may be said that for the most part the differences between them are theoretical alone without real practical effect.[42]

On the other hand, we should note a few more distinctions which are of practical importance for us.

Conditional References

Sometimes a particular legal result is conditional on the existence of certain legal consequences in another system. Thus under the *principle of reciprocity* Israeli law will recognize a certain legal result provided that the foreign law recognizes a corresponding result in relation to Israeli citizens or some other like proviso.[43] In the area of religious law we come

---

[40] Morelli, "Limiti dell'ordinamento statuale e limiti della giurisdizione," (1933), *Riv. Dir. Int.* 391; De Luca, *op. cit.*, pp. 63 et seq.; Bernardini, *op. cit., ibid. et passim.*

[41] This approach finds expression in the theory of automatic creation (produzione automatica) based on Perassi (cf. *Lezioni di diritto internazionale*, II, [Padova 1952], pp. 63 et seq.) For this theory and its various aspects see Bernardini, *op. cit.*, pp. 731 et seq. On the connection between it and the theory of "local law" as developed in the United States, see Rabel, *op. cit.*, p. 68. On the problem of the reception of foreign law by virtue of the rules of private international law in American literature, see generally Cheatham, "American Theories of Conflict of Laws: Their Role and Utility," 58 (1944–45) *Harv. L. R.* 361, 365.

[42] Bernardini, whom we have already cited several times, has a comprehensive analysis of the many viewpoints existing in Italy. It should be noted that Italian literature deals with this subject on the most abstract level and it is not easy to follow the subtle distinctions expounded. In not a few cases the matter appears to the present writer esoteric. Nonetheless we should not detract from the effort to clarify the theoretical foundations of the institution of reference. See, however, the comment of Rabel, *op. cit.*, p. 69: "After all, why can the foreign rule not simply come into court without crutches?"

[43] See, for instance, sec. 4(a) of the Foreign Judgments Enforcement Law, 5718–1958: "A foreign judgment shall not be declared enforceable if it was given in a state the laws of which do not provide for the enforcement of judgments of Israel courts."

across a conditional reference of a different kind. Section 3(b) of the Family Law Amendment (Maintenance) Law, 5719—1959, provides that: "A person who is not liable for the maintenance of his minor children or the minor children of his spouse according to the provisions of the personal law applying to him, ... is liable for (their) maintenance, and the provisions of this Law shall apply to that maintenance." The legislature has referred to religious law, the personal law of local residents, in order to establish the legal situation thereunder as a condition for the application of secular law. Here the condition is of a negative nature. The *conditional reference* is structurally akin to a fact reference but not identical with it.[44]

Univalent and Polyvalent References

Another distinction concerns the identification of the foreign system; it may be a single one or a number of systems chosen according to the factual context. By way of example, under section 2 of Rabbinical Courts Jurisdiction (Marriage and Divorce) Law, 5713–1953, marriage and divorce of Jews in Israel are to be performed in accordance with Jewish religious law; here is a reference to a particular religious law—a univalent reference. In contrast, a provision referring us to a person's personal law or the law of his domicile does not touch only one system, and is thus a *polyvalent reference*.[45]

Static and Dynamic References

Another important distinction relates to the status of foreign law as a living, autonomous system. It is possible to refer to another system in terms of its situation at the time of reference or some other specified moment. In this case the reference is to a "frozen" legal situation, a one-time photograph, as it were, of the foreign system. Thus, a reference to a particular statute is by its very nature a *static* reference.[46] Static references reduce the autonomy of the foreign system by not receiving it in its living and dynamic existence. Freezing the legal situation involves extrapolating the received norms from the living normative pattern. In Israeli law debate

---

[44] On the classification of references see in particular Perassi, *op. cit.*, pp. 51 et seq.; Betti, *op. cit.*, pp. 134 et seq. Both writers differentiate between fact reference and conditional reference. They specify different types of conditional reference.

[45] Cf. Bernardini, *op. cit.*, pp. 93 n. 59, 528 et seq. (*rinvio polivalente*).

[46] Triepel, *op. cit.*, pp. 161 et seq.; Walz, *Völkerrecht und staatliches Recht* (Stuttgart 1933), p. 16; Wengler, *op. cit.*, p. 51 ("*starre Verweisung*"); Bernardini, *op. cit.*, pp. 73, 77, 93 ("*rinvio fisso*").

goes on as to whether the reference to the common law in Section 46 of the Palestine Order in Council is static, and if so, what is the moment of "freezing" (the year of the State's establishment, 1948, or the year of the Order in Council, 1922)?[47] *Reference* is *dynamic* when a foreign system is received as it is from time to time.[48] The foreign system thus retains, in the eyes of the receiving system, its independent character, even after the act of reference, and every change in it will affect the content of what is received by the referring system.[49] The rules of private international law are *dynamic* references and so are generally references in local law to religious laws.[50]

Level of Abstraction

Another distinction concerns the level of abstraction of the foreign norm to which reference is made. At times the legislature will turn to the abstract and general foreign law and require the local judge to apply it to the facts of the case before him, that is, to carry out the process of its concretisation. At yet other times the legislature will turn to a concrete legal situation already crystallized in the foreign system itself.[51] These possibilities exist in both law and fact references. Let us give a few examples of fact references. The rule mentioned above, relating to *priests* or *heads of religious orders* in matters of oath-taking[52] assumes the crystallization of a concrete legal situation according to religious law; the fact that a person has the status in question results from the effectuation of the religious rules regulating

---

[47] On this problem see Tedeschi, "The Problem of Lacunae in the Law," *Studies in Israel Law* (Jerusalem 1960), pp. 166, et seq.; Silberg, *Talmudic Law and the Modern State* (New York 1973) pp. 213 et seq. It should be noted that reference to English Common law raises the special problem of its being case law. The question involves the changes which occur in the decisions and it is therefore connected with the questions of binding precedent and the significance of such changes in the Common law. On this last problem see, in particular, Tedeschi, *ibid.*

[48] Cf. Bernardini, *op. et loc. cit.* ("*rinvio mobile*"); Wengler, *op. et loc. cit.*, ("*elastische Verweisung*"); Walz, *op. et loc. cit.;* Triepel, *op. et loc. cit.*

[49] For a discussion of the problem whether a certain reference in internal law is static or dynamic see, Feller, "Reference and Reception Provisions" 25 (1969) *HaPraklit*, 320.

[50] See Tedeschi, "On the Choice Between Religious and Secular Law," *Studies in Israel Law,* pp. 238, 262.

[51] On this distinction see Bernardini, *op. cit.,* pp. 415 et seq., and particularly the sources given there.

[52] See above p. 59.

it. Similarly, when the law demands a marriage licence under a final judgment of a religious court as a defence to bigamy,[53] the reference is again to a concrete legal situation created in a religious system.[54] If, on the other hand, the court has to apply categories of the *Halakha*,[55] e.g., as regards the concept "Jew", the reference will be to the abstract norms of religious law and the task of implementing them falls on the civil judge.

Let us now turn to the significance of these distinctions in the relationship between state and religious law. It emerges from the examples given that references to religious law are not of one kind. Particularly important is the fact that they are not exclusively law references (for determining legal results) but include fact references (for completing the fact situation). Accordingly the technique of the rules of private international law, which are legal references, is not identical with the technique in the area of the more variegated religious law. This is yet another reason why some writers have warned against dependence on theories developed in private international law because of the great difference in status between a foreign state and the church in domestic law.[56]

The special status of the church, in respect both of its internal independence and of its real influence within the state itself, has given prominence to the idea of autonomy in the reception of Canon Law. Writers on ecclesiastical law have largely confined their attention to the question of the degree to which religious law and with it the Catholic Church retain each its autonomous character after reception of the former.[57] They have in fact attempted a synthesis of legislative policy regarding church autonomy, the technical form of reception and its results in respect of the

---

[53] Sections 5 and 6 of the Penal Law Amendment (Bigamy) Law, 5719–1959. Cf. Cr. A. 112/50, *Yosifof v. A.G.* 5 P.D. 481, 500–501, in which Justice Silberg mentions a similar distinction under the previous legal situation.

[54] No regard is had here to the difficult problem of the autonomous status of the religious courts in Israel. For the purpose of the example we assume that they are institutions of a foreign normative system. Cf. p. 46 above and p. 111 below.

[55] In the framework of the Rabbinical Courts Jurisdiction (Marriage and Divorce) Law 5713–1953, see above p. 59.

[56] See above p. 50.

[57] D'Avack, "La posizione giuridica del diritto canonico nell'ordinamento italiano," (1939), *Archivio di diritto ecclesiastico;* Id. *Trattato di diritto ecclesiastico,* I, pp. 84 et seq.; Giacchi, *La giurisdizione ecclesiastica nel diritto italiano* (2a ed. Milano 1970), pp. 352 et seq.; Id., "L'ordinamento della Chiesa nel diritto italiano attuale," *Chiesa e Stato,* vol. II (Milano 1939), p. 345; cf. F. Margiotta Broglio, "La qualificazione giuridica delle relazioni fra lo Stato Italiano e la Chiesa Cattolica," 165 (1963), *Archivo Giuridico* 53; De Luca, *op. cit., passim.*

status of religious law within the secular system. In the light of the many aspects, it is no wonder that efforts to fashion systematic concepts of forms of reference have had little success.

Triepel's original distinction between receiving reference and formal reference, the latter characteristic of the rules of private international law, has exerted considerable influence. It will be recalled that Triepel gave prominence to two aspects of formal reference: legislative policy not to solve certain problems but to leave it to another system; and the application of foreign law "by itself", preserving its autonomous character. These two ideas accord with the view of those scholars who after examining the status of Canon Law within state law have concluded that *law references* to religious law are fundamentally *formal*.[58] The idea of autonomy has guided these writers, even when dealing with fact references. In their view, the lawmaker uses the technique of fact reference when he does not regard himself at all qualified to regulate a particular matter and therefore relies on the religious law involved,[59] accepting it as a given fact—thus the difference between law reference and fact reference is manifested in legislative policy. Whilst in formal references the legislature regards itself as being competent in principle to regulate and turns to religious law for reasons only of convenience or some other material consideration, in the case of fact references it has no alternative in view of its self-acknowledged "incompetence".[60]

As has already been mentioned,[61] the very concept of formal reference has met with sharp criticism and in private international law has been

---

[58] S. Romano, *Corso di diritto costituzionale* (6a ed. Padova 1941), p. 361; Id., *L'ordinamento giuridico*, p. 167; Jemolo, *Lezioni di diritto ecclesiastico* (2a ed. Milano 1957), p. 48; Id., "Il valore del diritto della Chiesa nell'ordinamento giuridico italiano," 90 (1923) *Archivio giuridico*, 3; Id., "La Chiesa e il suo diritto," 93 (1925) *Archivio giuridico*, 245; Del Giudice, *Manuale di diritto ecclesiastico* (10a ed. Milano 1964), pp. 41 et seq. It is worth mentioning that "formal reference" is used in various ways, and even those who use it in Triepel's original sense do not always agree on the details. See especially, De Luca, *op. cit.*, pp. 35 et seq.

[59] S. Romano, *op. et loc. cit.*; Jemolo, *op. et loc. cit.*; cf. De Luca, *op. cit.*, pp. 34 et seq.

[60] See the sources cited in note 58. Others have noted the seemingly paradoxical phenomenon that in the case of fact reference, in which the legislature does not regard itself at all qualified, it attaches to the fact situation an *independent legal consequence*, whereas in the case of law reference in which it views itself qualified to regulate the matter, it accepts the legal consequences of religious law. The paradox is only apparent, as Giacchi explains, see note 65 below.

[61] See above p. 65 n. 32.

replaced by more fully developed concepts. But in the area of ecclesiastical law writers continued to use it long after it was abandoned elsewhere.[62] Finally the concept of "instrumental reference" (creative reference) has come to penetrate this area as well.[63]

By means of this last concept, attempts were made to create a synthesis between the idea of autonomy and the modes of reception. According to one school,[64] the legislator's choice of fact references demonstrates his intention to preserve the full autonomy of religious law and the organs operating within it. Religious law is thus accepted as an independent datum since the legislator does not feel competent to prescribe its own ordering. In law references, on the other hand, it acts on the assumption that the matter does not lie within the exclusive jurisdiction of the church but belongs to the jurisdiction of the state, even though it chooses, for various reasons, to make the legal ordering compatible with that of the church.[65]

Another school has rightfully objected to this attempt to base the two types of reference on the idea of the mutual autonomy of state and church.[66] There is no necessary connection between a political idea (autonomy) and the technical form of the reference.[67] Israeli law also provides

---

[62] Cf. Bernardini, *op. cit.*, p. 67 n. 20.

[63] D'Avack, *Trattato*, pp. 149 et seq.; Id., *La posizione giuridica, op. et loc. cit.*; Giacchi, *op. et loc. cit.*; Petroncelli, *Manuale di diritto ecclesiastico* (Napoli 1961), pp. 81 et seq.; cf. De Luca, *op. cit., passim*; Bernardini, *op. cit.*, pp. 210 n. 36, 320 et seq.

[64] D'Avack, *op. et loc. cit.*; Giacchi, *op. et loc. cit.*

[65] The two authors try to prescribe general tests to determine when a reference *ought to be* a fact reference or a law reference. They suggest a preliminary test for determining the authority of the legislator. In D'Avack's opinion, every question of the internal organization of the institutions of the Catholic Church and of the fundamentals of its faith is not within the authority of the state and it may only relate to them by means of a fact reference. The situation is different with respect to the *activities* of the Church in state territory. Here the state may make such regulation as it thinks fit and in an appropriate case refer to the norms of the Church by a law reference. Giacchi disputes this distinction between organization and activities and proposes a distinction based on the *concept of autonomy*. On this debate see Margiotta Broglio, *op. et loc. cit.*; cf. De Luca, *op. cit.*, p. 52 n. 100.

[66] Checchini, "L'ordinamento canonico nel diritto italiano," *Scritti giuridici*, pp. 67 et seq.; cf. Margiotta Broglio, *ibid.*; De Luca, *ibid.*

[67] Checchini, *op. cit.*, p. 94: "Non quindi dalla valutazione politica della 'qualità', della 'natura' dei rapporti—valutazione che può diventare arbitraria—si potrà desumere *a priori* la loro concreta regolamentazione giuridica, ma dall'esame di tale concreta regolamentazione si potranno trarre conclusioni in merito ai motivi di ordine politico che l'hanno determinata."

examples to show that simply because the lawmaker chooses fact reference does not necessarily mean that he regards himself incompetent to regulate a matter. On the question "Who is a Jew?" the legislature has in one instance, within the framework of the Rabbinical Courts Jurisdiction Law, used a fact reference to the categories of the *Halakha;* in another instance, within the framework of the Law of Return, it has itself determined the substance of the term "Jew".[68] This difference of treatment demonstrates that the fact reference in the first case is no indication of a feeling of incompetence to decide who is a Jew. In principle, no impediment exists but for reasons of its own the legislature made a choice. It is possible that it will one day decide to define who is a Jew, even for the purposes of the jurisdiction of the rabbinical courts as well.[69]

The latter school proposes a different distinction between law and fact references, free of political considerations. The difference suggested is to be found in the measure of identity in the legal results in religious and state law.[70] In the case of fact reference in which religious law is a datum for the purpose of completing the fact situation of the secular norm, the legal result of the fact situation is not identical to that of the identical fact situation in religious law. In this kind of reference the legal result is entirely determined by the legislature itself. In the case of law reference on the other hand, the legal result corresponds to that determined by religious law, since state law turns to religious law in order to derive the legal result of the given fact situation. In our view, this distinction is of a quantitative rather than a qualitative nature. It is indeed true that in fact references the legal results are not identical in the two normative systems. (Even here it need not be so; the legislature may on its own motion determine that the same legal result follows without any reference to religious law.) But as regards the law references, the opposite is not

---

[68] See above pp. 59, 61. Even after the 1970 amendment, there is not complete identity between the statutory definition and that of religious law, particularly in respect of conversion. The National Religious Party requires a further amendment indicating that only conversion according to orthodox rites will be recognized.

[69] Cf. Article 51 (2) (b) of the Palestine Order in Council, 1922, as amended in 1939, which authorized the enactment of an ordinance for the purpose of "determining the circumstances in which a person would be considered a member of a religious community." See A. L. Globus, "Responsa in Matters of Family Law and Personal Status," (1954) 10 *HaPraklit,* 225, 242 n. 21.

[70] Checchini, *op. et loc. cit.; cf.* De Luca, *op. cit.,* pp. 129 et seq. We are not concerned here with Checchini's view of the technique of the reference, for which see De Luca, *ibid.*

true, since a mere reference to religious law cannot effect an identity of legal results in the two normative systems. There are many reasons why the final legal result in state law will be different[71] and we shall discuss some of them later.[72] It cannot be denied, however, that the legal results are of a kin, in contrast to the situation in the cases of fact reference.

Summing up this theoretical discussion, we have found that *a priori* neither a specific legal policy nor specific legal results are to be associated with the technical form of the reference. Nevertheless, even if that be so, each of these elements deserves attention for the purpose of clarifying the status of religious law within the law of the state. Considerable importance attaches to the degree of autonomy retained by religious law after its reception (in the broad sense) into state law. But two different aspects of this problem must be distinguished: the legislature's position as a pre-legal factor, that is, its general policy towards religious law and its institutions; and the actual autonomy enjoyed by religious law within the state system.

Within the framework of the first it is of interest to know whether the legislature did or did not intend to limit its own authority, and what its general approach is to religious institutions as autonomous bodies. The second aspect should be examined according to the way religious law is actually applied, keeping in view the practical problems which arise in this connection. Among these problems are the proof of religious law, its interpretation, and the limits of its application. We shall enlarge upon these questions in the following Part.

In Israeli law, the general question of the status of religious law in the law of the State has been little discussed. The views expressed have emerged largely in the course of dealing with some concrete problem without attention to the various kinds of reference.[73] A fundamental view was voiced by Professor Feinberg in his criticism[74] of Justice Agranat's

---

[71] This phenomenon was dealt with by many writers who have discussed the institution of reference. See note 4 above, and in particular Anzilotti *Corso di diritto internazionale* (Roma 1928), p. 59: "La recezione... implica necessariamente una trasformazione delle norme recepite, che va al di là del puro valore formale." For the relationship between fact and law references from this aspect, see Magni, *op. cit.*, pp. 146 et seq.

[72] Below, pp. 76, 104–108, 136 et seq.

[73] The judges have touched upon the question of the status of religious law in connection with the rule that religious law is subject to judicial notice. See below, pp. 76, 84.

[74] "An obiter dictum which calls out for interpretation," (1954), 10 *HaPraklit*, 289, 293.

approach in *Skornik*: "When today we come to consider the laws of the Torah we cannot define them other than as religious laws, even if they have been given governmental force. In other words, the application of Jewish law in certain areas of life, either by the Mandatory regime or by the State of Israel, has not taken from this law its religious character. Although its application stems from the source of State power, which is secular in its very nature, in applying religious law, the State does not intend to impair its essential character. As a result of obvious *self-restraint the State reconciles itself to the application of religious law and even to its 'sovereignty', since the State regards it an area in which it is not free to act independently.*" (Emphasis added)

Here we find an echo of the traditional idea of formal reference. But even in relation to the political aspect alone, this view does not strike us as correct for all cases of reception of religious law. The Israeli legislature does not consider itself unqualified in the areas of personal status, witness its continued intervention by providing its own independent solution. It should *not* be assumed as a general principle that the application of religious law in these areas is indicative of the State's view that it lacks authority to act as it wishes.

It is possible to find more specific indications of legislative policy. Historically speaking the grant of exclusive jurisdiction to the religious courts of the various communities clearly denoted the legislature's view that its own jurisdiction in these areas should be restricted and regulation of the matter left to religious law as applied by the religious courts.[75] We emphasize "historically speaking", since in the meantime decisive changes have occurred in the status of a number of religious courts, particularly the rabbinical courts. The latter have been integrated into the state system which prescribes their organization and maintains them financially. To the legislature they appear today to be in large measure organs of the State. Thus even a grant of exclusive jurisdiction to these courts is no longer expressive of a policy restrictive of State authority, as was the case when these courts were not dependent on the State.

On the other hand, if we examine the extent of the autonomy enjoyed by religious law in terms of its actual application, the judicial bodies which apply it are of decisive importance. Regardless of the legistature's

---

[75] See in particular, Tedeschi, "On the Choice Between Religious and Secular Law," *Studies in Israel Law*, p. 274; Id., "Note di diritto matrimoniale israeliano (in margine a una polemica altrui)," *Raccolta di scritti in onore di A.C. Jemolo*, Vol. IV, pp. 629, 633 et seq.

view, the grant of jurisdiction to religious courts (exclusive or concurrent) exerts great influence on the status of religious law. As Justice Silberg said in one of his well-known decisions,[76] "Jewish law applied in a civil court is not the Jewish law applied in a religious court." Here we limit ourselves to the application of religious law in the civil courts.

The general status of the religious law in the local system was considered from a different angle in *Yosifof*.[77] After observing [78] that the Mandatory lawmaker had divested himself of the power to prescribe new rules of his own in matters of personal status, and for well-known and understandable reasons had given over the regulation thereof to the religious laws of the different communities, Justice Silberg went on to say: "Did the Mandatory legislator leave a legislative vacuum and in respect of these matters employ foreign legal norms which have no place in his own legal system, or did he take over these legal norms and make them an integral part of his own general system of law?"

Justice Silberg relied on the fact that the term "law" as defined in the Interpretation Ordinance includes religious law and answered the question he had posed in these words:

"The legislature has (here) expressed its opinion in unmistakable language that the religious law, to the extent that it is in force in Palestine, constitutes an integral part of the law of the State. That is to say, if a District Court deals, for example, with the obligation of a Jewish husband who is a citizen of Palestine to pay maintenance and applies, as it must, Jewish law, the part of that law which treats of the matter is deemed to have been enacted as one of the laws of the State. This, moreover, is the only possible reasonable approach to the matter. Religious law is not a foreign branch engrafted into the trunk of the tree from outside but, to the extent that is recognized, is inextricably interwoven with the boughs of the tree and forms a part thereof."

This form of analysis gives rise to a few doubts. The lack of clarity seems to be due in the absence of conceptual tools for an exact study of the problem and its solution.

Justice Silberg puts the question in the form of a choice: either a vacuum and the use of religious norms which have no place in the local system, or complete integration of the religious norms. How is this alternative to

---

[76] C.A. 238/53 *Cohen-Buslik* v. *A.G.* 8 P.D. 4, 19. (English translation in 2 S.J.S.C. 239, 254). See also his *Personal Status in Israel*, pp. 5–6 (in Hebrew).
[77] Cr. A. 112/50 *Yosifof* v. *A.G.*, 5 P.D. 481.
[78] At 501.

be understood? It reminds one somewhat of the old, traditional distinction between formal reference and receiving reference, a distinction which emphasized the degree of autonomy enjoyed by the received law.[79] But his conclusion refutes this assumption. In his view the second alternative exists, whilst according to the accepted criterion religious law retains a large measure of autonomy. As Professor Tedeschi rightly points out,[80] it is appropriate (on the assumption that the distinction mentioned is supportable)[81] to classify the reference to religious law as a formal reference.[82] It appears that Justice Silberg attached undue significance to the inclusion of religious law in the definition of "law" in the Interpretation Ordinance.[83] His conclusion regarding religious law raises the question of the nature of the distinction he proposes: What is the theoretical or practical difference between a foreign law which constitutes an integral part of state law and a foreign law which does not? What is the difference between laws which are deemed to have been enacted as part of the law of the State and laws which are not? Justice Silberg did not elucidate, and it is difficult to grasp the full implications of his remarks.

---

[79] See above pp. 64–65 and also Tedeschi, *op. cit.*, p. 272.

[80] *Ibid.*, p. 274.

[81] Professor Tedeschi himself raises the question concerning its correctness, see the following note. As noted above, the distinction has not stood the test of criticism. The new concept "creative reference" (above p. 66) not only shakes the foundations of the concept of formal reference but even brings about a substantial change in the significance of the receiving reference.

[82] *Ibid.*, p. 274: "What is the status of these norms in our legal system, and generally what is the status of these norms of Jewish law which are recognized by our legislator? We have already said that it is the status of a second and collateral system which is linked with the principal system. Can we say that the Jewish law has become merged into the law of the state? If by 'merged' as distinguished from 'linked up' we mean that the norms in question have been plucked, as it were, from the system to which they belong and fused into another system, or that their sources, their special character, the principles of interpretation peculiar to them, etc., are rejected, in short, that their autonomy is denied, the answer is in the negative. This autonomy makes the reference in question a kind of non-receiving reference, as this has been called by the writers mentioned (though with them this expression is bound up with a certain doctrine which is questionable)." See also A. Vitta, "Religious Courts and Their Jurisdiction in Palestine and Their Legal Nature," 3 (1946) *HaPraklit*, 70 reprinted in 25 (1969) *HaPraklit* 174, 177–178.

[83] Vitta, *op. ult. cit.*, p. 178, and see below pp. 84–85, 94.

PART THREE

THE APPLICATION OF RELIGIOUS LAW

Chapter I

INTRODUCTION

In this Part we deal with the application of religious law in the civil courts. Our concern is not with the general operation of religious law in the different religious courts in the State of Israel which have been accorded jurisdiction by the legislature. As we have mentioned,[1] essential differences exist between the religious judicial institutions and the civil courts in their manner of applying religious law. Our attention is directed to the special features which characterize the application of religious law in civil courts.

"Application" is here taken in its broadest sense, that is, as any reliance on or consideration of religious law provisions in the Israeli legal system. This use of "application" is wider than that common among many writers who confine it to reliance on norms *for the purpose of determining legal results*,[2] with the consequence that *application* of foreign law occurs only in cases of *law reference* as distinct from *fact reference*. In other words, the application of foreign law means, in the strict technical sense, the determination of the legal result of a certain fact situation according to that law.[3] According to these writers, fact reference does not involve "application" but merely taking into account the foreign norms.[4]

As far as concerns the status of a foreign legal norm as a *rule of conduct* in the domestic system, the distinction between "application" and "taking into account" is without doubt significant (particularly so in conditional references,[5] such as the requirement of reciprocity, where the relationship

---

[1] Above, p. 76.
[2] Bernardini, *Produzione di norme giuridiche mediante rinvio* (Milano 1966), p. 364; F. Rigaux, *Droit international privé* (Brussels 1968), no. 136: "Comme la règle de droit attache à une hypothèse certaines conséquences juridiques, *appliquer* cette règle consiste à déduire à propos d'une situation particulière l'effet juridique qui lui appartient."
[3] Rigaux, *op. et loc. cit.*: "*Applique* le droit étranger, le juge qui emprunte à ce droit la conséquence juridique postulée par la partie à laquelle il donne gain de cause."
[4] Rigaux, *op. cit.* nos. 137–138. As to the distinction between a fact reference and a law reference see above pp. 58–63.
[5] For this concept, see above pp. 67–68.

with the foreign system is without substance with respect to the facts of the case). But if we look at the mental process involved in applying a norm, the distinction is not so material. Even in fact references the judge is sometimes called upon to give body to an abstract foreign provision in respect of a given fact situation, a process which is characteristic of any application of law. The only difference is that here reliance on foreign law is only one stage in resolving the matter in question. The final legal outcome is determined by a domestic rule since reliance on foreign law in fact references is intended to complete the fact situation. In truth what is called a fact situation may itself sometimes constitute a legal result in relation to an earlier fact situation. For example, a person being a "Jew" is the fact to which the legal result that the rabbinical court has jurisdiction is connected but is itself the legal result of prior facts, such as religious conversion.[6]

The broad use of the concept of application does not import any denial of the existence of important differences between the two kinds of reference mentioned.

The fundamental question is whether a basic difference exists between, on the one hand, applying norms which belong to another normative system and are effectuated by means of reference,[7] and, on the other hand,

[6] For the relation between the fact situation and the legal consequences, see in particular Larenz, *Methodenlehre der Rechtswissenschaft* (Berlin 1969), pp. 186 et seq.: "Man gelangt auf diese Weise zu einer gewissen Relativierung der Begriffe 'Tatbestand' und 'Rechtsfolge'. Die Rechtsfolge des einen Rechtssatzes erscheint in einem anderen Rechtssatz als Tatbestandselement."

[7] Certain problems, particularly of construction, are apt to arise as a result of the direct reception of religious law (for this concept, see above p. 53), but a problem of *principle* exists with respect to reception by reference alone. As to the question of construction, see H.C.J. 163/57, *Lubin* v. *Municipality of Tel Aviv-Jaffo*, 12 P.D. 1041, where the question was the interpretation of "pork or pork products destined for food" which appeared in the Local Authorities (Special Enablement) Law, 5717–1956. This Law authorized a local authority to enact by-laws limiting or prohibiting the raising or keeping of pigs and the sale of pork and derivative products. The petitioner's argument was that not all parts of the pig are included in the term "pork," which term was to be construed in its ordinary sense, including the tender parts suitable for consumption only, and not other parts. This argument was rejected by the three judges who heard the case. Olshan P. explained: "If it is true... that the enabling legislation was intended to enable local authorities to prohibit the sale of pork having regard to the sensibilities of a part of the population—and no one disputes that—it is impossible to avoid interpreting the term 'pork' in the light of that tradition which was known to the legislator when the law was being drafted" (at 1048). Justice Silberg said (at 1067): "There is no doubt

INTRODUCTION

applying norms which were formulated entirely by a domestic legislature. The question has arisen in many systems in relation to foreign norms given effect to in the domestic system by the rules of private international law. The problem is usually formulated in terms of the effect on the *status* of the foreign rule—is it a *question of fact* or a *question of law?*[8]

The tendency is first to define the status of foreign rules as fact or as law and then to deduce the various consequences regarding proof of the foreign law, its interpretation, etc. This approach might perhaps be justified if it were possible to find an unambiguous criterion to distinguish between fact and law, and if in addition this criterion could with certainty classify the foreign law as being within one or the other category. Neither of these conditions appears to exist. Apart from dispute over the significance of the distinction between fact and law,[9] there is no consensus as to whether foreign law is a question of fact or a question of law.[10] Moreover, the legal ordering of a number of matters is sometimes based on a pragmatic approach which does not completely correspond to either viewpoint. There is accordingly no point in trying to classify foreign law on the basis

---

that the *indirect* object of the Law—and frequently the indirect object is the 'direct' aim of the legislator—was to reduce the *consumption* of pork... It is therefore clear that, in using the term 'pork' it had in mind all the parts which fall under religious prohibition." And see (at 1077), the remarks of Justice Sussman, who joined in the conclusion but disagreed with Justice Silberg concerning the status, as a matter of principle, of the English rules of construction with respect to Israeli legislation. In general, it should be noted that the debate centred on the interpretation of a *term*. See also, Mo. 98/51, *Mitova B.M.* v. *Kazam*, 6 P.D. 4, and see above, p. 61 n. 19. On the other hand, it would appear that no one would doubt that in the case of a reference one must apply the religious norm in accordance with the independent rules of construction of the religious system.

[8] The literature is extensive, see the bibliographies in C. David, *La loi étrangère devant le juge du fond*, (Paris 1965); Zajtay, *Zur Stellung des ausländischen Rechts im französischen internationalen Privatrecht*, (Berlin 1963); Id., "The Application of Foreign Law," *International Encyclopedia of Comparative Law*, vol. III, ch. 14. (1972); M. Giuliano, "Le traitement du droit étranger dans le procès civil dans les systèmes juridiques continentaux," 14 (1962), *Rev. int. de droit comparé* 5; S.L. Sass, "Foreign Law in Civil Litigation, a Comparative Survey," 16 (1968) *A.J.C.L.* 332; A. Nussbaum, "The Problem of Proving Foreign Law," 50 (1940–41) *Yale L.J.* 1018.

[9] Cf. *Le fait et le droit, Etudes de logique juridique* (Brussels 1961); cf. Paton, *Jurisprudence* (4th ed., Oxford 1972), pp. 204 et seq. On the present theme, see particularly I. Zajtay, *Zur Stellung*, pp. 7 et seq.

[10] See the sources referred to in note 8 above.

of an *a priori* determination. Maury[11] has rightly noted that "the determination that application of foreign law is a question of fact does not constitute an argument which justifies the solutions but a formula which summarizes them."

Israeli law which follows the traditional Anglo-American approach regards the application of foreign law as a question of fact.[12] This approach finds its main expression in procedure, in the manner of pleading and proving foreign law. It also held sway in relation to religious law, although from the beginning of the British Mandate there existed special provisions concerning the proof of religious law in the civil courts which deviated to some extent from the traditional inflexible rules appertaining to the proof of foreign law.[13]

An important change in the status of religious law occurred as a result of a 1945 amendment to the Interpretation Ordinance which extended the meaning of "law" to include religious law, in contrast to foreign law which applies in Israel by virtue of the rules of private international law. This amendment is without doubt important, as we shall see more amply in what follows with regard to the procedural status of religious law. It appears, however, that the local courts have exaggerated its importance in respect of the general status of religious law in the local system;[14] ultimately, the Interpretation Ordinance is nothing more than a compilation of definitions for the convenience of the lawmaker. The tendency of the courts to attach significance to the inclusion of religious law under "law" and to infer from that alone the nature of the reception of religious law into the local system is inacceptable.[15] The status of religious law is

---

[11] *Derecho Internacional Privado* (Puebla, Mexico 1949), p. 50, cited by W. Goldschmidt, "Jacques Maury et les aspects philosophiques du droit international privé," *Mélanges Maury* (Paris), t. 1, pp. 152, 157.

[12] C.A. 118/51, *New Zealand Insurance Co. Ltd.* v. *Youval* 7 P.D. 518, 527 (English translation 1 S.J.S.C. 332, 344); C.A. 406/62, *Zilcha* v. *Romili* 17 P.D. 904, 907–909. See A. Salant, *The Law of Evidence*, (Tel Aviv 1963), p. 181, 188 (1969 Supplement) (in Hebrew); Vitta, *Personal Status in Palestine* (Tel Aviv 1947), pp. 141 et seq.

[13] See below, pp. 88 et seq.

[14] See, for example, the remarks of Justice Silberg in Cr.A. 112/50, *Yosifof* v. *A.G.*, 5 P.D. 481, 501–502; see above, p. 76. Cf. also C.A. 99/63, *Peleg* v. *A.G.*, 17 P.D. 1122, 1127, on the question of binding precedent in the construction of religious law, and particularly below pp. 130 et seq. See also A.H. Shaki, "The Confusion of Spheres and the Restriction of the Religious Jurisdiction" 21–22 (1965) *Gevilin*, 38, 46; M. Shawa, "Error in the Determination of Jewishness which Denies Jurisdiction," 25 (1970) *HaPraklit*, 617, 628–630, 639.

[15] Cf. Vitta, "Religious Courts and Their Jurisdiction in Palestine and Their Legal

to be deduced from the substantive provisions of the Interpretation Ordinance (or of other laws) which explicitly concern "law" and thus also religious law.[16]

We begin our discussion therefore with the existing solutions of specific questions touching on the application of religious law in the local system, and not with any *a priori* determination based, as it were, on the special *nature* of a foreign system.

But even had we chosen to examine the status of religious law in the Israeli system according to the detailed rules which determine its mode of application, we would still have to ask whether there is not a material difference in the general approach of the judges when called upon to apply foreign legal provisions. In other words, status is special as a matter not of dogma but of reality. This aspect of the problem has been particularly emphasized by Batiffol who sees an essential difference between the judge's approach to domestic law and to foreign law. In the one case he plays a creative role in determining the content and meaning of the law, since he lives within his system and seeks to find a logical, effective and just solution within the terms of the law. In the case of foreign law, he approaches his task as a kind of observer from the outside who is satisfied with finding what "exists".[17] Clearly there is great justice in Batiffol's observations. The judge concerned with foreign law has no feeling of identification with the foreign normative provisions; he lacks that sense of

---

Nature," 3 (1946) *HaPraklit*, 70, reprinted, 25 (1969) *HaPraklit*, pp. 174, 178; cf. above p. 76.

[16] Most important is section 33 of the Interpretation Ordinance which deals with judicial notice and which we will examine in the next chapter. Apart from this section there are practically no provisions which deal substantially with religious law.

[17] Batiffol, *Aspects philosophiques du droit international privé* (Paris 1956), pp. 108 et seq.: "Il ne s'agit plus de raisonner sur le juste, l'utile ou le caractère contraignant de l'impératif législatif, mais de constater un état de fait. Selon la juste expression de W. Goldschmidt (*Sistema y folosofia del derecho internacional privado*, I, p. 18; cf. aussi *ibid.*, II, p. 6 et Beziehungen zwischen Ontologie und Logik in der Rechtswissenschaft, *Oesterreichische Z. für öffentl. Recht*, III, p. 197), les juges ont vis-à-vis du droit étranger la position d'observateurs sociologiques." *Id., Droit international privé* (5e ed., Paris 1970), tome 1, p. 392: "La cause de cette différence se trouve dans ce que le juge est *extérieur* au système juridique étranger: au lieu de contribuer à le créer, il l'observe du dehors, comme un sociologue selon la juste observation de W. Goldschmidt, c'est à dire qu'il le regarde comme un fait extérieur a constater, et non pas comme une notion à élaborer;" cf. *ibid.*, p. 386; Kegel, *Internationales Privatrecht* (3. Aufl. München 1971) p. 202.

responsibility for the integrity of the system and its orderly working in society as is largely the case in the application of his own law.[18]

Is this also true of religious law in Israel? It seems that a great difference exists between the attitude of a Jewish judge to Jewish law and his attitude to other religious laws. The Jewish judge—and we mean one versed in Talmud and the rabbinic literature—has an ideological relationship to Jewish law and attributes it with religious or national value. He identifies with Jewish law and treats it with deference. The result is well reflected in the judgments. Those judges learned in *Halakha* plunge deep into the sea of the Talmud, sometimes with conspicuous independence of approach, and bring up solutions which seem to them desirable.[19] The same judge will have a different approach to another religious legal system. Here his position is like that of any judge referring to foreign law.[20] But this dif-

[18] But see Zajtay, *Zur Stellung des ausländischen Rechts im französischen internationalen Privatrecht*, pp. 27 et seq. Id., "The Application of Foreign Law," s. 23. The author disagrees with Batiffol, asserting that the technique of construction in the application of foreign law is no different from that used with respect to the local law. The arguments of Zajtay are not convincing. It would seem that he confuses the authority, as a matter of principle, of the judge to apply foreign law just as he does local law, with the reality that the judge does not act in this manner. The fact that the judge has no sense of identification with foreign law makes it difficult for him to play a creative role in the application of that law. This is not a matter of theoretical principle but a psychological and social reality. In this regard, see the same author's analysis of the position of the French Court of Cassation which avoids review of the application of foreign law out of reluctance to participate in the creation of foreign law, which is involved in the judicial process. See, *Zur Stellung*, pp. 118–120, 206.

[19] See, for example, C.A. 88/57, *Rosenberg* v. *Kremeraz* 12 P.D. 1096 (Justice Cheshin); H.C.J. 301/63, *Streit* v. *The Chief Rabbi of Israel*, 18 P.D. (1) 598, 616 (Justice Silberg); C.A. 164/67, 220/67, *A.G.* v. *Avraham*, 22 P.D. (1) 29 (Justice Silberg). There is no need to add examples. Research should, we believe, centre on the treatment of Jewish law in the secular courts. Such research would evaluate the application of Jewish law and its development from the internal Jewish point of view; it should be carried out by scholars versed in Jewish law.

[20] In reality reliance on Jewish law is out of all proportion to reliance on the other religious law, as may be seen from an examination of the indexes to the Supreme Court reports. By way of example, see H.C.J. 143/62, *Funk Schlesinger* v. *Minister of the Interior*, 17 P.D. 222, 250–251 (Justice Sussman, Canon Law); H.C.J. 235/68, *R.B.* v. *The Chief Rabbis of Israel*, 23 P.D. (1) 449, 467–470 (Justice Silberg, various religious laws). The approach is cautious and that of an external observer: "I will not continue to develop further this idea, of examining the procedure of the Sharia Court to see whether or not it is in accordance with the requirements of section 130; I do not wish, nor am I

ference, which exists in practice, is not recognized by the legislature which places all religious systems on the same footing.

In what follows we shall discuss specific questions of the application of religious law: the proof of religious law; religious legal precedents (including their binding power); limitations on the application of religious law (the principle of public policy and the distinction between substance and procedure); the question of adaptation in the combining of religious and civil law.

qualified, to involve myself with the authorities on the matter, the judges of the Sharia Court of Appeal." H.C.J. 111/63, *Abu Chorash* v. *Sharia Court of Acco*, 18 P.D. (1) 589, 593 (Justice Silberg). Cf. also 839/67, *Havra* v. *Havra*, 73 P.M. 183, 184; 99/66, *Arshid* v. *Arshid*, 68 P.M. 331, 337–339 (Byzantine Law); 54/69 *Shauah* v. *Halabi*, 73 P.M. 61–62 (Druse Law).

Chapter II

ASCERTAINMENT OF RELIGIOUS LAW

The British Mandatory Government was from the outset aware of the problem of applying different legal systems in matters of personal status. In particular it foresaw that the civil courts, obliged to apply the "personal law" in these matters, would encounter the problem of knowing what this law is. Reference to personal law is polyvalent[1] and relates fundamentally to two main groups of laws: religious laws concerning citizens, members of the different communities[2] and national laws concerning foreigners.[3]

The Mandatory legislator who doubtlessly knew the accepted English legal position that foreign law is treated as a fact question laid down special rules regarding knowledge of personal law in the civil courts.

As regards religious law, the Palestine Order in Council, 1922, originally[4] provided in art. 47: "Where in any civil or criminal cause brought before the Civil Court a question of personal status incidentally arises, the determination of which is necessary for the purposes of the cause, the Civil Court may determine the question and may to that end take the opinion, by such means as may seem most convenient, of a competent jurist having knowledge of the personal law applicable."

---

[1] For this concept, see above, p. 68.

[2] This was the original situation. In the meantime, important changes have occurred, particularly with respect to Jews, as a result of the Rabbinical Courts Jurisdiction (Marriage and Divorce) Law, 5713–1953. See in general Silberg, *Personal Status in Israel*, (Jerusalem 1957) (in Hebrew).

[3] See Article 64 of the Palestine Order-in-Council. We ignore here the extent of the reference. It is noteworthy that in recent years the tendency has been to replace national law by the law of the domicile. See generally A. Shaki, "The Criterion 'Domicile' and its Preference over the Criterion of Nationality in Israel Private International Law," *Scripta Hierosolymitana*, Vol. XVI (Jerusalem 1966), pp. 163 et seq.

[4] The provision has been repealed by section 48(8) of the Courts Law, 5717–1957. As to the significance of the repeal, see below p. 102.

A slightly different rule was prescribed for the national law of a foreigner in matters of personal status:[5] the court is empowered to invite the consul or a representative of his to sit as a judicial-assessor to advise on the personal law.

Both provisions display some deviation from the rules of English common law regulating the status of foreign law[6] in British courts. According to these rules foreign law is considered purely as a *question of fact,* and the court has no need to take any initiative in acquainting itself of its content. The burden of proof is upon the litigant who wishes to rely on the foreign law and proof is by *expert witness.*[7] In English law, however, it is possible to find statutory modification of the traditional rule allowing the court to obtain an opinion from a foreign court.[8] These provisions, which were formally applicable also in Palestine,[9] are limited in their application and appear to be little used.[10]

The Mandatory legislator's deviation from the common law rule is easily understood in view of the great difference between the role of personal law in matters of personal status and the role of foreign law applied by virtue of the ordinary rules of private international law.

What is the typical situation in private international law? A fact situa-

---

[5] Article 64 (iii), Palestine Order-in-Council. Compare the possibility of including a religious judge on the Special Court in accordance with Article 55 of the Order-in-Council.

[6] With the exception of the ecclesiastical (Anglican) law of England, which is considered a part of the internal legal system and not as an autonomous normative system. See, in particular, 115/54, *Grenzburg v. Bulein,* 12 P.M. 129, 132–133.

[7] For English Common law, see Dicey and Morris, *Conflict of Laws,* (9th ed. London 1973), pp. 1124 et seq.; Cheshire, *Private International Law,* (8th ed., London 1970), pp. 123 et seq. The historical background of the English approach is treated in S.L. Sass, "Foreign Law in Civil Litigation," 16 (1968) *A.J.C.L.* 322, 335 et seq.

[8] British Law Ascertainment Act, 1859; Foreign Law Ascertainment Act, 1861; cf. Dicey and Morris, *op. cit.,* pp. 1132–33.

[9] By means of Article 35 of the Palestine Order-in-Council, 1922.

[10] Foreign Law Ascertainment Act of 1861 makes its application to treaty making conditional. It appears that not a single treaty has been made to date. See Dicey and Morris, *op. cit.,* p. 1133. In the United States there is a tendency to depart from the traditional approach of English Common law, which has found expression in the legislation of a number of states, and in the Federal Rules of Procedure. See Sass, *op. cit.,* pp. 340 et seq., 346 et seq.; Miller, "Federal Rule 44.1 and the 'Fact' Approach to Determining Foreign Law," 65 (1967) *Michigan L.R.* 615; Zajtay: "The Application of Foreign Law," *International Encyclopedia of Comparative Law,* vol. III, ch. 14, s. 20–21.

tion arises in which there is a foreign element. The question is one of choice of law, which in the simplest instance involves "competition" between the solution available in the domestic system and that provided by the foreign system. Indeed, the problem of the status of the foreign law in the local system is greatly influenced by the coexistence of a solution in both systems.[11] In these cases the role of private international law rules is to enable a choice of substantive solution, having regard to the international aspect of the problem.

The situation is completely different in matters of personal status in Israel, when the lawmaker turns to religious law. The problem is not a choice between two "competing" solutions,[11a] but reference to personal law because of the *absence of substantive solution* in the State's own law (in the narrow sense—norms the content of which is fully determined by the Israeli legislator, as distinct from rules applying by virtue of a reference). The State's system lacks substantive self-created rules for solving the dispute.

This fact is of great importance for the question of the proof of religious law. Israeli law, in the narrow sense, cannot serve as a substitute for ignorance of religious law.[12] Thus, if the court has no knowledge of the content of the personal law, the only possibility is to decide a matter on the formal grounds that the burden of proof in respect thereof has not been discharged.[13] By contrast, under private international law there is no need to resort to such formal dismissal of the action but the court will decide

---

[11] Cf. generally, David, *La loi étrangère devant le juge du fond, passim;* Zajtay, *op. cit., passim.*

[11a] We do not refer to cases in which the individual is given a choice to resort, at his discretion, either to religious law or to the law of the state. As to this possibility, see generally Tedeschi, "On the Choice between Religious Law and Secular Law in the Legal System of Israel," *Studies in Israel Law* (Jerusalem 1960), p. 238. In the case of a reference to religious law no internal solution usually exists. But cf. note 16.

[12] On this function in private international law generally, see David, *op. cit.*, pp. 94 et seq. (*La vocation subsidiaire de la lex fori*); Batiffol, *op. cit.*, no. 349; Zajtay, *op. cit.*, s. 22, p. 26.

[13] Cf. C.A. 37/49 *Rappaport* v. *Feldbrovski* 4 P.D. 645, 647: "If there is a need to prove foreign law in a local court, that is, if the rights of one party or another are dependent on the provisions of foreign law, and no evidence is brought before the court as to the substance of that law, two alternatives are open to the court: (a) to rule against the party who is required to prove the foreign law, that is, the party upon whom the burden of proof of the foreign law lies in order to establish his rights, since that party has not discharged his burden of proof, or (b) to rule in accordance with the local law known to the

ASCERTAINMENT OF RELIGIOUS LAW

according to substantive domestic law. Such, indeed, is the practice in Israel, on "presumption of the identity of laws" [14] the source of which is English common law.[15] But in matters of personal status in which Israeli civil law lacks its own proper rules,[16] this possibility does not exist and

> court, on the fictitious assumption that the foreign law is identical with it."
> It follows that if local law lacks substantive provisions, only the first alternative is available. We need not consider the question whether such a situation of the absence of substantive provisions can occur in local law, in view of Article 46 of the Palestine Order-in-Council concerning *lacunae*, or, more precisely, whether the absence of a solution is established before or after having recourse to English Common law. Cf., C.C. 41/45, *Craig* v. *Corbett*, (1946), S.J.D.C. 105, 108: "I have not been told what the law of that country is on this subject, but I think that as no evidence has been adduced to the contrary I am entitled to presume it is the same as English Law... It occurs to me that if there is no law at all in this country in respect of the celebration of marriages we might be entitled to introduce the English Common Law upon the subject." Cf. also, Silberg, *op. cit.*, pp. 259 et seq., who deals with the question of the personal law of an Israeli citizen who is not a member of one of the recognized religious communities.

[14] As to the principle in Israel and its limitations, see C.A. 281/53 *Pacific Mediterranean Line, Panama*, v. *Palestine Industries B.M.*, 9 P.D. 1779; C.A. 109/56 *Maror* v. *Zordick*, 11 P.D. 904; C.A. 291/61, *Tzisis* v. *Barshel*, 15 P.D. 2087, 2094 et seq. In the last case Justice Cohn expressed the opinion—current in Anglo-American literature—that this is not a "presumption" in the usual sense of the term, but that the foreign law which is not pleaded and proved is rejected in favor of the *lex fori*. Cf. David, *ibid;* Zajtay, *ibid*. The most important limitation on the application of the presumption from our point of view occurs in matters of personal status. See note 18 below. The use of local law where the foreign law is not known has been criticised by many, and in our opinion properly so. Cf. Currie, *Selected Essays on the Conflict of Laws* (Durham 1963), pp. 3 et seq. The writers recommend that the judges show more initiative in ascertaining foreign law and, if necessary, giving judgment in accordance with universal legal principles or those close to the foreign system. See in this context, David, *op. cit.*, pp. 105 et seq., 123 et seq.; Kegel, *op. cit.*, § 15; cf. Batiffol, *ibid.*, nn. 45–46; Cappelletti, "Jura novit curia," *Scritti in memoria di Antonio Giuffrè*, II (Milano 1967), pp. 143 et seq.

[15] Cf. Morris and Dicey, *op. cit.*, p. 1133; A. Nussbaum, *op. cit.*, pp. 1035 et seq., David, *op. et loc. cit*. The last writer reviews comparatively the various approaches. It should be noted that the courts do not always resort to local law, even when this alternative is open to them. See in particular the *Walton* case in New York, 233 F.2d 541 (2d Cir. 1956) and the criticism thereof in Currie, "On the Displacement of the Law of the Forum," 58 (1958) *Col. L.R.*: 964; Ehrenzweig, *Conflict of Laws* (St. Paul 1962), pp. 366 et seq.; David, *op. cit.*, pp. 97 et seq.; Cappelletti, *op. cit.*, pp. 143, 148 n. 9, 152 et seq.

[16] We have in mind principally the legal situation existing at the beginning of the Mandate. Since then there have been many changes in the direction of intro-

the only solution would be to dismiss the action. This solution is, however, extremely undesirable, since the determination of personal status is a matter of public interest.[17]

These considerations seemingly moved the Mandatory legislator to enable the courts to take the initiative in ascertaining religious law.[18] During the Mandatory period the civil courts usually turned to some religious authority for an authoritative opinion, or based their decisions on the expert evidence of the parties.[19] Most noteworthy was the initiative taken by the Court of Appeal in putting questions of religious law to the heads of the religious communities, *in addition* to the expert testimony taken in the lower court.[20]

> ducing secular law to regulate matters which were originally defined as matters of personal status (maintenance, adoption, etc.).
>
> [17] Cf. C.A. 179/54 *Provalski* v. *Silber,* 11 P.D. 626, 631. The Supreme Court remitted the case for hearing of evidence on foreign law, rather than dismiss it.
> [18] The truth is that a similar situation exists in matters of the personal status of foreign citizens and the provisions of Article 64(iii) are to be understood against this background. If it happens that the personal law is not known to the court, reliance on Israeli law (in the wide sense, including religious laws) is not a satisfactory solution. Indeed, Israeli courts have expressed reservations about applying the presumption of identity of laws in matters of personal status. See C.A. 37/49 *Rappaport* v. *Feldbrovski* 4 P.D. 645; C.A. 51/49, *Yazdi* v. *Yazdi,* 4 P.D. 762; C.A. 291/61, *Tzisis* v. *Barshel,* 15 P.D. 2087, 2094 et seq. The reason given for not applying the presumption of identity (that is, *lex fori*) is that local law is not uniform, but in matters of personal status refers to the various religious laws, see C.A. 291/61, at 2091 (Justice Cohn). The courts incline to initiate ascertainment of foreign law (see C.A. 179/54) or to resort to local law as expressive of universal legal principles (such as the right of the wife to maintenance, to succession, etc.). See C.A. 51/49 at 767; C.A. 291/61, at 2091. Cf. Nussbaum, *op. et loc. cit.,* n. 116; Ehrenzweig, *op. cit.,* pp. 364–365. On the other hand, it appears that the local courts utilize the presumption of identity of laws as to the rules of choice of law, even in matters of personal status. See Cr. A. 141/60, *A.G.* v. *Yagoda,* 14 P.D. 1355, 1356.
> [19] Cf. Cr.A. 11/40, *Marashli* v. *A.G.,* 7 Ct. L.R. 118; C.A. 65/34, 2 P.L.R. 348. It is an interesting question how far the local courts must initiate ascertainment of foreign law under Article 64(iii). It seems that nowadays the courts are not greatly assisted by the consuls. V. Shawa, "The Nature and Manner of Proving Foreign Law in Anglo-American Law and in Israeli Law" (1974) 3 *Iyune Mishpat* 725, 742. In Mandatory times there were a number of cases in which the court did not content itself with an opinion from the consuls, but demanded further proof. C.A. 176/26, 3 *Rotenberg,* 985; C.A. 20/29, 1 P.L.R. 420. The significance of Article 64(iii) was dealt with in C.A. 51/49, at 764–765; and the argument that the testimony of the consul was the only way to prove foreign law was rejected.
> [20] Cr.A. 85/38, *A.G.* v. *Melnik,* (1939) 1 S.C.J. 15, 16–17: "Although evidence

The courts, however, continued in principle to regard the application of religious law as a question of fact to be proved by evidence.[21] But the line between fact and law was often blurred, especially when the judge had personal knowledge of religious law which allowed him direct and independent access to the legal material.[22]

An important change in the status of religious law occurred in 1945 with the amendment of the Interpretation Ordinance. The definition of "law" was extended to include—in addition to internal legislation and certain British statutes—"Ottoman Law, religious law (whether written or unwritten), and the common law and doctrines of equity of England, which is or are now, or has or have heretofore been, or may hereafter be, in force in Palestine." The main importance of the amendment relates to the ascertainment of religious law in court, and this under section 35 (now section 33 of the New Version): "Judicial notice shall be taken of every law, unless the contrary is expressed by law."

It is interesting and characteristic that Jewish jurists accepted the amendment with some hesitation and even opposition. They were interested in having the interpretation of religious law entrusted to a *halakhic* institution, the Chief Rabbinate. Opposition arose out of religious and national considerations. Some objected in principle to any interpretation of religious law by secular judges or members of other religions;[23] others were concerned with an autonomous renaissance of Jewish law.[24] Both views preferred that the content of the law be determined by authorized persons of religion.

---

as to the law applicable was taken before the District Court we thought fit to take the opinion of Chief Rabbi Herzog in this matter."

[21] Cf. C.A. 139/38, *Shomar* v. *Shomar,* 4 Ct. L.R. 91–92; C.A. 65/34, 2 P.L.R., 348.

[22] Cf. C.A. 51/30, *Frankenthal* v. *Leibel,* 1 P.L.R. 639, 641: "Two witnesses gave evidence in the Court below as to the meaning of this clause. Our learned brother Frumkin has consulted authoritative text-books on this question and we have no hesitation in holding . . ."

[23] Klug, 2 (1945) *HaPraklit* 209.

[24] Dickstein (Dykan), "Jewish Law in the Framework of the Law of Palestine," 2 (1945) *HaPraklit,* 291, 298. The author proposed that the secular courts should turn to the Chief Rabbinate with specific questions; "particularly since Jewish religious law of the family is not to be regarded as ossified. It is a living law with its currents and shifts and we are interested that the Chief Rabbinate should have the opportunity of developing it according to its understanding and adapting it to the needs of the country, the people and our times." See also Freiman, "Maintenance of the Child Born out of Wedlock Under the Religious Law of Israel," 2 (1945) *HaPraklit,* 163, 172–173.

The creation of the Jewish State a few years later changed the setting of the entire problem. The civil courts, whose judges are now Jews, are no longer thought of as institutions of a foreign power, and national considerations urge that Jewish law should be entrusted to them for development and modernization.[25] From the viewpoint of the Jewish religion, the coexistence of civil courts and rabbinical courts in the State has created new problems, but this is not the place to discuss them.[26]

The inclusion of religious law in the term "law" resulted in its receiving equal status with domestic law in respect of its ascertainment by the courts.[26a] But in contemplation of the courts the change has not been restricted to the practical procedural aspects of proof of religious law but has effected a change in its status generally. The application of religious law is no longer a question of *fact* but of *law*. If hitherto the whole problem had been considered from the perspective of religious law as fact[27] —an approach which still applies to foreign law[28]—the desire now is to make it comparable to domestic law in every respect.[29]

Before discussing this change in its relation to the ascertainment of religious law, we must clarify the scope of the new rule. Does it affect every religious law applied in Israel, or did the legislator have in mind only the law of the recognized religious communities?

The definition itself now contains a general limitation: "all as in force in Palestine before the establishment of the State or as in force in the State." The question, however, remains, what does this limitation mean. It is possible to understand it as referring to every religious law applied in Israel, in which case the test is formal: every religious law applied in Israel by virtue of Israeli legislative intent. This approach would have section 33 of the Interpretation Ordinance apply not only to the religious law of the recognized communities but to every religious law relied upon for solving any dispute. For example domestic law provides that matters of the personal status of a foreigner are to be decided in accordance with

---

[25] Compare the position of Justice Zmoira, above pp. 27–28 note 37.

[26] Cf. Englard, "The Problem of Jewish Law in a Jewish State" 3 (1968) *Is. L.R.* 254.

[26a] See C.A. 247/64, *Roshtash* v. *Roshtash,* 18 P.D. (4) 264, 269.

[27] The situation found expression inter alia in the non-interference of the Supreme Court in the findings of the lower courts in matters of religious law where these rest on sufficient valid evidence. Cf. C.A. 65/34, 2 P.L.R. 348 but see also C.A. 85/38, *ibid.*

[28] As noted, Article 64 (iii) of the Palestine Order-in-Council enables an opinion of a foreign consul to be received in matters of personal status. See n. 19 above.

[29] For example, the doctrine of *stare decisis,* see pp. 130 et seq. below.

his national law. Assuming that the national law refers us to some religious law (in India,[30] say), will the latter also come under judicial notice? In our view this was not the legislative intention. A limited number of religious systems were in mind, those which "permanently" apply to residents *in matters of personal status,* that is, the laws of recognized communities. The expression "as in force in the State" appears to have no formal technical meaning but expresses the idea of permanent reference.

This brings us to the second question: Is judicial notice taken of the law of a recognized community in every possible respect or only in matters of personal status? We believe that the legislator had in mind only matters of personal status. We infer this from the words, "as in force in the State" in the definition, which point to a permanent application of religious law and not to a fortuitous one.[31]

Nevertheless where the matter is one of personal status in a recognized community, no distinction should be made between a fact and law reference. Every question of religious law is a matter of "law" within the

---

[30] Cf. Derrett, 7 (1958) *A.J.C.L.* 380–393; Id., "Statutory Amendments of the Personal Law of Hindus since Indian Independence," *Rapports généraux au Ve. Congrès international de droit comparé,* I (Brussels 1960), pp. 101–124.

[31] Support for this conclusion can be found in a similar limitation in the case law with regard to English Common law. The latter, as we know, is also included in the definition of "law." The Supreme Court has held that English law which is subject to judicial notice is the law which applies by virtue of Art. 46 of the Palestine Order-in-Council, that is to say, by virtue of a permanent and general reference. Accordingly in every case of a one-time reference to English law (for example, when it is the national law of a foreign citizen), the party who relies on that law has the burden of proving it and must do so by expert opinion. See C.A. 118/51, *New Zealand Insurance Co. Ltd.* v. *Youval,* 7 P.D. 518, 527 (English translation 1 S.J.S.C. 332, 344): "We have to be careful not to be confused by, and to avoid the mistake of relying purely on, outward similarities. If by following the rule proposed by Wolff and Dicey, we have to ascertain the law which is in force in England on the subject, this will not be the English common law which, through article 46 of the Order in Council, has become our 'own' local law, but the English law as a foreign law consisting of both common law as well as statutes. This law we have to apply by reason of the principles of Private International Law.... This English law as a 'foreign law' and especially the statutory part of it, cannot be considered as 'a notorious fact that requires no proof.' Even though it is 'English' it has to be proved like all foreign law by evidence of experts and not by reference to text books. For the content of a foreign law is a question of fact and not a question of law." Cf. 77/66, *Davis* v. *Woodall,* 59 P.M. 151. The specific references to English law in local legislation, such as the Civil Wrongs Ordinance, the Criminal Law Ordinance and others, should be regarded as permanent references.

meaning of the Interpretation Ordinance and it makes no difference whether the reference to that law is for the purpose of determining the legal result of a norm or its fact situation. Thus should a question of the validity of a marriage arise in a criminal case, judicial notice is taken of the relevant religious law and it need not be proved.[32]

In conclusion, section 33 of the Interpretation Ordinance is subject to two limitations, one relating to the particular religious law and the other to the subject matter of litigation. Judicial notice is taken of religious law if it is the law of a recognized community and the question before the court involves a matter of personal status, as defined in art. 51 of the Palestine Order in Council, 1922.

Accordingly, in the case of a citizen of India where his national law refers us to his personal religious law judicial notice will not be taken of religious law and the problem of its proof must be resolved according to the rules concerning foreign national law (art. 64(3) of the Order in Council).[33] Likewise, if a matter should come before an Israeli court involving a Catholic religious order whose rules require the matter to be determined by Canon Law, no judicial notice will be taken of the rules of Canon Law under section 33, and the parties must prove them like any other foreign law.

These questions have not been explicitly discussed in Israeli case law.[34] Jewish law is in reality the principal religious law on which parties base their case. In addition national and religious considerations encourage those judges expert in *Halakha* to refer of their own motion to its provisions in all areas of law.[35] It is therefore not surprising that the civil

---

[32] As, for example, in the framework of the Penal Law Amendment (Bigamy) Law, 5719–1959; cf. pp. 27, 59 above and Cr. A. 485/65, *Amash* v. *A.G.*, 20 P.D. (1) 378. The term "law" also includes the religious laws of the recognized communities to which the legislator has referred by conditional reference. See, pp. 67–68 above.

[33] See nn. 18 and 19 above.

[34] But cf. C.A. 216/65, *Artan* v. *"The Four Carpenters,"* 50 P.M. 352. Here the judge took the position that the doctrine of binding precedent applied only to those religious laws as to which the legislature has provided "in unequivocal language" that they apply to particular subjects "as it did in matters concerning the personal status of Jews." On the problem of precedent, see pp. 126 et seq. below.

[35] Among many examples, see H.C.J. 290/65, *Altgar* v. *Municipality of Ramat-Gan*, 20 P.D. (1) 29 (Justice Kister); C.A. 110/53, *Jacobs* v. *Kartuz* 9 P.D. 1401 (Justice Silberg), and the further examples in M. Elon, "Jewish Law in the Law of the State", 25 (1969) *HaPraklit*, 27, 44; S. Meron, "Jewish Law in the Law Reports of 1968–1969," *Dine Israel, an Annual of Jewish Law*

courts show no tendency to limit the possibilities of self- and independent reliance on religious law. But however understandable this sympathetic approach to Jewish law, which confers on it a special status, we must not overlook the fact that the statutory provisions refer to *all* religious laws.[36] There is no doubt that the question of the scope of section 33 will arise, if at all, in connection with the religious laws of other communities, access to which is more infrequent and more difficult.

The problem is in the circumstances the *meaning* of section 33 of the Interpretation Ordinance. In the case of the personal status of a person belonging to one of the recognized religious communities, what does it mean that "judicial notice shall be taken"? Does it bar the judge from hearing expert testimony on the content of the religious law? How should a judge act when he does not know the content of that law?

The British Mandatory judges were the first to be faced with the problem of judicial notice after the amendment of the Ordinance, when called upon for the most part to decide *halakhic* questions. The new provision that judicial notice is to be taken of religious law did not fit the true state of their knowledge. One of these judges reacted quite negatively by laying down in absolute terms that "the court is not required to know the religious law, despite the provisions of Section 33 of the Interpretation Ordinance, 1945. In my opinion one cannot expect the Palestinian judge to know the laws of all the religious communities at the same time that English courts are not required to know the Roman Catholic laws in England."[37] Although understandable, the reasoning lacks all basis in law.[38]

---

and *Israeli Family Law* (Z. Falk, ed.) vol. 1 (Jerusalem 1969), pp. 101–106 (in Hebrew).

[36] In this context, however, it should be noted that the courts are not completely consistent concerning foreign law. Despite the prevailing view (see p. 84 above) that foreign law is treated as a fact, the courts frequently rely of their own initiative on foreign law and decisions as a source of inspiration for their conclusions about Israeli law. Reliance on American law is particularly common. Cf. M. Wolff, *Private International Law* (2nd ed. Oxford 1950), p. 220; Shawa, *op. cit.*, pp. 736–737.

[37] The judgment is summarized in 3 (1946) *HaPraklit* 153, and is cited in 115/54, 12 P.M. 129, 136.

[38] See the more balanced position taken in C.C. 38/44, 1946 S.J.D.C. 41, 43: "Having regard to the recent amendment of the Interpretation Ordinance it falls upon the court to take judicial notice, among other systems of law, the applicable Jewish Law. That, of course, puts any judge, who has not had the advantage of studying that system of law, in considerable difficulty."

After the establishment of the State, which led to a change in the composition of the courts, a new situation was created in which knowledge of Jewish law was more widespread among the judges. In these circumstances we can understand the following categorical observation of an Israeli judge, which expresses a sympathetic approach to Jewish law: "I am unwilling to regard Jewish law as foreign law; it is impossible for a Jewish judge to have to listen to expert witnesses for knowledge of what Jewish law requires."[39] Yet this view as well—between which and that of the Mandatory judge a characteristic difference exists—is not sufficiently well-based in law. Israeli law, as we have seen, grants equal status to all recognized religious law. The truth is also that even in Israel not all judges are expert in Jewish law and only a tiny minority have any expertise whatsoever in other religious laws.

What then will a judge, without knowledge of religious law or doubtful of its solution of a particular problem, do? The precise meaning of section 33 is involved. Clearly this section allows the judge to rely on his personal knowledge, exactly as in the case of any domestic legal provision.[40] The question should go the other way: in the absence of such knowledge may the judge be assisted by experts?

The latter question was discussed extensively in a District Court judgment.[41] One of the parties sought to aid the judge with expert evidence to which the other party objected. Relying strictly on the words "Judicial notice shall be taken of every law," the judge said: "It is provided that 'judicial notice shall be taken', not that evidence may not be given. The emphasis is upon 'judicial notice shall be taken'." The judge concluded that the court may rely on its personal knowledge, but it if lacks sufficient qualifications in this area, it will be dependent on an expert witness to advise it, but without the evidence being received as a fact in relation to the religious law.[42]

---

[39] C.A. 216/65, *Artan v. "The Four Carpenters,"* 50 P.M. 352, 354.
[40] C.A. 267/64: "The term 'law' also includes religious laws and therefore the rule of *jura novit curia* clearly applies."
[41] 115/54, *Grenzburg v. Bulein,* 12 P.M. 129.
[42] *Ibid.,* at 137. The court reached similar conclusions in other cases; see 60/64 *Korlandski v. Zioni,* 49 P.M. 13, 17: "I would not hesitate... to hear the evidence of a rabbi who would instruct us in the law and answer the questions of the parties and of the court, in order to assist the court to reach the correct conclusion in accordance with *Halakha.* I say this despite the fact that under the definition of 'law' in the Interpretation Ordinance, the legislature assumes that the law is known to the court and need not be proved as a fact."; 2542/62/8, *Hassan v. Benjamin,* 35 P.M. 243, 253: "Indeed the rule is that under the

Although this conclusion is acceptable, we do not agree with its reasoning. That judicial notice is taken of some law means that it is within the judicial knowledge of the court and is not amenable to proof at all: "Judicial notice covers the provisions of law which is not a matter of evidence at all."[43] The law *is not considered to be a fact in issue,* and therefore does not lend itself to a process of proof. A matter which needs no evidence is not amenable to proof.[44] But, as we have said, that does not derogate from the correctness of the conclusion. For just as the judge may, and even must, be assisted by his own personal knowledge, which means that he may take steps to acquire knowledge independently about the religious law (by reading the literature, consulting with associates, and so on),[45] logic likewise requires that he should be at liberty to be assisted by other people in the court room. Why should he be prevented from doing in public what he may do in his chambers?

In the normal case involving a point of domestic law, the judge is assisted by lawyers representing the parties. The citing of precedents and the submission of legal argument are indeed in the nature of a duty placed on

---

Interpretation Ordinance there is no need for evidence of religious law and the court takes judicial notice of religious matters; however, ... in practice this provision only means that the court is not required to hear expert witnesses and may rely on the books, but one should not expect judges in the secular courts to be familiar with all the laws of the religious communities with which they are required to deal, and it is therefore preferable to hear the experts, although the court is not bound by their opinion"; 99/66, *Arshid* v. *Arshid*, 58 P.M. 331, 337–339.

[43] Phipson, *Evidence* (11th ed. London 1970) § 47; Walker, *The Law of Evidence in Scotland* (Edinburgh and Glasgow 1964) p. 48: "Evidence regarding these matters is excluded."; David, *op. cit.,* no. 223. We refer to judicial notice in matters of law. "Judicial notice" is more extensive and there are cases in which the judge is assisted by witnesses. There is no need to consider here the problem whether this testimony is in the nature of evidence. Cross and Wilkins, *An Outline of the Law of Evidence* (3rd ed. London 1971), p. 38.

[44] The approach of English law which regards knowledge of the law as being part of the topic of judicial notice blurs somewhat the difference between the *duty* of the court to know the law (*jura novit curia*) and its *right* to acquire information of the facts which are the subject of judicial notice (*notoria non egent probatione*). The two are not identical and in other systems are viewed as separate matters. Cf. Ch. T. McCormick, "Judicial Notice," 5 (1951–52) *Vanderbilt L.R.* 296, 304: "As to domestic law generally, the judge is not merely permitted to take judicial notice but required to do so."

[45] Cf., *e.g.*, C.A. 63/69, *Joseph* v. *Joseph*, 23 P.D. (1) 804, 811, in which Justice Cohn noted that his colleague, Justice Kister, who was not sitting in that case, had called his attention to a source of Jewish Law.

the lawyer, despite the fact that domestic law is a matter of judicial notice which does not require proof.[46] We see no reason therefore, to prevent the judge who is not expert in a particular religious law from requesting the parties to assist him by producing expert opinion or from obtaining such an opinion on his own initiative.[47]

Since, however, *proof of a fact* is not involved, such an opinion is not testimony in any technical sense; it is a form of assistance to the court, similar to the continental conception of expert opinion testimony.[48] Nonetheless, even if such an opinion is not evidence in the strict sense, some of the rules which apply to the taking of evidence should properly be observed. In particular, the judge should give both sides a chance to present their positions. Further, where the judge has himself initiated the expert opinion, it should be put to the parties so that they can react to it either by argument or by submission of a further opinion. The same applies where one party has submitted an expert opinion; the other party should be given an opportunity to present his position with respect thereto.[49]

---

[46] Cf. Walker, *op. et loc. cit.* We should understand in this sense the statement of Justice Witkon in H.C.J. 359/66, *Gitea* v. *The Chief Rabbinate*, 22 P.D. (1) 290, 301: "Had the petitioner succeeded in showing that the respondents erred in their decision and that there is some means under *Halakha* to regard the conversion of his mother as proven, I would grant him relief; he did not do so and therefore... we have no choice but to dismiss the order nisi." The judge did not have in mind *proof* of religious law but its *reasoning*. Therefore, the criticism of Shawa is not well founded: 25 (1970) *HaPraklit*, 617, 628–629.

[47] As for the role of the judge in ascertaining the foreign law applicable by virtue of the rules of private international law, see in particular David, *op. cit.*, pp. 141 et seq.; Batiffol, *op. cit.*, no. 330; Rigaux, *op. cit.*, pp. 212 et seq. See also the situation in German law and in other systems in which a duty to ascertain the law is placed on the judge: Sass, *op. et loc. cit.*, pp. 141 et seq.; Zajtay, *op. cit., passim;* Giuliano, *op. et. loc. cit.;* Kegel, *op. cit.*, pp. 200 et seq.; Cappelletti, *op. cit.*, pp. 150 et seq., and in particular the last author who deals with the relationship between the principle that judicial notice is taken of law and the right to be assisted by expert opinion. Cf. Sapienza, "Il principio 'iura novit curia' e il problema della prova delle leggi straniere," (1961) *Riv. trim. dir. proc. civile* 41.

[48] It appears that in England as well expert opinion was not treated at first as evidence. See Harnon, "The Judge's Initiative in Calling Witnesses," 19 (1963) *HaPraklit* 246–258, and the sources there cited. See, in general, David, *op. cit.*, pp. 212 et seq., 244 et seq.

[49] Cf. David, *op. cit.*, pp. 190 et seq., 231 et seq.; Motulski, "L'office du juge et la loi étrangère," *Mélanges Maury*, pp. 337, 368. Local courts have in practice respected this principle; see 155/54 at 140: "Finally I wish to note that if counsel

Obviously, the judge is not bound by the opinions and is free to reach his own conclusions in law. This is also the situation to some extent in the case of foreign law[50]—which is considered to be a question of fact in domestic law—and *a fortiori* when religious law which is regarded as a question of law falls to be determined.[51]

Thus far we have considered the situation where the judge is interested in obtaining information. What is the rule where the parties themselves wish to present expert opinion, but the judge sees no need therefor? Have the parties any rights? The answer appears to be no. Since religious law is not *subject to* proof, the parties cannot require the judge to receive any expert opinion.[52] They may, however, *argue* the question of the law's content. In the final analysis there is no great difference between the two situations.

On the other hand, if the judge does not know religious law and the parties do not give him the necessary assistance, either because they do not rely on that law at all or because they do not present expert opinion, then the judge must clarify the matter by himself.[53] Here the position of religious law is equivalent to that of the law enacted by the legislature itself in view of the explicit provision of the Interpretation Ordinance: "judicial notice shall be taken of every law," including, as above-mentioned, religious law.

It follows that from the practical point of view of the judge's knowledge religious law is in an intermediate position between a question of law and a question of fact. It needs no proof and the parties do not bear the

---

for the respondents sees fit, on his part, to call an expert on Jewish law, I will not prevent him, although evidence has already been concluded, in order that I may have a full and clear picture of Jewish law in so far as it relates to the matter in hand."; 99/66, *Arshid* v. *Arshid*, 58 P.M. 331, 338.

[50] The English courts have reserved to themselves freedom to criticise, even where the testimony of the expert is uncontradicted. See the sources cited in Dicey and Morris, *op. cit.*, p. 1129 nn. 57–61; Cheshire, *op. cit.*, pp. 126–127; David, *op. cit.*, pp. 258 et seq.; Ehrenzweig, *op. cit.*, p. 365.

[51] See 2542/62/8, *Hassan* v. *Benjamin*, 35 P.M. 243, 253–256; see the sources cited in n. 42.

[52] 115/54, at 137: "... in as far as a judge hearing a matter involving questions of Jewish Law has actual knowledge of that law, he will rule in accordance therewith without resorting to the aid of any expert witness."

[53] Regarding the duty of the judge to ascertain the content of foreign law see n. 47 above. As to the similar question of application of Canon Law in Italian Law, see in the same spirit Falco, *Corso di diritto ecclesiastico*, vol. 2 (Padova 1938), p. 41.

burden of persuasion. The court may, and even must, take steps when necessary to ascertain the content of religious law and, in doing so, to observe certain of the rules of evidence.

To sum up the meaning of section 33 of the Interpretation Ordinance —in the light of the 1945 amendment which expanded the term "law" to include religious laws—we can say that the principal change was in the role of the court. Whereas under the original Article 47 of the Palestine Order in Council the court was entitled to initiate inquiry into religious law but the parties continued to bear the burden of proof, under the amendment the inquiry has become the duty of the court and is not a matter requiring proof. This difference raised the problem of the relation between the two provisions which continued to exist side by side,[54] but it disappeared in 1957 when the legislature quietly repealed Article 47.[55] The repeal was indeed justified since, in the foregoing, Article 47 did not add anything to powers which the court already enjoyed under the Interpretation Ordinance.

---

[54] The problem was mentioned in 115/54, but the court saw no need to resolve it in the circumstances of that case.

[55] The provision was repealed by section 48(8) of the Courts Law, 5717–1957. See the observations of the chairman of the Constitution, Law and Judiciary Committee of the Knesset about certain reservations in respect of another matter, which indicate that the Committee did not discuss the repealing provision at all (22 *Divre HaKnesset*, p. 2507).

CHAPTER III

ADJUDICATION OF RELIGIOUS LAW BY THE COURTS

The purpose of this study is to examine the status of religious law in Israel and our point of departure, the autonomous character of the two normative systems. The central problem in the application of religious law by secular courts is what is the relationship between the autonomous character of religious law and the adjudicatory process by which the courts apply it in accordance with legislative prescript. The problem has various aspects—the treatment of religious norms by the secular judge, that is, the judicial process as such; the relationship between secular adjudication and adjudication by religious institutions; the question whether the doctrine of the binding precedent applies to decisions on the content of religious law.

1. *The Judicial Process*

In the previous chapter we dealt with the ascertainment of religious law in general. In practice, however, the judicial process is composite and two stages are discernable. The first is to ascertain and comprehend the legal provisions relevant to the matter in hand; the second is to apply these provisions to the circumstances of the case.[1] Although the two stages are closely related, they are distinguishable by the degree of concretization of the legal norm. In the first stage the aim is to understand the meaning of the legal norm in its own terms, be it a legislative act or a binding precedent. Here the norm is treated as having a general, abstract character. In the second stage the task is to evaluate the actual circumstances of the case

---

[1] It is usual in the literature to designate the first stage as *interpretation* and the second as *application* of the legal norm. See David, *op. cit.*, nos. 345 et seq.; Larenz, *Methodenlehre der Rechtswissenschaft* (2. Aufl. Berlin 1969), pp. 228 et seq., 291 et scq.; Engisch, *Einführung in das juristische Denken* (5. Aufl. Stuttgart 1971), pp. 43 et seq.; cf. Hart, *The Concept of Law* (Oxford 1961), pp. 121 et seq.

in the light of the relevant norms.[2] This is a process of concretization, since the abstract norm is applied to existing facts which are unique.[3]

The judge who applies religious law must carry out both tasks, but considerable room is left for his creative role.[4] We will not deal here with the limits on the freedom of the judge to arrive at a result acceptable to him in the framework of the existing norms. The question has engaged many scholars,[5] and the last word has not yet been said.

Here, however, special importance attaches to the existence of this judicial freedom, because it touches on a foreign normative system. As was pointed out at the beginning of this Part,[6] there is a difference between the judge's approach to his own system and his approach to another system. The difference will in practice manifest itself in both of the aforementioned stages: the stage of *interpreting* the religious provision and the stage of *applying* it to the specific case. The judge who is called upon to apply a foreign system does not identify himself with it as he generally does with his national normative system. The absence of this feeling greatly diminishes the impulse to play a creative role in the judicial process. Another factor which contributes to the passive attitude of the average judge is his unfamiliarity with religious law and his necessary dependence on the opinion of experts.[7] We have already noted the different attitude towards Jewish religious law of those judges who are experts in it; a creative initiative is displayed comparable to that shown in respect of Israeli secular law.[8]

When, however, judges utilize the creative possibilities of fashioning religious norms in an independent manner, their initiative is apt to result

---

[2] In the German literature this process is called "Subsumtion." See the sources cited in the previous note, and particularly Larenz, *op. cit.*, p. 255 n. 1. On the relationship of the two stages, see R.B. Seidman, "The Judicial Process Reconsidered in the Light of Role-Theory," 32 (1969) *M.L.R.* 516, 520 et seq.

[3] The process of concretizing the norm and the role of the judge are discussed in Kelsen, *Pure Theory of Law,* pp. 236 et seq.; 348 et seq.

[4] In general see Kelsen *ibid.*, pp. 346 et seq., and also Hart, *op. cit.*, pp. 121 et seq.

[5] See the sources cited in n. 1 and Esser, *Grundsatz und Norm in der richterlichen Fortbildung des Privatrechts* (Tübingen 1956); Id., *Vorverständnis und Methodenwahl in der Rechtsfindung,* (Frankfurt/M 1970); Stone, *Legal System and Lawyers' Reasoning* (London 1964) passim.

[6] See p. 85 above.

[7] Cf. 99/66, *Arshid v. Arshid,* 58 P.M. 331, 337–339; Note the questions put to the experts.

[8] Above p. 86.

in a divergence between the substantive solutions of the secular courts and those of the religious judicial system. The phenomenon of different outcome in the two jurisdictions is well known.[9] One of the reasons is that the law of the State does not receive religious law in its entirety but distinguishes, for example, between substantive law and procedure, a distinction which we will examine later.[10] In our opinion, even apart from these external limiting factors, the possibility of divergence is inevitable because of the religious character of the norms. The larger the judge's role in the judicial process, the greater the prospect of divergence. The feature particular to Jewish law—the absence of codification and the existence of many points still in dispute—lend weight to the role of the religious judge in the process of law determination.[11] Even apart from this factor, there is an essential difference in the ideology of the secular judge. The difference is of particular significance where one poses it against the religious outlook in respect of a religious norm. The tension is not so accentuated when the relationship between the legal systems of two *states* is involved, since very possibly no substantial difference exists between the social background of the two systems; there are reasonable prospects that the conclusion of the local judge will not be very distant from that which the foreign judge would reach in applying his own law.[11a] The situation is otherwise with respect to religious law based as that is on transcendent presuppositions which are not acceptable to persons who are not of the same faith.

This difference is especially in evidence where the religious norms themselves leave scope for judicial discretion as when a general concept involving a value judgment is to be construed. It is, for example, a principle of Jewish religious law that the decisive test regarding custody is "the child's welfare".[12] What will appear to be best for a child's welfare to a judge of a religious court will almost certainly not accord with the tests applied

---

[9] Above p. 76.
[10] Below, pp. 177 et seq.
[11] For further details, see the present writer's treatment of the incorporation of Jewish law in the Israeli legal system, "The Problem of Jewish Law in a Jewish State," 3 (1968) *Is. L.R.* 254.
[11a] The truth is that here too there is no identity in the outcome of the case. See specially Ehrenzweig, *op. cit.*, pp. 361–362, 366: "We must acquiesce in the fact that what we are applying as foreign law is nothing but a 'domestic jus gentium'."
[12] See *Shulhan Arukh,* Eben Ezer, 82, 7 and Rema's comment thereon. S.T. 1/60, *Winter* v. *Beeri,* 15 P.D. 1457, 1477 et seq. (per Rabbi Goldschmid); Shereshevski, *Family Law* (2d ed. Jerusalem 1967), pp. 376–381 (in Hebrew).

by a secular judge who does not regard himself bound by the yoke of religious commandment.[12a]

A number of Israeli judgments exemplify the conflict between secular and religious decisions resulting from the difference in outlook. One of the cases concerns the status of a Jewish couple who had married abroad in a civil ceremony. Such a marriage is not valid in the view of the Jewish religious courts, yet formal religious divorce proceedings are required to terminate the marriage so as to remove the remotest doubt of validity because of the seriousness with which Jewish law regards adultery.[13] On the other hand according to the rabbinical courts the man is not to be compelled to legitimate the union by religiously marrying the woman. If the wife therefore does not consent to accept a *get*, the man may be allowed to marry another woman.[14] The basis of this approach is the view that cohabitation following a civil ceremony alone is contrary to religious commandment. It is thus not surprising that a completely different attitude was adopted by the judges of the Israeli Supreme Court when the question came before them.[15] [16]

[12a] See Shifman, "Child Welfare in the Rabbinical Court," 5 (1974) *Mishpatim* 421, 427 et seq.

[13] For the approach of Jewish Law to civil marriage, see Shereshevski, *op. cit.*, pp. 85 et seq.; Levinger, "Will Civil Marriages Split the Nation?", (1966) *Ovnaim* 65, 67 et seq. (in (Hebrew).

[14] Appeal 89/5720, 3 *Law Reports of the Rabbinical Courts*, 369, 374: "And thus in this case there is in law certainly no more than a doubtful marriage, and if they are to live together he should marry her in a valid ceremony and if he is not willing to do so, he cannot be forced against his will to wed her. Accordingly the law requires the wife to accept a divorce in order that the man be set free.... Even though we have made it sufficiently clear that the wife is to be compelled to accept a divorce, in accordance with *Halakha*, nonetheless, a simple judgment that the wife should be so compelled is apt to lead to her imprisonment, if she refuses to obey the judgment for some period of time and in accordance with law.... There are differing views about the proper manner of exerting compulsion on women.... It is possible to permit (the man) to take another woman as his wife in lawful Jewish marriage, since the first marriage is of doubtful validity and divorce is required only out of caution... and see Responsa Ahi'ezer, Part I, 10."

[15] H.C.J. 301/63, *Streit* v. *The Chief Rabbi of Israel*, 18 P.D. (1) 598, 615 (per Justice Silberg): "This couple have cohabited for more than thirty years, and they may continue to do so in the future, if only the husband is willing to celebrate a lawful Jewish wedding ceremony. On (the woman's) part, as emerges from all the circumstances of the case, there is nothing to prevent the ceremony, but *he* is not willing to do so. Because of *his* refusal to legitimate their life in common it is impossible to regard her as a woman who properly

The great importance which attaches to the philosophy of life, the faith of the judge when applying religious law has not been overlooked by the scholars. It has aroused heated controversy among Canon Law jurists in view of the fundamental argument that lawyers who do not believe in the Catholic faith are incapable of grasping the essence of the Canon Law. According to this view, the modern representatives of which include Del Giudice[17] and Baccari,[18] personal identification with the fundamentals of the Catholic faith (*sentire cum Ecclesia*) is a precondition of any profound understanding of the Canon law.[19] Many have criticized this view[20] for the reason that even if it is true that a religious outlook plays an important part in the Canon law, that does not prevent a non-believer understanding the system from a scientific point of view.

In our opinion, an understanding of religious law must be distinguished from its application, knowledge of it from its development. The non-believer may understand and describe the religious law, even if he does not accept the religious assumptions on which it rests but it will be hard

---

requires divorce and to permit him, for that reason, to marry another woman!"; and see also the observations of Justice Silberg, *ibid.*, at 627.

[16] Another matter in which conflict between the approach of the secular and the religious judges has manifested itself is that of a private marriage ceremony in the case of a prohibited marriage (between a *cohen* and a divorcee). See H.C.J. 80/63, *Gorfinkel, Chaklai* v. *Minister of the Interior*, 17 P.D. 2048, 2068–2069 (Justice Landau), and Cf. 465/5724 of the District Religious Court, Tel Aviv-Jaffo, 5 *Law Reports of the Rabbinical Courts*, 219, 222–223. In this connection, cf. H.C.J. 130–32/66, *Segev, Reichert* v. *The Rabbinical Court and the Chief Rabbinate of Safed*, 21 P.D. (2) 505, 534–535, and more particularly H.C.J. 51/69, *Rodnitzki* v. *The Rabbinical Court of Appeal*, 24 P.D. (1) 704. See also below pp. 170 et seq.

[17] V. Del Giudice, *Nozioni di diritto canonico* (11a ed., Milano 1962), p 12; Id, "Note conclusive circa la questione del metodo nello studio del diritto canonico," (1940) *Arch. di dir. eccl.* 3 et seq.

[18] R. Baccari, "Il sentimento religioso nell'interpretazione del Diritto Canonico," in *Studi in Onore di Vicenzo Del Giudice*, I, (Milano 1952), pp. 1 et seq.

[19] Del Giudice, *Nozioni*, p. 12: "Se e vero sempre che 'solo chi ama comprende,' è tanto più vero che l'aderenza spirituale alla verità cattolica—cioè, classicamente, il 'sentire cum Ecclesia'—è condizione per la 'conoscenza' profonda del diritto canonico."

[20] Fedele, "Il problema del metodo nello studio del diritto canonico," *Lo spirito del diritto canonico* (Padova 1962), pp. 35–40; Id., *Enciclopedia del diritto*, Vol. XII, (1964), pp. 896 et seq.; D'Avack, *Corso di diritto canonico*, Vol. I, (Milano 1956), pp. 70 et seq.

for him to play a creative role.[21] Religious faith has an important part in the actual application of religious law.

Indeed, one great contemporary Italian jurist in the field of ecclesiastical law—Arturo Carlo Jemolo—raises the question of the application of Canon Law by a secular judge in the following words, "When the Italian judge requires to apply foreign law, he need not in general rely on concepts which are essentially different from those to which he is accustomed, and he certainly need not adopt a new mental attitude; his efforts are generally completed with interpreting the foreign norm. In contrast, when our judge is required to apply the law of the Church, he must rely on such unique institutions as the *aequitas canonica* and the *epieicheia*." [22]

In Jewish tradition also we find many sources which stress the importance of God-fearingness and acceptance of the Torah and the commandments when determining the *Halakha*.[23] As the Talmud well says, "Every person who possesses learning without fear of Heaven is like the treasurer who has been given the keys to the house, but not to the outer gate." [24]

This problem of the difference in adjudication between secular and religious judges, for all its importance, is insoluble. Nor can it be avoided as long as jurisdiction is in the hands of a secular institution. Since the legislature is not prepared to grant exclusive jurisdiction to religious institutions,[25] we can only note the existence of the phenomenon.

[21] Cf. the examples in Baccari, *op. cit.,* pp. 17 et seq. The author stresses his view by means of the concepts *rationabilitas* and *aequitas canonica;* the determination of the content of these concepts is conditioned by the religious sense of the interpreter. The examples concern the practical application of religious law. Even the non-believer can discern that in the interpretation of these concepts the interpreter's philosophical outlook is important. His difficulty is to apply them to concrete reality. For the concept *aequitas canonica*, see n. 22 below.

[22] Jemolo, "Un caso di abuso di astrattismo giuridico," *Pagine sparse di diritto e storiografia* (Milano 1957), pp. 265, 271 et seq. The author goes on to emphasize the difference between the state courts and the church courts, noting that the latter have wider powers in that they are to some extent both legislative and executive institutions. As to this question, see pp. 118–119 below. For *aequitas canonica*, see Lesage, *La nature du droit canonique* (Ottawa 1960), pp. 135 et seq.; Fedele, "Certezza del diritto ed aequitas canonica," *Lo spirito del diritto canonico,* pp. 197 et seq.; Id., "L'equità canonica," *Discorsi sul diritto canonico* (Roma 1973) 59; Eichman, Mörsdorf, *op. cit.,* vol. 1, p. 113, and the authorities cited by these authors.

[23] See England, "The Problem of Jewish Law in a Jewish State," *cit.,* nn. 11 and 44.

[24] Babylonian Talmud, *Shabbat,* 31a and Rashi's comment, *ibid.*

[25] Cf. Tedeschi, "Paralipomena on Stare Decisis," 17 (1961) HaPraklit 244.

2. The Relationship between Secular and Religious Judgments

The problem of the autonomous character of religious law is not exhausted by the phenomenon just considered, the part played by the judge's outlook on adjudication. The question also has its implications at the formal level. What is the relationship between religious and secular legal interpretation? In more concrete terms, what is the binding force of religious precedents (that is, judgments of religious institutions) on the secular courts? Must the latter accept religious interpretations as binding, as being the authoritative expression of religious law? The problem can in principle be put as follows: does the autonomy of religious law in contemplation of the law of the State extend to the concretizing of norms by religious judicial institutions? Examination of a similar problem in private international law regarding the application of foreign law may be helpful. Here the question is to what extent a domestic court applying foreign law is bound by decisions of the foreign court in interpreting the provisions of a particular law. Is the domestic court free to deviate from such interpretation and exercise an independent approach to the foreign normative material? The accepted opinion is that the starting point must be the status of case law in the foreign law itself. If it has binding force there, then the rules which emerge are general norms of a binding nature. The domestic legislator, in referring to foreign law, refers to the complex of legal sources and thus also to such foreign case law as is of binding force.[26] What justification is there to reject a binding rule of another system, when the task is to apply the provisions of that system in their entirety? The domestic court must follow the binding interpretations of the foreign court.[27]

---

[26] Nussbaum, "The Problem of Proving Foreign Law," 50 (1940–41) *Yale L. J.*, 1018, 1032: "A valid legal limitation upon the forum's power may result from the force of foreign judicial decisions. In the first place, it is obvious that a civil law (or any other) forum applying the rules of a common law legal system must respect the rule of precedent even though the forum itself does not possess such a rule." Niboyet, "Qu'est-ce que la loi étrangère aux yeux des juges d'un pays déterminé", (1928) *Revue de droit international et de législation comparée*, 753, 791 et seq.; cf. Carbonnier, "Loi étrangère et jurisprudence étrangère," 62 (1935) *Clunet* 473, 478–79, 483 et seq.; David, *op. cit.*, pp. 275 et seq.; Kegel, *op. cit.*, § 15; cf. Wolff, *Private International Law* (2d ed., Oxford 1950), pp. 215 et seq.

[27] Cf. *Buerger v. N.Y. Life Assurance Co.*, (1927) 96 L.J.K.B. 930, 934: "a Court in this country cannot by putting its own construction upon the term 'interpretation' as it understands it, make a law for Russia which the Russian legal system does not recognize." (per Bankes, L.J.); cf. *Guaranty Trust Co. of N.Y. v. Hannay & Co.*, [1918] 2 K.B. 623, 638–39 (per Pickford, L.J.), 658–59 (per

The situation is different when court decisions do not constitute a source of law officially recognized under the doctrine of binding precedent. The accepted opinion is that judgments of foreign courts should be given great persuasive weight, particularly when they issue from the highest judicial authority, the functional concern of which is the consistency of the law, even if the doctrine of binding precedent does not apply.[28] It follows that the domestic judge will follow foreign judicial decisions in applying foreign law but is not absolutely bound to do so. He may for good reason deviate from rules laid down in foreign precedents.[29] No greater weight need ultimately be given to foreign case law than it enjoys in its native system.[30] Clearly a domestic court will not lightly reject a rule of a foreign system since the presumption is always that for-

---

Warrington L.J.), 667–670 (per Scrutton L.J.). It appears that Scrutton L.J. in these two cases recognizes the authority of the local court to deviate from the decision of the foreign court (See *Guaranty Trust* at 667). He does not, however, deal with the doctrine of binding precedent; see in particular his attitude towards the American precedents (at 669). Cf. also, David, *op. cit.,* pp. 280 et seq. See in this context the rule in *Erie R. Co. v. Tompkins,* (1938) 304 U.S. 64, 114 A.L.R. 1487, concerning the application of the laws of the various states of the United States in the federal courts: "The law to be applied in any case is the law of the State. And whether the law of the State be declared by its Legislature in a Statute or by its highest court in a decision is not a matter of federal concern" (at 78). On the problem of binding precedent in this context, see Moore, *Federal Practice* (2d ed. New York 1965), Secs. 0.402(1) nn. 15, 35; 0.307(1); Note, "How a Federal Court Determines State Law," 59 (1946) *Harv. L. R.* 1299; "Authority in State Courts of Lower Federal Court Decisions on National Law," 48 (1948) *Col. L. R.,* 943. Cf. also the problem of the interpretation of national law by the International Court; C.W. Jenks, "The Interpretation and Application of Municipal Law by the Permanent Court of International Justice," 19 (1938) *B.Y.I.L.* 67, 92–95; David, *op. cit.,* pp. 302 et seq.

[28] Nussbaum, "The Problem of Proving Foreign Law," *op. et loc. cit.;* Wolff, *op. cit.,* p. 215; Niboyet, *op. cit.,* pp. 799 et seq.; David, *op. cit.,* pp. 275 et seq.; Zajtay, *op. cit., International Encyclopedia of Comp. Law,* s. 24.

[29] Cf. Niederer, *Einführung in die allgemeinen Lehren des internationalen Privatrechts* (2. Aufl. Zürich 1956), p. 343: "Von der im fremden Staate üblichen Auslegung des fremden Rechts darf der inländische Richter nur abgehen, wenn die ihm aus guten Gründen in einem besonderen Falle als unrichtig erscheint." As to the grounds which justify a deviation from the interpretation accepted in the foreign state, see in particular David, *op. cit.,* pp. 278 et seq., who emphasizes the need for coordination between the various systems. In his view this consideration gives the judge a certain independence in interpreting the foreign law.

[30] Cf. David, *op. cit.,* p. 278.

eign courts understand their own law and rightly apply the directives of their own legislator; as one writer has said, "It behoves a judge to walk humbly." [31]

These principles of private international law are equally applicable to the religious law referred to by the Israeli legislator. The religious system is autonomous and the legislator in referring to it does not distinguish between its different legal sources. If, therefore, precedent has binding force in the religious system, it will retain the same status in Israeli law. It may be urged that religious law is different because it is deemed to be "law" of which judicial notice is taken, in contrast to foreign law which is treated as a question of fact.[32] The answer lies in the treatment of English law. That law is also deemed to be "law", yet, as Professor Tedeschi points out, "insofar as English law (or certain parts of it) has to be imported for filling the gaps in the Palestinian system—whether generally, by way of Article 46 of the Palestine Order in Council, 1922, or specifically under various Ordinances—it is clear that it is accepted as it is, according to the sources, and among them the precedents."[33]

Although the principle for solving the problem seems clear, it is difficult to apply to the status of Jewish law in Israel. One reason is that religious institutions, particularly the Jewish, are interlocked with the State's legal system, which complicates the question of the significance of their activities for the secular courts. Another reason is the definition of the functions of the religious courts within the religious system itself. As we shall see, these two matters are closely connected.

As was noted earlier,[34] the status of religious courts in Israel, and particularly the Rabbinical courts, is ambivalent. The State tends to view them as its own judicial institutions; in the eyes of the judges who sit in them and a part of the religious public, they are essentially autonomous

---

[31] Kegel, *op. cit.*, p. 202: "Allerdings, je mehr man von einer Sache versteht, um so freier darf man sich äussern, und vom ausländischen Recht wird man meist weniger verstehen als vom eigenen. Takt is also am Platze."

[32] On this problem, see pp. 93 et seq. above.

[33] Tedeschi, "On the Principle of *Stare Decisis*", *Studies in Israel Law* (Jerusalem 1960), pp. 114, 130. Controversy over the question whether we should follow new law introduced in England after the establishment of the State does not detract from the correctness of our conclusion since the controversy is whether the reference is "static" or "dynamic" (see above pp. 68–69); in any event no one disputes that in principle we must resort to English precedents, see Tedeschi, "The Problem of *Lacunae* in the Law and Art. 46 of Palestine Order in Council, 1922," *op. cit.*, pp. 166.

[34] P. 46 above.

institutions of the normative religious system. The practical test, of course, is found in the relationship between the secular and the religious courts.

First, the question may arise whether the secular courts (or more specifically the High Court of Justice) are empowered to review decisions of the religious courts and to reverse them if it is thought that they have erred *in the application of religious law*.

This question is close to our problem, but not identical with it. Indeed, if such power were recognized, it would mean the denial of autonomy to the religious judicial system. In this situation, the decisions of the religious courts would obviously lack binding force, even if the religious courts themselves accepted the doctrine of *stare decisis,* since in contemplation of the State the secular court functions as a kind of appellate tribunal for the religious judicial system. The accepted rule is, nevertheless, that the High Court of Justice does not review decisions of the religious courts as to their consistency with religious law.[35] Its function is to see that the religious courts do not exceed their authority, which also includes observance of the principles of natural justice in judicial proceedings.[36]

---

[35] See H.C.J. 301/63, 17 P.D. (1) 598, 636: "I agree with my colleagues that we cannot assume the powers of an appellate court with respect to the judgments of [the rabbinical courts] and express any opinion on their decisions from the *halakhic viewpoint*" (per the President); *ibid.,* at 608: "Counsel for the petitioner submitted that the decisions of the [rabbinical] courts disclose, on their face, legal errors; he exercised himself to discover religious sources which are not at one with the view of the law as expressed in the judgments of the rabbinical courts in this case. It is however, an established rule and a firm practice of this court that we do not sit in appeal on religious courts: Whatever they decide is their religious law and the secular court may not begin to doubt the nature and character of the religious court" (Justice Cohn); at 629: "The rabbinical court judges decide in accordance with its law and the secular court judges in accordance with its law and neither reviews the law of the other" (Justice Sussman). See also H.C.J. 130–132/60, *Segev, Reichert* v. *Rabbinical Court and Chief Rabbinate of Safed,* 21 P.D. (2) 505, 520. Justice Witkon took a different approach in H.C.J. 359/66, *Gitea* v. *The Chief Rabbinate,* 22 P.D. (1) 290, 297–298: in his opinion there is no fundamental obstacle to the intervention of the secular courts. See the criticism of this viewpoint by M. Shawa, "An Error in the Determination of Jewishness which Negates Jurisdiction," 25 (1970) *HaPraklit* 617, and in particular the sources cited at pp. 626–627, n. 44. We have considerable reservations about Shawa's approach as will become clear hereafter.

[36] See H.C.J. 130–132/66, at 518–519 and the sources there cited. In *Gitea,* at 295, Justice Landau suggested that it might be argued that an error concerning Jewish law should be considered an excess of jurisdiction. But he did not express an opinion and to the best of our knowledge such an argument has not yet

This situation, which results from an interpretation of the statutory provisions governing the role of the High Court of Justice (section 7 of the Courts Law, 5717–1957),[37] is, however, not decisive for the question regarding the relationship between secular and religious case law. The *absence* of a power to review religious court decisions does not necessarily mean that the secular courts will accept them as binding.[38]

Indeed, the unmistakable tendency of the secular courts is to treat the religious courts as judicial institutions of special expertise in matters of religious law, but not as autonomous organs of the entire religious system. Accordingly the binding force of religious-court decisions appears to the secular courts to be a question of the extent to which *res judicata* applies, just as in the case of any other decision of special courts which function in the State. This approach can be described in technical legal terms as a reference by the legislature to the *abstract norms* of the referred religious system. Decision-making, as the concretization of abstract norms, is a process in which there is no essential difference in status between the secular and religious courts. Both apply abstract norms to concrete circumstances and the religious courts have no normative priority in the exercise of this function—as distinguished from a possible qualitative superiority because of their special expertise. It follows that the secular courts are not bound by the interpretation of the religious courts. Although decisions of the religious courts have persuasive force deriving from the expertise of the religious judges, the secular court is in principle free to adopt a different interpretation as it thinks requisite according to existing abstract religious norms.

This view was expressed by Justice Witkon in *Gitea*:[39] "It is inconceivable for any question of *Halakha* to be a closed area to an Israeli [secular] court. Certainly, I agree that only in very rare cases will this Court disagree with the rabbinical courts on a matter of *Halakha*. Those

---

been accepted. For the concept of excess of jurisdiction cf. also H.C.J. 202/57, 12 P.D. 1528, where it was held that a religious court judgment which ignored the provisions of a law of the state which were binding upon it constituted a jurisdictional defect. See the criticism of Shawa, *op. cit.* p. 621 n. 16.

[37] See H.C.J. 301/63 at 619–620; H.C.J. 359/66 at 298, and in particular Shawa, *op. cit.*, and the authorities cited by him.

[38] It should be recalled that the High Court reviews specific cases, that is, the individual norms issuing out of the religious court. The question of the relation between religious and secular precedents extends to the binding force of rules established by religious precedents as general norms. See the discussion immediately following.

[39] H.C.J. 359/66, at 297.

courts are presumed to be expert in Jewish religious law, and, as in other areas requiring special expertise, we will not quickly dispute the opinions of experts. Religious courts are in this respect like other special courts and tribunals.... Religious law, whether written or oral, is also within the definition of 'law' (see section 1 of the Interpretation Ordinance) and the presumption is that a court of the State of Israel, which deals with the laws of various lands, is not a stranger to Jewish law." [40]

The conclusion is that the binding effect, if any, of a religious court decision rests solely on the doctrine of *res judicata*.[41] The decision is binding *qua individual normative ruling*, as distinguished from a general norm expressed by the principle of binding precedent.[42] Hence the binding

---

[40] Justice Witkon's remarks relate mainly to the possibility of review by the High Court of specific judgments of religious courts. It is clear, as we have said, that such review of the judgments of the supreme religious court would deny, at least from the point of view of the State, the doctrine of *stare decisis* as to decisions of the religious courts. Justice Berinson said so expressly in F.H. 23/69, *Joseph* v. *Joseph*, 24 P.D. (1) 792, 810: "It is reasonable to assume that in deciding on a matter covered by a decision of a religious court, a secular court will attach great weight to that fact and in general be guided by it... It is, however, clear that the decision of a religious court does not bind the courts of the State in a matter falling within their jurisdiction, even when it should be decided in accordance with religious law.... Even if, as we have said, a secular court properly respects the decision of a religious court in a matter within its jurisdiction, it may decide in an independent manner, according to the best of its knowledge and understanding."

[41] Cf. C.A. 54/65, *Mekitan* v. *Mekitan*, 19 P.D. (2) 651, 656: "Indeed, in the matter of the divorce, the finding of the rabbinical court that the wife was 'rebellious without cause' is final; however, the further finding of the rabbinical courts, at both levels, that the husband is not liable for her maintenance, was not necessary for the matter of the divorce and in point of law is to be deemed a mere expression of opinion, which has no *res judicata* effect in the technical sense." This case dealt with the difficulties which arise from the concurrent jurisdiction in matters of maintenance and the exclusive jurisdiction of the religious courts in matters of divorce. For the binding force of a judgment of the rabbinical court as *res judicata* see the decision in the previous case between same parties; C.A. 634/61, 16 P.D. 945, 948; cf. also C.A. 353/65, *Haham* v. *Haham*, 20 P.D. (2) 199, 207–208.

[42] As to this distinction in the framework of the application of foreign law (by virtue of the rules of private international law) cf. Niboyet, "La loi étrangère d'un pays déterminé," *cit.*, pp. 794 et seq. The author differentiates between *lex specialis* (a decision as an individual norm) and *lex generalis* (a decision as a precedent).

force of the decision is treated not as flowing from its internal authority but largely from considerations of legal efficacy.[43]

In our view, this reasoning does not afford a complete answer to the main question regarding the binding force of religious-court decisions. Even if we accept that the religious courts are part of the State's judicial system, we must still ask what is their status in the religious normative system. If in point of religious law itself, the rules of these religious courts have binding force, then the secular courts which must apply religious law whatever its source are not free to ignore this particular source. The matter is comparable to the status of enactments of the authoritative organs of the religious system which in any view bind the secular judicial system[44] operating a dynamic reference process.[45]

An examination of the status of religious courts in the religious system reveals that it is fundamentally different from the status of courts in a modern state. In the conception of Jewish Law a court is not only a judicial organ but also a legislative,[46] and to some extent an executive body.[47] The idea of the separation of powers has no place in traditional Jewish law,[48]

---

[43] See the observations of Justice Cohn in C.A. 54/65 at 657, in which he emphasizes the possibility that Jewish law does not recognize *res judicata* and adds: "However, the approach of the rabbinical courts in this matter, or the law under which they judge, is irrelevant to the law binding the secular court which is to give *res judicata* effect and not to allow the parties to contest a matter which has already been finally decided between them." As to the question whether Jewish law recognizes *res judicata*, see A. Mechlowitch, "Finality of Judgments in Jewish Law," *Dine Israel, an Annual of Jewish Law and Israeli Family Law*, vol. 1 (Jerusalem 1969), p. 7; cf. S.T. 1/60 *Winter v. Beeri* 15 P.D. 1457, 1487–1488.

[44] See H.C.J. 80/63, *Gorfinkel, Chuklai v. Minister of the Interior*, 17 P.D. 2048, 2061; H.C.J. 359/66, 294–295.

[45] As to this concept, see p. 68 above.

[46] Cf. Maimonides, *Hilkhot Sanhedrin*, XXIV, 4, and see generally Gulak, *The Foundations of Jewish Law*, Vol. 4, pp. 3 et seq. (in Hebrew), and in the field of criminal law, Y.M. Ginzburg, *Law for Israel* (Jerusalem 1956), pp. 1 et seq (in Hebrew).

[47] See Gulak, *op. cit.*, p. 43 and the sources there cited.

[48] See in particular the role of the High Court of Seventy-One (the Great Sanhedrin) as it appears in the sources of Jewish law; cf. Maimonides, *Hilkhot Mamrim* I, 1, and the sources cited in the *Encyclopedia Talmudica*, vol. 3, "The High Court" (Hebrew). The historical role of the Sanhedrin lies outside the present study. Our concern is purely dogmatic, the *halakhic* understanding of the Court, since that is a decisive factor in the shaping of the religious courts of today. The historical aspects are treated in Mantel, *Studies in the History of the Sanhedrin* (Tel Aviv 1969), pp. 64 et seq. (Hebrew). See also, *ibid.*, pp. 259 et seq., on the court of the President (Nasi).

and it appears that in the Canon law it exists only to a limited extent.[49] It is clearly possible to distinguish functionally between a legislative act and a judicial act, and this distinction is not overlooked by Jewish law; even if the religious court fills a legislative role, the legal basis for and the legal technique of a legislative act are different from those of a judicial act.[50] It would therefore be wrong to infer from the legislative power of the religious court that its judicial decisions are binding precedents, since precedent is a result of judicial authority.[51] Analytically therefore, whilst the legislative acts of a religious court are very conceivably binding as general norms, its judicial decisions may lack binding force.[52]

Thus we come to the main question: Does the doctrine of binding precedent apply in existing Jewish law? We emphasize the word "existing" because we are not concerned with establishing whether or not in the distant past there was a supreme judicial organ of authority. Even if it is assumed that the rules declared by the Sanhedrin, the court of seventy-one judges sitting in the Chamber of Hewn Stones in the Temple in Jerusalem, were indeed binding on all other religious courts,[53] the question today is

---

[49] The central concept of *potestas iurisdictionis* has three functions: legislative, judicial, and executive. Cf. Del Giudice, *Nozioni di diritto canonico* (11th ed. Milan 1962), pp. 90, 94 et seq.; Jemolo, "Un caso di abuso," etc., *cit.*, p. 272: "...uno ordinamento che solo recentemente ed in forma molto attenuata ha accettato una certa divisione dei poteri, ma ove la nozione dominante e quella della *iurisdictio*, che contiene in sè tre funzioni, legislativa, executiva e giudiziaria."

[50] The legal tools of legislation are *"Takkana"* and *"Gezera."* See Elon, *Jewish Law*, pp. 391 et seq. and the sources there cited.

[51] On our reservations concerning the views of Shawa, *op. et loc. cit.*, with respect to the status of the Rabbinical Court of Appeals in the State of Israel, see p. 117 below.

[52] Compare the talmudic principle: "One court cannot reverse the act of another court unless it is greater in wisdom and number." (M. Eduyot, I, 5) as explained by Maimonides, *Hilkhot Mamrim* I, 1, 2: "Where the High Court has decided a question of law according to one of the rules of interpretation and a subsequent court finds other grounds for arriving at a contrary conclusion, the latter can reverse the earlier decision, as it deems proper. Where a court has issued a prescript or made a regulation and a later court wishes to annul and set aside what the first has done, it can only do so if it is greater in wisdom and numbers." Cf. *Tosafot* to *B. Gittin 36b*. See also Cohn, "On those who immerse themselves in the Halakha," *Mishpat Wekalkala* (*Law and Economics*) vol. 3, pp. 129, 137–138 (in Hebrew).

[53] According to the sources it appears that the rules pronounced by the High Court bound all other courts. A *halakhic* pronouncement of the Great Sanhedrin was conceived as an *authentic interpretation* thereof. See the sources cited in

whether in the absence of this institution the doctrine of *stare decisis* applies.[54] More precisely for our purpose, does the doctrine apply in the religious judicial system in Israel?[55]

The accepted view is that the Jewish law does not today recognize the doctrine of *stare decisis*,[56] in contrast to *res judicata*.[57] It has been well put by Rabbi S. Israeli, "It follows that every religious court and scholar of [*halakhic*] authority is at once similar to and different from the High Court [that is, the Sanhedrin]. The High Court had the power to determine the law itself, and its determinations were binding, and every other court was thenceforth required to act accordingly. This power was given only to the High Court. As for other courts, though they decide cases by a majority, their decisions have no binding effect on other courts nor are they determinative of the law itself. This is so as regards the substance of the law, and other courts or scholars have authority to decide as seems proper to them. But as regards the particular case or problem before it, the decision of a court stands and the public must act accordingly as if it were an indisputable *halakhic* ruling in that case on that problem."[58]

From the viewpoint of Jewish law the authority of every rabbinical organ, it would seem, derives today from public consent to accept and

---

n. 48 above and Gulak, *op. cit.*, pp. 14 et seq., 18; H. Cohn, *op. cit.*, p. 133. Cf. I. Herzog, *The Main Institutions of Jewish Law* (2nd ed. London 1965), Vol. I, p. 15. We repeat that we are making no historical judgment, see n. 48.

[54] We disagree with Shawa who compares the status of the Rabbinical Court of Appeal today with that of the Great Sanhedrin (*op. cit.*, pp. 624, 625, 628). See also below on the Council of the Chief Rabbinate. See also H. Cohn, *op. et loc. cit.*, and see n. 61a below.

[55] Shawa's approach is puzzling. On the one hand he agrees that *stare decisis* does not exist in Jewish Law (*op. cit.*, pp. 625–626) and on the other hand argues that no one is entitled to differ from a judgment of the Rabbinical Court of Appeal (*ibid.*, p. 628). See the statement of Rabbi Israeli cited in the text at n. 58 below.

[56] See H. Cohn, *op. et loc. cit.*, and the sources cited; I. Herzog, *op. cit.*, p. 13; Elon, *op. cit.*, pp. 800 et seq. As to the question of *stare decisis* in the Canon law, see n. 88 below.

[57] Jewish law even limits the *res judicata* effect of a judgment; see the sources cited by Gulak, *op. cit.*, pp. 179 et seq., and by Mechlowitch, *op. et loc. cit.*; see n. 43 above and particularly regulations 116 and 117 of the Procedural Rules of Rabbinical Courts in Israel, 5720.

[58] Israeli, *Amud HaJemini* (*The Right-Hand Pillar*), (Tel Aviv 1966), pp. 45, 47–48 (in Hebrew). A series of judgments of a rabbinical court may, however, constitute a binding custom. See in particular the statement of Justice Kister in 377/56, *In re Bloom, deceased*, 12 P.M. 154, 160–161; 779/59, *Kerz v. Estate of Kerz*, 21 P.M. 400, 406–407.

abide by such authority, a fact which may be explained, as we have already observed,[59] by the absence over many generations of any central authority. Rabbinical authority is now based on the idea of the "local Master," an idea which relies not on any institutional hierarchy but on community consensus which results in a spatial division of authority. The rule is: "One may not rule on prohibitions or permissions, nor seek or exercise authority in the locality of a colleague."[60]

Nonetheless, any attempt to apply these principles to the real situation in Israel will demonstrate that new patterns have been created which do not correspond to the traditional approach. Hence the difficulty in answering the questions which concern us. The integration of rabbinical institutions into the normative system of the State has brought about a splitting up of functions. Judicial authority was granted to the rabbinical courts, organized hierarchically, with a Rabbinical High Court of Appeal and district courts. Residuary powers—not explicitly defined—were entrusted to the institutions of the rabbinate, headed by the Chief Rabbinical Council. This tendency to separate functions, which was strengthened after the establishment of the State,[61] does not accord with the approach of the *Halakha*. The latter views the religious court as the central body with varied powers. If therefore, we ask today what authority attaches under *Halakha* to the decisions of the Rabbinical High Court of Appeal, we immediately encounter the difficulty of defining the relationship between this body and the Chief Rabbinical Council.[61a] Rabbinical circles are certainly aware of the difficulty and we understand that the practice has developed of deciding issues of principle in joint sessions of the two bodies.[62]

---

[59] Above p. 29.

[60] *Shulhan Arukh, Yoreh Deah,* 245, 22 and Rema's gloss thereon.

[61] Under sections 4 and 8(a) of the Dayanim Law, 5716–1955, only the two Chief Rabbis are members of the Rabbinical Court of Appeal ex officio. But see the amendment of section 8(3) in 1969, that "where there are two town rabbis both qualified to be *dayanim*, both shall act as chief presiding *dayanim*."

[61a] From the *halakhic* viewpoint the problem exists of the relationship between the Rabbinical *District* Court and the Rabbinical Court of Appeal. The institution of a court of appeal is unusual in Jewish law. On the establishment of the Chief Rabbinate in Palestine in 1921 by the British government, considerable pressure had to be exercised on the Chief Rabbis to obtain their consent to the setting up of a Rabbinical Court of Appeal. For a case where a Rabbinical District court refused to abide by this appellate jurisdiction, see H.C.J. 214/64 *Bassan* v. *Rabbinical Court of Appeal,* 18 P.D. (4) 309, 310.

[62] Recently, for example, both institutions met to decide on the question of the registration of Jewish nationality. See also the Procedural Rules of Rabbinical

The present structure of two separate authorities, Courts and Rabbinate, is viewed by the State as an expression of the separation of the judicial function from the administrative and legislative functions, along the lines of institutions of the State. The extent to which this conception is in conflict with the outlook of the religious institutions can be seen from the facts of *Gitea*.[63] This case concerned the Jewishness of a member of the Falasha community. The person was referred to the Rabbinical District Court which in turn referred him to the Chief Rabbinate which gave its decision. The (secular) High Court of Justice, when called upon to review the matter, was astonished at the manner in which the rabbinical institutions had handled it. As Justice Landau observed, "I assume that the religious court acted as it did because it regards the Chief Rabbinate as the supreme authority in matters of religious law. It could be argued that in this the religious court erred, since the Chief Rabbinate, as distinct from the rabbinical courts system, no longer possesses judicial authority."[64] The Justice recognized, on the other hand, the Chief Rabbinate's legislative authority.[65] Justice Witkon also expressed wonder at the course taken by the religious institutions. "In this case the religious institutions acted in confusion. The petition passed from the authorized rabbi to the religious court, which in turn transferred it to the Chief Rabbinical Council, apparently because of its public importance. The reasons and the legal basis for these peregrinations are not clear to me."[66]

From the *halakhic* viewpoint there is nothing surprising in the religious court turning to the Chief Rabbinical Council or referring the petitioner to it. In *halakhic* literature the referral of legal questions to noted rabbis is the rule.[67] It would not be at all surprising for a rabbinical district court to put a question to a leading *halakhic* scholar living abroad who is an expert in some area of Jewish law. To the secular court the passage from a judicial authority (the religious court) to an administrative one (the Chief Rabbinical Council) is strange.[68] But the implied differentiation does not accord with the outlook of the religious institutions.

Courts in Israel, 5720 (1960), which were adopted in a joint session of the Council of the Chief Rabbinate and the judges of the Rabbinical Court of Appeal.

[63] H.C.J. 359/66, *Gitea v. The Chief Rabbinate and the Religious Council of Jerusalem*, 22 P.D. (1) 290.
[64] At 294.
[65] *Ibid*.
[66] At 296.
[67] Cf. Gulak, *op. cit.*, p. 18.
[68] See Justice Witkon in *Gitea* at 297.

From the foregoing it follows that "determination of the *Halakha*" is not identical with "judicial decision," and this is patently demonstrated by the duality of the religious courts and the Chief Rabbinate. If we now return to the question of the binding force of precedent in the religious system, we must come to a negative conclusion regarding the religious courts. Religious law does not give binding force to judicial decisions of the rabbinical courts, as such, in the manner known to English law. Even decisions of the Rabbinical High Court of Appeal have no binding force as precedents.[69] Formally that also solves the problem for the secular courts. If the decision of a religious court is not a source of law for the religious system, it is not by itself binding in the state system.[69a] Such a decision is persuasive and in practice the secular courts often rely on rabbinical court judgments.[70] All this, of course, from the viewpoint of the state law, which examines the sources of the religious law to which it refers. It may be assumed that a different answer would be given to the question of the relationship between religious and secular decisions if the question were posed from the *halakhic* viewpoint. Jewish law might well give a different answer to the question whether the secular courts may depart from the decisions of the rabbinical courts.[71] But that is not the question before us, since our point of departure is state law.[71a]

---

[69] Cf. rule 116 of the Procedural Rules of the Rabbinical Courts in Israel, 5720, which authorizes the court to rehear a case if it suspects that it is in error.

[69a] See, in this spirit, F.H. 23/69, *Joseph v. Joseph*, 24 P.D. (1) 792, 810, (per Justice Berinson); "As far as I know, even in the rabbinical courts one court does not regard itself bound by the ruling of another court. All the more is that the case as between a secular court and a religious court." On the other hand, the reasoning of Justice Cohn, at 809, is unacceptable. See the judgment of Justice Kahan at 810–812; see also C.A. 61/71, *Cohen v. Cohen*, 25 P.D. (2) 327, 331.

[70] See, for example, H.C.J. 130–132/66, *Segev, Reichert v. The Rabbinical Court, etc.*, 21 P.D. (2) 505, 518, 533; C.A. 13/66, *Plonit v. Plonit*, 20 P.D. (2) 512, 516; C.A. 166/66, *Goldman v. Goldman*, 20 P.D. (2) 533, 536; C.A. 231/66, *Hakhari v. Hakhari*, 20 P.D. (2) 685, 687; C.A. 63/69, *Joseph v. Joseph*, 23 P.D. (1) 804, 808–809.

[71] A religious court may regard a secular court incompetent to rule once a *halakhic* decision has been given by a rabbinical court.

[71a] Accordingly the reasoning of Justice Kister in F.H. 23/69 at 805 is very doubtful: "In my opinion we must accept the ruling of the rabbinical courts of Israel.... The reason ... may be found in the laws of the Torah which command obedience to the words of those learned therein of every generation, 'And Jephthah in his generation is as Samuel in his.'" This reasoning is based *on the viewpoint of Jewish religious law*. From the viewpoint of the law of

The integration of the institutions of religion into the state system and the special significance of the concept of *halakhic* decision [72] raise two additional questions worthy of consideration. One relates to the Chief Rabbinical Council and the other to the judicial institutions of the Catholic Church outside the State of Israel.

The Chief Rabbinical Council stands at the apex of the rabbinical system in Israel. The Council is the supreme *halakhic* institution in the State and it issues regulations and *halakhic* decisions on various questions of Jewish law. We may therefore ask how far such decisions bind the secular courts? The question has two aspects, first, the authority of the Chief Rabbinical Council in the eyes of the *Halakha* itself, and secondly its authority in the eyes of the State.

It is not easy to answer the first question. According to Rabbi Israeli,[73] one of the few who has concerned himself with the matter, "the majority of the public in Eretz Israel has accepted the Chief Rabbinate *as its Rabbis*.... It follows that the Chief Rabbinate enjoys the status of "the local Master" throughout Israel and the local rabbis act only as its agents. As a result, the rule of REMA (Rabbi Moses Isserles) applies,[74] one may not decide contrary to it, unless it has erred with respect to a Mishnaic rule, and not merely in a matter of discretion."[75]

Whatever the authority of the Chief Rabbinate under the *Halakha*,[76] we must nevertheless ask whether the State views it as a supreme *halakhic*

the State, this command does not prevail. It should be remembered, as noted by Justice Kahan in a slightly different context in the same case, that there are secular judges in the State of Israel who are not Jewish.

[72] That is, not only a judicial decision but also an authentic *halakhic* determination.

[73] Israeli, *op. cit.*, p. 51.

[74] See n. 60 above.

[75] As to the distinction between a mistake as to fundamental law and an error of discretion, see the sources cited in n. 57 above. See also Rabbi Israeli, *op. cit.*, p. 51, regarding that part of the public which has not accepted the authority of the Chief Rabbinate (for example, certain circles of Agudat Israel, which have a separate institution, the Council of the Great in the Torah): "It must be held that that does not involve a violation of the rule against establishing two religious courts in the same city." Cf. B. *Yebamoth*, 13–14; Maimonides, *Hilkhot Avodat Kokhavim* XII, 14 and the commentary of *Kesef Mishne,* thereon.

[76] In practice, the question may also arise with respect to the rabbinical courts. A *halakhic ruling* of the Council of the Chief Rabbinate, which it normally hands down in association with the judges of the Religious Court of Appeals binds, in our opinion, the religious courts in accordance with the view of Rabbi Israeli: "But as to that public, and it is the majority of the community in Israel, which chose the Chief Rabbinate and regards them as its Rabbis, *and*

institution with complete autonomy. Prima facie this is a curious question. Why does the State have to grant a religious institution a status higher than that which it enjoys in the framework of its own system? Although the matter may seem strange in respect of the relations between the legal systems of different states, it is not so with respect to a religious system operating within the area of a state itself. A state may be interested in dealing only with a single body representing exclusively a particular religion. Indeed this was the situation under the Ottoman Empire, when the heads of the respective religious communities were recognized as the exclusive representatives vis-à-vis the regime.[77] At the beginning of the Mandate the Chief Rabbinical Council was recognized as the supreme *halakhic* institution,[78] and there is reason for holding that this status has been preserved in the State of Israel.[79] On the other hand, there is nothing

---

to the rabbis who serve that community under appointment and authorization by the Chief Rabbinate, it is clear that [the Chief Rabbinate] has the status of the 'local Master' whose judgments and rulings are binding, even on questions of Biblical prohibitions, so long as no mistake of fundamental law is disclosed" (emphasis supplied).

[77] Englard, "The Status of the Council of the Chief Rabbinate and the Review Authority of the High Court of Justice," 22 (1964) *HaPraklit* 68.

[78] See the public notice of the Secretary of State, of March 18, 1921, cited *ibid.,* pp. 71–72. See also H.C.J. 69/25, *Federman* v. *Governor of the Southern District,* 1 P.L.R. 57, 63. The notice became ineffective upon the entry into force of the Knesset Israel Regulations, 1928, but in our opinion the status of the Chief Rabbinate as supreme authority in Jewish law was unchanged. See, however, A. Rubinstein, *The Constitutional Law of the State of Israel* (2nd ed. Tel Aviv 1974), pp. 116–119 (in Hebrew).

[79] See Englard, *op. cit.,* pp. 72–74; although it is true that this is not set out expressly in the Laws of the Knesset, the historical background to the creation of the institution and its name testify to its status in the eyes of the State. See the letter of appointment of Rabbi Yitshak Nissim on the occasion of his election in 1955 as *Rishon LeZion* and Chief Rabbi of Israel. The letter is signed by the President of the State, the Prime Minister and the Minister of Religious Affairs and states inter alia: "[He] has been appointed to shepherd the people of the Lord and lead it to the fountains of the Torah, and he shall be regarded as one who gives judgment and direction in all respects in accordance with the law of the Torah. What he says shall not be disputed and all his utterances shall be observed." But see Rubinstein, *op. cit.,* p. 119 n. 48. In our opinion there is no fundamental contradiction between the view that Jewish law draws its binding force in Israel from the law of the State (or, as Rubinstein puts it, "Jewish law is a part of the law of Israel") and our conclusion that the State views the Chief Rabbinate as the supreme *halakhic* institution. Both are the will of the Israeli legislature.

in Israeli law which recognises that the Rabbinical High Court of Appeal has a similar status; it is treated as an appellate tribunal and no more.[80]

If we are right in thinking that the Chief Rabbinical Council is the supreme *halakhic* institution in the eyes of the State, then its *halakhic* declarations are in principle binding on all authorities of the State, if and to the extent that these authorities must apply Jewish law according to the will of the Israeli legislature.

The scope of authority of the Chief Rabbinate has not, however, been sufficiently defined. It is not a judicial institution in the view of the State.[81] The secular courts have expressly recognized its legislative authority and have applied regulations which were promulgated by it in matters of marriage and divorce.[82] But the secular courts' attitude towards its *halakhic* decisions, which are functionally not legislative acts, has been considerably more reserved. In particular, the secular courts tend to regard *halakhic* decisions relating to specific problems as acts of concretizing existing religious norms. For the secular courts such decisions are either quasi-judicial or administrative acts as to which the Chief Rabbinate is not sovereign.[83] Accordingly they are not binding. The primary difficulty arises from the fact that the functional division between administrative, judicial and legislative acts is not easily adaptable to an institution which is thought of as a supreme *halakhic* authority. As we have emphasized above,[84] the preliminary and primary question is whether the State really recognises the Chief Rabbinical Council as a supreme *halakhic* authority. If it does,[85] then every decision on the content of *Halakha* binds the

---

[80] Hence our reservations as about the view of Shawa, *op. et loc. cit.*, and see n. 55 above.

[81] See the *Gitea* case. The judges hint that the High Court of Justice might have intervened to prevent the Council of the Chief Rabbinate from taking a judicial decision on a concrete dispute pending before a rabbinical court.

[82] H.C.J. 359/66 at 294; see Englard, *op. cit.*, n. 26.

[83] See H.C.J. 359/66. But see C.A. 238/53, *Cohen, Buslik v. A.G.*, 8 P.D 4, 23 (English translation 2 S.J.S.C, 239, 260–261): "This ruling of a high religious authority, expert in the matter, cannot be questioned by us tar as the religious aspect is concerned, so that for the purposes of this case, we have to assume that the appellant was indeed prohibited from having the solemnization performed." The religious authority mentioned in that case was the Chief Rabbinate of Tel Aviv.

[84] P. 121; cf. Englard, *ibid.*

[85] No *express* opinion has as yet been found which denies this status to the Chief Rabbinate. In *Gitea* Justice Witkon implied as much but did not deal with the matter explicitly, and we cannot know how the court will solve the problem of the status of the Chief Rabbinate. See also H.C.J. 195/64, *The Southern*

authorities of the state, and it is immaterial whether the decision is functionally judicial, legislative or administrative. The State can of course decide that in certain matters the Rabbinate is subject to the norms of the State and must give them priority to the norms of Jewish law,[86] or that the State does not receive Jewish law in this or that matter, in which event the *halakhic* decision has no normative validity in the law of the State.[87]

To sum up: the intervention of the secular court in the *halakhic* decisions of the Chief Rabbinate or its deviation therefrom may mean (a) that the Chief Rabbinate is not recognized by the State as the supreme and sovereign *halakhic* institution, either in general or as to a particular matter, or (b) that in a specific matter the Chief Rabbinate is not authorized to act on the basis of Jewish law alone but must take into account the norms of the State as well, or (c) that in a specific matter no reference is made to religious norms and therefore the independent norms of the State apply. If we apply these principles to *Gitea*, the *halakhic* decision of the Chief Rabbinate that the members of the Falasha community are not Jews and require conversion is a rule of Jewish law binding all the authorities of the State, on the double assumption that the Rabbinate is the supreme *halakhic* institution and that the matter is to be decided, under Israeli legislation, according to Jewish law.

Up to now we have considered Jewish law and the rabbinical institutions. Fundamentally the principles which guided us in the search for a solution of the problems concerning these institutions should also apply with respect to other religious laws. Unfortunately, our knowledge of the other religious laws is incomplete.[88] It is, however, appropriate to note that the various Christian courts are more independent in their organization, since

---

Company "Marbek" B.M. v. Council of the Chief Rabbinate, 18 P.D. (2) 324, and our comments in the cited article.

[86] For example, in administrative acts such as appointments and the like. See in greater detail Englard, *op. cit.,* pp. 74–77.

[87] In principle, three alternatives are open to the State in its relation to religious norms (including rulings of law by the Chief Rabbinate): to adopt them, as in matters of marriage and divorce; to ignore them or be indifferent to them (as in ritual matters which are of no concern to the State); to forbid compliance with them (as in the case of religious norms which violate public policy). On these alternatives, see expecially Del Giudice, *Manuale di diritto ecclesiastico* (10a ed. Milano 1964), pp. 40 et seq.

[88] On the question of binding precedent, however, see can. 17 of Codex Juris Canonici. Canon Law distinguishes between general authentic interpretation (by a legislative organ) which is binding as a general norm and special inter-

they do not depend on statutory provisions of the State for the appointment of judges and for their structural organization.

The supreme religious institutions of the Catholic Church are located in Rome. Under Israeli law there is no doubt that to the extent that reference is made to Catholic law, the legislative acts of the competent institutions under that law are received in Israel. But the question is, what is the status in Israeli law of the supreme judicial organs in Rome?[89] Must a judgment of a Vatican court in an appeal from the decision of a local Catholic court be recognized? True, this problem lies somewhat outside the scope of our subject, which is the application of religious law in the secular courts, since in the given instance an appeal from a decision of a religious court within the religious system is involved and from the point of view of the secular court the matter is restricted to the question of jurisdiction and *res judicata*. Nonetheless, the problem basically concerns the autonomy of religious law, the principle which is at the centre of our discussion. The question had already arisen during the Ottoman regime but its solution was in dispute.[90] One view rejected any recognition of the judicial decisions of Vatican institutions on the basis that all jurisdiction is territorial and that the Sultan did not intend to grant jurisdiction to institutions outside the Ottoman Empire.[91] The other view advocated direct recognition of these institutions and in 1894 it was adopted in a decision of the Mixed Court in Egypt.[92] Nor was the matter finally decided during the Mandatory period.[93] Some judges tended to recognize this

---

pretation in a specific instance—as in a judgment—which is only of binding force for the parties concerned. See in general Abbo, Hannan, *The Sacred Canons* (1952), Vol. I, pp. 31 et seq.; cf. Motu propr. *Cum iuris*, Sept. 15, 1917 (AAS, IX, 483, 484).

[89] The supreme judicial authority is the Pope himself, but he acts largely through two established courts, the Sacra Romana Rota and the Signatura Apostolica. See, cann. 1597–1605.

[90] Cf. Sidarouss, *Des Patriarcats* (Paris 1907), pp. 332–338; Rosetti, "L'autorité judiciare du Pape dans L'Empire Ottoman," *L'Egypte Contemporaine* (1912) pp. 371 et seq.

[91] Cf. Sidarouss, *op. cit.*, p. 333; Rosetti, *op. et loc. cit.*

[92] G. Privat, "Des Patriarcats catholiques d'Orient et de la juridiction suprême de la sainte Cour de Rome en pays Ottoman pour les procès matrimoniaux," 22 (1895) *Clunet* 994, 1002–1017; for an intermediate view, Sidarouss, *op. cit.*, pp. 334, 337.

[93] E. Vitta, *Conflict of Laws in Matters of Personal Status in Palestine* (Tel Aviv 1947), pp. 119 et seq.; Goadby, *International and Interreligious Private Law in Palestine* (Jerusalem 1926), pp. 135 n. 21.

possibility of appeal;[94] others denied any effect to such decisions as were made by religious courts outside the borders of the state.[95]

In the absence of specific statutory provisions it is difficult to answer the question in an unambiguous manner.[96] The fact that a religious court is situated outside the State does not of itself necessarily exclude the possibility of recognition. That fact must be balanced against *the unity of the religious system,* which bears special weight in matters of marriage, since in Catholic law the marriage institution possesses transcendent religious significance.[97] To ignore a judgment which is binding in a religious system would seriously impair the integrity of its law.

One serious argument against recognition is the lack of judicial review of tribunals situated abroad. It would, however, be possible to meet this argument by granting the High Court of Justice review powers—not indeed over the foreign tribunal itself but over the recognition of the foreign judgment and its execution in Israel. Those grounds which serve the secular court for interfering directly in the activities of a religious court would here form the basis for review.[98]

3. *Decisions on Religious Law by the Supreme Court and the Doctrine of Stare Decisis*

Let us now turn to the adjudication of religious law by the secular courts. What is the status of the Supreme Court in applying this law? In the light of the express provision of the Interpretation Ordinance that religious law is subject to judicial notice, there can be little doubt of the Supreme Court's power to review the proper application of religious law by lower courts.[99]

---

[94] H.C. 11/43, *Abu Khalil* v. *C.E.O.* 1943 A.L.R. 143; H.C. 103/42, 9 P.L.R. 579; cf. Vitta, *ibid.*

[95] Goadby, *ibid.;* Vitta, *ibid.;* cf. H.C. 36/37, *Karam* v. *C.E.O. Jerusalem,* (1937) S.C.J.; 302 C.A. 84/40, *Wilner* v. *Barkat,* 7 P.L.R. 401; H.C.J., 171/68, *Hanzalis* v. *Ecclesiastical Tribunal of the Greek Orthodox Patriarchate,* 23 P.D. (1) 260, 280.

[96] The fact that the Palestine Order in Council, 1922, refers only to religious courts possessing jurisdiction in Israel does not, in our opinion, exclude the possibility, that decisions of religious courts outside the State will be recognized. But see Vitta, *ibid.*

[97] Marriage is considered a *sacramentum.* See Privat, *op. cit.,* p. 1012.

[98] Cf. the provisions of the Foreign Judgments Enforcement Law, 5718–1958, which may possibly be applicable by way of analogy, since it is very doubtful whether a judgment of Vatican institution is to be considered a *foreign judgment* within the meaning of the Law.

[99] As to foreign law applied by virtue of the rules of private international law

The question is whether the doctrine of *stare decisis*, in the form it takes in section 33 of the Courts Law, 1957, also applies to decisions concerning religious law by the Supreme Court? One thing is clear: so long as religious law is treated as a question of fact[100] to be proved in its entirety, no foundation lies for applying *stare decisis*. The Court relies primarily on the evidence adduced by the parties and its conclusions as to the law need not bind other litigants who may bring other evidence about the content of the religious law. This was the situation regarding all religious law until the 1945 amendment of the Interpretation Ordinance, and, indeed, this is the situation in England with respect to decisions involving foreign law which is considered a question of fact.[101]

The conclusion that *stare decisis* can only apply to decisions of law of which judicial notice is taken still has some importance in the application of religious law in Israel. As was noted above[102] section 33 of the Interpretation Ordinance is confined to the religious laws of the recognized communities in matters of personal status. Hence those laws in matters unconnected with personal status, and the laws of unrecognized communities are required to be proved and *stare decisis* will not apply. In these instances, the decisions of the Supreme Court are not in the nature of "established precedent" within the meaning of section 33 of the Courts Law.

That was the conclusion reached by a District Court in a case involving the duty of a Jew to be sworn before giving evidence.[103] In the terms of the regulation then governing the matter, every witness must take an oath, unless it is contrary to his religious principles, in which event he may give evidence upon affirmation.[104] The Supreme Court had held earlier that

there is a problem in some states about the reviewing power of the supreme court as to its application. A detailed analysis of this question is found in Zajtay, "The Application of Foreign Law," *International Encyclopedia of Comp. Law*, ss. 25 et seq., Id., *Zur Stellung, passim;* Batiffol, *op. cit.*, vol. I, nos. 335 et seq.; Kegel, *op. cit.*, p. 203; Wolff, *op. cit.*, pp. 223 et seq.; Nussbaum, *op. et loc. cit.* For the situation in the United States, see Note "Proof of the Law of Foreign Countries: Appellate Review and Subsequent Litigation," 72 (1958–59) *Harv. L. Rev.* 318.

[100] Until the Interpretation Ordinance, 1945, see above p. 93.
[101] Cf. *Lazard Bros.* v. *Midland Bank* [1933] A.C. 289, 297–301; *Ottoman Bank of Nicosia* v. *Chakarian* [1938] A.C. 260, 279–281; cf. Wolff, *op. cit.*, p. 219.
[102] Above pp. 95–96.
[103] C.A. 216/65, *Artan* v. *"Four Carpenters"*, 50 P.M. 352.
[104] Rule 182(a) of the Rules of Civil Procedure, 5723–1963: "Every person shall be examined under oath unless the court finds that giving an oath is contrary to the principles of the religion of the witness or that he has no religion at

the taking of an oath was not contrary to Jewish religious principles,[105] relying on a number of Biblical passages but not at all on many of the later sources.[106] The District Court in question held that it was not bound by this earlier decision of the Supreme Court, one of its reasons being that "one should not regard a view taken by a superior court as binding precedent where Jewish law is concerned, when the legislator does not unambiguously provide that Jewish law shall apply to a certain matter, as it has done in matters of personal status involving Jews." [107]

Even if this formulation is not quite precise,[108] it is in essence accurate. As we have said, a distinction must be drawn between the application of religious law in matters of personal status and its application in other matters. Only the first category is considered "law" not requiring proof. The fact that the Supreme Court did not have recourse to testimony on the content of religious law (and this is its customary procedure in matters of Jewish law)[109] cannot affect the status of that religious law which is taken to be a question of fact requiring proof.

Even where religious law comes under "law", within the meaning of the Interpretation Ordinance, it is not certain that *stare decisis* applies and that a decision of the Supreme Court on religious law is to be considered an "established precedent" within section 33 of the Courts Law. First of all, as a formal matter the word "law" does not appear in the binding Hebrew text of section 33(b), which translated provides that "A precedent established by the Supreme Court binds every Court, except the Supreme Court." The definition of "law" (including religious law) in the Interpretation Ordinance cannot therefore of itself be decisive in

    all; in each of these cases a witness may be examined on his solemn affirmation alone." In 1966 this provision was amended to read "the witness shall be sworn to tell the truth, but he may, on giving notice that he is doing so for reasons of religion or conscience, instead of being sworn declare by solemn affirmation, unless the court is convinced that the reasons of the witness were not given in good faith."

[105] C.A. 269/64, *Martsefot P.P., B.M.* v. *Alfasi*, 18 P.D. (4) 63.

[106] See England, "The Witness' Oath—A Requirement of the Torah?" 21 (1965) *HaPraklit* 435.

[107] *Ibid.*, p. 354.

[108] The question is not whether the statutory language is ambiguous or not. It seems that the judge intended to distinguish between a univalent and a polyvalent reference (on these concepts, see above p. 68), but even this distinction is not satisfactory. The difference is between a permanent and a non-permanent reference, as we concluded from the definition of the term "law". See above p. 95.

[109] As to the special approach of the court to the Jewish law, cf., p. 96 above.

the matter which concerns us here.[110] Hence solution of the problem must be based on more general considerations of a substantive nature, bearing on the status of religious law.

Among these considerations clearly is the fact that as a result of the inclusion of religious law in the category of "law," judicial notice must be taken of it. But the question is whether this fact is decisive for the application of the doctrine of *stare decisis*. It would appear not to be so. The rule that judicial notice is taken of law means that the court is *required* to know the religious law and no burden of proof rests on the parties. But this rule does not necessarily lead to the conclusion that a judicial decision is a binding "established precedent." That may be demonstrated by the treatment of foreign law! As we have noted[111] there is a tendency, particularly in the United States, to relax the traditional rule that foreign law is a question of fact and to ease proof thereof. Thus there is no necessary connection between *stare decisis* and extending judicial notice to foreign law. Nussbaum correctly notes that the absence of binding force of a decision concerning the content of foreign law is not a result of regarding it as a question of fact. The rejection of *stare decisis* is mainly due to historical reasons and considerations of judicial policy.[112] The extension of judicial notice to foreign law means that the judge is entitled to rely, among other things, on decisions of the Supreme Court in previous cases (as a source of information) but not that there is a duty to follow such earlier decisions as binding precedents.[113]

Thus we cannot find any express or unambiguous answer to our question, neither in the term "law" nor in the principle of judicial notice. We have turned full circle—did the Israeli legislator intend to include religious law under "a precedent established by the Supreme Court" in section 33 of the Courts Law?

The question has been canvassed both in the judgments and in the

---

[110] See in the same spirit A.C. Shaki, "The Confusion of Spheres and the Restriction of Religious Jurisdiction," 21–22 (1965) *Gevilin* 38, 46 (Hebrew).

[111] Above p. 89 n. 10.

[112] Nussbaum, *op. cit.*, pp. 1034 et seq.: "It is true that a statement of the highest court on a point of foreign law lacks the effect of precedent, not because foreign law is regarded as a fact, but because the rule of precedent has been limited to domestic law for historical and policy reasons."; Note "Proof of the Law of Foreign Countries, Appellate Review and Subsequent Litigation," 72 (1958–59) *Harv. L. Rev.* 318, 324 et seq.; cf. A.R. Miller, "Federal Rule 44.1 and the 'Fact' Approach to Determining Foreign Law," 65 (1966–67) *Mich. L. Rev.* 615, 690 n. 295.

[113] Cf. Nussbaum, *ibid.;* Note, *cit.*

literature. The arguments against applying *stare decisis* can be divided into two groups: general arguments relating to religious law as a separate normative system and those relating to the application of religious law in Israel in the context of the coexistence of religious and secular courts.

We will first consider the general arguments as they were vigorously presented by Justice Kister in *Kerz*.[114] Justice Kister denied the binding nature of Supreme Court decisions in the following words: "When the court is faced with a question which it must decide in accordance with a law enacted not by the Israeli legislature but by an institution outside the legislative institutions of the State, whether the law be foreign law or public international law or religious law, it must find the law in the sources of that law itself and interpret it in accordance with the principles which that law has prescribed for the purpose. If the court does not do so but regards itself bound by a decision of a domestic court inconsistent with the sources of that law, then it does not decide in accordance with the law which it is bound to apply."[115]

A similar idea has been expressed in the United States concerning *stare decisis* in the application of foreign law: "It is arguable that a litigant is entitled to have his rights determined by direct reference to the applicable law and not by reference to an elaboration of that law by the forum upon the basis of its own prior decisions."[116]

This argument was utterly rejected by Justice Cohn who held that "the 'law' which courts interpret and execute includes under section 1 of the Interpretation Ordinance not only secular laws but also written and unwritten religious laws."[117] Justice Cohn created, therefore, an identity

---

[114] C.C. 779/59, *Kerz* v. *The Estate of Kerz* 21 P.M. 400, 405.

[115] Justice Kister relies on the decision of the Privy Council in *The Zemora* [1916] 2 A.C. 77, 91. Although it is true that this decision well defines the difference between the autonomous application of international law and the application of domestic law, it does not seem to address itself directly to the question of binding precedent. The decision indeed speaks of the difference between relying on domestic law, which purports to express the rule of international public law, and direct reliance on international law, but it is doubtful whether the English court would for that reason have rejected the rule of *stare decisis* with respect to a judicial interpretation of one of the provisions of international law. See, however, in the spirit of Justice Kister's views, C.W. Jenks, "The Authority in English Courts of Decisions of the Permanent Court of International Justice," 20 (1939) *B.Y.I.L.* 1, 28, 31–32. For the question of the application of *stare decisis* to customary international law, see note 120 below.

[116] Note, *cit.*, 72 *Harv. L. Rev.* 324.

[117] C.A. 99/63, 17 P.D. 1122, 1127.

between a binding precedent in the sense of Section 33 of the Courts Law and the concept "law" as defined in the Interpretation Ordinance. As we have noted, however, this identification is not compelling formally, since the term "law" does not appear in section 33, and it is also doubtful whether the conclusion is correct in point of substance. First, the legal provisions enumerated in the definition of the term "law" possibly do not exhaust all types of norms to which the rule of *stare decisis* may apply, for example, a *custom* which has become generally accepted[118] or customary public international law.[119] These are not included in the concept "law", and yet very possibly decisions of the Supreme Court with respect to them would be considered binding precedent.[120] Secondly, Justice Cohn gives no material reason why the boundaries of *stare decisis* must be restricted by the scope of the definition of "law" in the Interpretation Ordinance. Is it indeed so clear that the "rules of the Common Law" and the "principles of English equity" are exclusively determined by the case law of the local Supreme Court (assuming that such case law

---

[118] Cf. as to severance pay prior to the Law of 1963, C.A. 160/58, *Mendelovitz v. Porath*, 14 P.D. 666.

[119] On the assumption that this law applies in Israel "since Israel is a sovereign state and exists in its own right" (per Justice Cheshin in 174/54, *Staempfer v. A.G.*, 10 P.D. 5, 15), and not by means of English Common law.

[120] Particularly with respect to custom; the matter is not so clear as regards customary public international law. See the general considerations set forth below. Cf. the judgment of Justice Kister, cited at note 114 above. But see Tedeschi, "Paralipomena on Stare Decisis" 17 (1961) *HaPraklit*, 244, who notes international laws as being subject to binding precedent. There are divergent views in English law as well over the question of binding precedent in international law. See *Chung Chi Cheung v. The King* [1939] A.C. 160, 168 (per Lord Atkin): "The Courts ... will treat [International law] as incorporated into the domestic law, so far as it is not inconsistent with rules enacted by statutes or finally declared by their tribunals." A less rigid view was expressed in *The Odessa* [1915] P. 52, 62: "Precedents handed down from earlier days should be treated as guides to lead, and not as shackles to bind. But the guides must not be lightly deserted or cast aside"; F. Morgenstern, "Judicial Practice and the Supremacy of International Law," 27 (1950) *B.Y.I.L.*, 42, 80–82; Jenks, *op. et loc. cit.;* cf. O'Connell, *International Law,* Vol. I, (London 1965), p. 59. It should, however, be noted that according to the English approach which regards customary international law as part of domestic law, the central question is whether reference to international law is "dynamic" or "static" (as to these concepts, see above p. 68). And, indeed, study of the cited sources reveals that this question is indirectly introduced into the discussion of binding precedent, that is to say, the question is, among other things, how are changes in customary international law to be treated.

exists), without the lower courts being able to cull the content thereof directly from English law?[121]

Professor Tedeschi has provided a conceptual basis for the extension of *stare decisis* to findings of religious law.[122] Referring to the observations of Justice Kister cited above, he argues that if this reason is accepted, it could lead to a total denial of *stare decisis,* since erroneous precedent would falsify the law in every area, and why should the foreign system be preferred to the internal law of the legislature? The latter has agreed that the decisions of the Supreme Court are decisive of the interpretation of its own enactments; there is no reason to doubt the ability of the Supreme Court to interpret other legal systems.

On the face of it, this argument is very persuasive in Israeli law, based as it is primarily on legislative acts in contrast to the common law created by the judges. In our system many precedents are no more than interpretations of statutes, but the legislature apparently denies the lower courts the possibility of referring directly to the primary source—the statute—and forces them to accept the interpretation of the law given by the Supreme Court. In the very words of Professor Tedeschi (who is certainly no supporter of the rule of *stare decisis*):[123] "the binding precedent turns the judge away from the text of the law, they cease to be 'servants of the legislator' and become 'servants of his servants'."[124] Hence his conclusion that if this obtains with regard to domestic law, it is proper also to religious law.

The argument, however, is not decisive. There are a number of differences between domestic law and religious law as an autonomous normative system, which render questionable the application of *stare decisis* to religious law. First a practical consideration: we have seen that the domestic judges are not expert in all the religious laws which apply in Israel and must at times resort to expert opinion.[125] We need not be

---

[121] The question is particularly pertinent, since English law itself recognizes *stare decisis.* Niboyet discusses a similar question in *op. cit.,* p. 807, from a purely theoretical point of view and leaves it open. In Israeli law the question takes a special form in the light of the view expressed in several decisions that English case law since the establishment of the State does not have binding effect in Israel. In accordance with this view, we are faced with a *static* reference. On the problem, in general, see p. 69 above.

[122] Tedeschi, "Paralipomena on Stare Decisis", *ibid.*

[123] See his conclusions, *ibid.,* pp. 249–250.

[124] Tedeschi, "On the Principle of *Stare Decisis*", *Studies in Israel Law,* Jerusalem 1960, pp. 114, 150.

[125] Above pp. 100–101.

exercised to convince ourselves that in such cases no justification exists for giving binding or even persuasive force to the decisions of the court. Moreover, even in those cases in which the judges directly determine religious law provisions, the possibilities of error are much greater than in the cases in which the domestic law is applied.[126] It is not a coincidence that the rejection of Justice Kister's view occurred in the course of a case dealing with Jewish law and by a judge who is an expert in that law. But does the same feeling of confidence exist with respect to other religious law? In any event, the fact that the legislature relies on the Supreme Court for the interpretation of its own laws is not decisive since it does not necessarily follow that the legislature also intended so to rely upon the court regarding laws which it did not itself create.

The rule of *stare decisis* is an expression of the explicit recognition of the creative role of the court. The legislature upholds case law as a legal source. The courts, for their part, are an integral part of the domestic legal system. The legislature is ready to entrust to the Supreme Court the power to give binding interpretations of its laws, since it retains the ultimate competence itself to review the rules which have been declared and change them when necessary by statute. This relationship between case law and legislation is as clear as may be in the minds of the judges, and even if they have placed excessive reliance on this relationship,[127] there is no doubt that it is the foundation of the statutory ordering of the rule of *stare decisis.*

The situation is completely different with respect to religious law. The legislature turns to it in a general manner, without putting its mind to the details of the law. Those who possess religious legislative authority do not on their part pay constant attention to the decisions of the secular courts in Israel, or at least most of them do not see any connection between these decisions and their own religious law. It follows that an erroneous decision of religious law by a secular court will be perpetuated unrectified. It would appear that the legislature did not intend this result in providing that matters of personal status be regulated by religious law.

According to Professor Tedeschi *stare decisis* is based on the legislator's

---

[126] Cf. Note, *cit.,* 72 *Harv. L. Rev.* 324.
[127] See the criticism of Tedeschi ("Recent Trends in *Stare Decisis*" 22 (1966) *Ha-Praklit* 320–323) of the observations of Justices Cohn and Witkon, which suggests that legislative silence indicates approval of the case law. See F.H. 13/60, *A.G.* v. *Matana,* 16 P.D. 430, 462 (Justice Cohn); C.A. 446/63 *Gutman* v. *Shen,* 18 P.D. (1) 371, 374 (Justice Cohn); C.A. 346/63, *Trifman* v. *Victor,* 18 P.D. (1) 366, 368 (Justice Witkon).

view that to follow precedents is a better guarantee that the law will be properly applied than it is a danger that it will be distorted.[128] The legislator may indeed so believe, but it seems that the rationale for the adoption of *stare decisis* is to be found in the desire for stability of the law and its uniformity.[129] Desire for uniformity explains, in our opinion, why binding force has been given to the precedents of the Supreme Court, since there is only one supreme court in the state standing at the apex of the regular judicial system. It also explains the institution of the *Further Hearing*[129a] which enables uniform rules to be determined by a fuller bench of the Supreme Court.

In considering whether *stare decisis* should apply to religious law, we must enquire whether in the legal reality of Israel it achieves the goals of stability and uniformity.[130] At this point we come to the duality which exists in the jurisdiction on matters of personal status, with the secular system facing the religious system. Indeed, very serious objections have been levelled against the application of *stare decisis* in the secular courts. First of all, it is clear that the decisions of the Supreme Court do not bind the courts of the religious system.[131] Moreover, the religious courts are regarded as experts in religious law and in this respect their decisions have great persuasive effect on the secular courts. Imagine a case in which the Supreme Court has decided a question of religious law in one way, whilst a contrary decision was reached in the religious jurisdiction. Is there any reason to require the secular courts to follow the secular precedent? Here *stare decisis* would contribute to a lack of uniformity, and thereby to a lack of stability of Israeli law in the wider sense; the result would therefore be the opposite of what the rule of *stare decisis* seeks to achieve.[132]

---

[128] Tedeschi, "Paralipomena on *Stare Decisis*," *op. cit.*, p. 244.

[129] Cf. *Mirehouse* v. *Rennel* (1833) 6 E.R. 1015, 1023 (*per* Parke J.); cf. Allen, *Law in the Making* (7th ed., Oxford 1964), pp. 232 et seq.; cf. Stone, *Legal System*, pp. 211–212.

[129a] See sec. 8 of the Courts Law, 5717–1957.

[130] For similar considerations with respect to the application of precedents in international law, see Jenks, *op. et loc. cit.*

[131] Section 33 of the Courts Law does not apply to religious courts but deals expressly with the civil secular courts. Cf. Shawa, *op. cit.*, p. 639 n. 95a.

[132] In this respect there is a difference from the situation obtaining in the application of foreign law. In the latter case, a binding interpretation of the foreign law in domestic law would at least bring about uniformity in the domestic system. On the reluctance of the French Court of Cassation to rule on questions of foreign law, see Zajtay, *Stellung*, *passim*. On uniformity of local law, see Shaki, *op. cit.*, pp. 46–47. Section 35 of the Courts Law, 5717–1957, which provides that in the case of proceedings under incidental jurisdiction the deci-

The truth is that in principle the problem of *stare decisis* is not critical in our system since the Supreme Court may deviate from its own precedents.[132a] The problem is thus confined to the lower courts. In the light, however, of the Supreme Court's clear tendency to follow in practice, if not in theory, its own precedents,[133] real importance may well attach to a decision in principle that *stare decisis* does not apply to religious law.

To sum up the discussion, in the absence of any express legislative provision concerning the application of *stare decisis* to religious law, we must examine its operation, having regard to the concepts which lie behind the rule, that is to say, the ideas which have guided the legislature in adopting it. From this point of view, we are doubtful whether it is appropriate for a foreign normative system as a general matter, or for religious law in particular, in respect of which two separate judicial systems operate within the State.

---

sion is "for the purposes of that matter," is not in our opinion in point. Contrary to Shaki, we think that the nature of the jurisdiction (main or incidental) does not affect the question of binding precedent. Accordingly a ruling under incidental jurisdiction is as binding as any other rule decided by the Supreme Court. The limitation ("for the purposes of that matter") refers to the relations between the parties to the suit in point of *res judicata*.

[132a] See above p. 128.
[133] Tedeschi, "Recent Trends in *Stare Decisis*" cit. pp. 324–325.

CHAPTER IV

LIMITATIONS ON THE APPLICATION OF RELIGIOUS LAW

1. *Defining the Problem*

We have already had occasion to mention that the civil courts do not apply religious law in its entirety and that as a result their substantive solutions differ from those of the religious judicial system.[1] Thus far, however, attention has been focussed on the "internal" factors of the matter, such as the effect the judge's philosophic outlook and his personal faith has on his treatment of religious norm. This chapter deals with the "external" factors, the fixed principles of law which are intended to delimit the application of religious law in the civil courts. This clearly does not exclude the internal factors but the characteristic feature of an external factor is precisely the official recognition of its operation and expression in legal concepts.[2] Justice Silberg in a well-known dictum[3] has set out three principal limitations to the application of religious law: the modes of procedure, the law of evidence and the rules of private international law. In the result, "Jewish law as applied in the secular courts is unlike Jewish law as applied in the religious courts."[4] Justice Silberg begins by comparing the outcome of a case in the secular jurisdiction with that in the religious jurisdiction. From this viewpoint the three matters mentioned are of equal significance. Just as differences in procedure and in the law of evidence are likely to lead to a different conclusion in a specific case, so the application or non-application of the rules of private international law has a decisive effect on the outcome. It follows that the religious courts' "exemption" from applying these conflict rules[5] which are binding on the secular courts is an additional element contributing to a possible

---

[1] See pp. 76, 105 above.
[2] Cf. the Introduction to this study.
[3] C.A. 238/53, *Cohen, Buslik* v. *A.G.*, 8 P.D. 4, 19 (English translation 2 S.J.S.C. 239, 254).
[4] *Ibid.;* cf. Silberg, *Personal Status in Israel*, pp. 4–6 (Hebrew).
[5] See note 11 below.

difference between the decisions of the two judicial systems in the same matter.

In respect, however, of *limitation* of application of religious law, the three areas are not of the same texture. The rejection of religious and the preference for secular procedural and evidentiary rules is based upon the distinction between substantive law and procedural rule. When a secular court is required to apply religious law it chooses therefrom the substantive part as distinct from the procedural. Religious courts on the other hand always act in accordance with the provisions of religious law as a whole, both substantive and procedural. The situation is different with conflict rules. One of the characteristic features of religious law is its universal applicability. It spreads its net—retroactively and without qualification—over acts done by foreign subjects outside the boundaries of the state,[6] particularly so with Jewish law in matters of strictly religious commandment.[7] In general it may be postulated that it is in the nature of all religious law to deny recognition to the provisions of other legal systems which are contrary to the religious order. Religious rules concerning the conflict of laws are scarce.[8] In any event, there is no relationship between the conflict rules applied in Israeli law (which in many matters

---

[6] C.A. 238/53, see Levontin, *Marriages and Divorces out of the Jurisdiction*, (Jerusalem 1957), (Hebrew) p. 18: "In point of Jewish marriage law there is no such thing as 'abroad'. Its rules are personal and not territorial and as long as a person is a Jew, no significance attaches to the place of the marriage (just as no significance attaches to the nationality of a Jew). One who goes abroad has not done anything, since the revelation at Sinai extends to all Jews everywhere, and there is no magic in the present borders of the State of Israel."

[7] See in particular, Shaki, "Effect of Civil Marriages between Jews contracted outside Israel—in Rabbinical Courts in Israel," 20 (1964) *HaPraklit*, 385, 391, 394–396. Shaki disputes the sweeping propositions that religious law never recognizes foreign law and that it completely lacks conflicts rules. In an analysis of rabbinical judgments, he shows that, at least in civil matters, there is a tendency to recognize rights acquired under foreign law, even in matters of marriage. Nonetheless, he agrees that in matters of purely religious significance religious law is careful to uphold its own precepts and to ignore all other law. See also Id., "Civil Marriage contracted between Jews outside Israel—A Cause for Granting a 'Permit to Marry' to the Husband," 22 (1966) *HaPraklit* 347, 358–360.

[8] For examples of recognition given by rabbinical courts to foreign laws, see the cited articles of Shaki, note 7 above, and for references to foreign legal systems by other religious legal systems, and religious conflicts rules, see Vitta, *Conflitti interni ed internazionali*, Vol. 2 (Turin 1955), p. 8 nn. 90–91. Szászy, "Interpersonal Conflicts of Laws," *op. cit.*, p. 803. On the relationship between different religious laws in general, see Wengler, "Grundprobleme des interreligiösen Kolli-

refer us to English Common law) and the principles to be found in religious law.[9] Religious law asserts exclusive and retroactive competence whilst completely rejecting all foreign law.[10]

In the religious courts, the religious-law approach naturally reigns supreme. The secular courts on the other hand have held that they are bound by the rules of private international law even when the application of religious law is involved. The civil courts apply ordinary choice-of-law rules even as between religious law and the law of a foreign state. That does not in principle constitute any special limitation on the application of religious law, since precisely the same principles limit the application of the domestic secular law of the state. The secular courts do not view this as a qualification of the application of religious law but rather as an equalization of its status with that of the other rules of substantive domestic law. This equalization is, without doubt, of unique significance since religious law claims universal and retroactive application and its claim is fully realized in the religious courts which have been granted jurisdiction by the state. The civil courts, which themselves apply the rules of conflict of laws, expressly recognize the right of the religious courts to act exclusively in accordance with their religious law even in a case which contains a foreign element.[11]

This approach has created a rift in the law in matters of personal status. The present is not the occasion to examine the correctness of the approach taken by the civil courts nor its detailed rules.[12] For our purpose it is enough to posit that the elimination of religious law on the basis of the rules of conflict of laws does not constitute a special limitation on its application; the limitation is not related to the special status of religious law in the law of the state. But this is only true formally. Materially there is

---

sionsrechts", *Aphieroma eis Charalampon N. Phragkistan* (Thessaloniki 1967) pp. 483–502.

[9] See also Shaki, *op. cit.*, p. 395: "It is true that the religious courts do not have recourse to the rules of private international law applying in the secular courts. This is not because they are denigratory of their content and substance but because they have their own clear principles for achieving the same results, subject to certain limitations." Although we agree that it is possible to find examples in Jewish law of recognition of foreign law, we do not believe that this recognition has its source in a desire to achieve the results which are sought by the rules of private international law.

[10] See, in general, Tedeschi, "Transition from Secular to Religious Matrimonial Status and the Retroactive Application of the Latter," *Studies in Israel Private Law*, (Jerusalem 1966), 212, 213.

[11] H.C.J. 301/63, *Streit v. Chief Rabbi of Israel*, 18 P.D. (1) 598, 608, 620, 621.

[12] See, in general, Levontin, *ibid.*

a very significant relationship between the content of religious law, particularly Jewish law, and its rejection on the basis of formal rules.[13] The judge's inability to agree to the solution offered by religious law because it is inconsistent with his philosophy of life is likely to be an important consideration in his deciding not to have recourse to religious law in a case involving a foreign element.

This brings us to another problem in the limitation of religious law, though it was not mentioned in the dictum of Justice Silberg, that is the *principle of public policy*. Is an Israeli court entitled to disqualify religious law to which it generally refers, on the grounds that its content is contrary to Israeli public policy. The problem is on the same level as the rejection of religious procedural rules, since the acceptance of the public policy principle implies a special limitation on the application of religious law as distinct from secular law of the legislator's own making. Both limitations are familiar in the application of foreign law in the context of private international law. The question of their application to religious law brings us back to the central issue of this study: the status of religious law in Israeli law as compared with domestic Israeli law on the one hand and with foreign law on the other.

We begin the discussion with the principle of public policy and shall thereafter consider the distinction between substance and procedure.

2. *Public Policy*

A. General

Israeli law recognizes the principle, found in other legal systems as well, that foreign law, otherwise applicable according to normal conflict rules, will be rejected, if it is contrary to public policy.[14] This principle applies equally to the enforcement and to the recognition of foreign judgments.[15]

---

[13] Cf. *ibid.* p. 50.

[14] See H.C.J. 143/62, *Funk-Schlesinger* v. *Minister of the Interior*, 17 P.D. 231: "Every country which wishes to live in harmony in the family of nations must forego the execution of part of its legal rules, when a foreign element arises and intervenes in a legal act.... But there are cases, exceptional cases, in which giving effect to foreign law and the results flowing therefrom, would adversely affect the public order by which we live. Only where the foreign law is contrary to the feeling of justice and morality of the Israeli, must we reject it."

[15] Section 3(3) of the Foreign Judgments Enforcement Law, 5718–1958: "A court in Israel may declare a foreign judgment enforceable if it finds that the tenor of the judgment is not repugnant to the laws of the State of Israel or the public policy of Israel." But see *Addendum*.

From a technical legal point of view, however, public policy serves two different functions, positive and negative.[16] The negative function is more prominent, since foreign law is rejected after an examination of its content and the effect of its application in a specific case. The rejection is a judicial act, the judge being authorized to inquire into the compatibility of the foreign solution with the basic principles of the society which he serves.[17] The positive function of public policy is less apparent, since the outcome is the preference of local law to foreign law at a preliminary stage. The foreign law is not rejected because of its specific content but because of the binding nature of domestic law. The public policy provisions of the latter are considered to be "rigid" and do not yield to the provisions of the foreign law. Here public policy points in advance to a solution of the problem by local law without recourse to any foreign law.[18] It has been observed that this function of public policy is in fact only a hidden rule of

[16] On the distinction in general, see M. Wolff, *Private International Law* (Oxford 1950), p. 171; Neuhaus, *Die Grundbegriffe des internationalen Privatrechts*, (Tübingen 1962), pp. 257 et seq.; Betti, *Problematica del diritto internazionale*, (Milano 1956), pp. 282 et seq.; Vischer, *Schweizerisches Privatrecht*, I (Basel 1969), pp. 509, 532; Niederer, "Ordre Public in der neueren Rechtssprechung des Bundesgerichts," 62 (1943) *ZSR*, 1, 11 et seq.; Meise, *Zur Relativität der Vorbehaltsklausel im internationalen und interlokalen Privatrecht* (Hamburg 1966), p. 194; Raape, *Deutsches Internationales Privatrecht*, I (Berlin 1938), para. 12, p. 60.
[17] Cf. Batiffol, *Droit international privé* (5e éd., Paris 1970), no. 355 et seq.; Maury, *L'éviction de la loi normalement competente: l'ordre public et la fraude à la loi* (Valladolid 1952), *passim*. On the application in private international law of the public policy principle to foreign religious law, see in general Elgeddawy, *Relations entre systèmes confessionnel et laïque en droit international privé* (Paris 1971) pp. 117 et seq. This work is mainly concerned with Moslem Law (as applied in Egypt) and French Law. Despite its promising title it has to be read with caution. The author tends to employ oversimple generalizations.
[18] Maury, *op. cit.*, pp. 69 et seq.; cf. W. Goldschmidt, "Système et philosophie du droit international privé," 45 (1956) *Revue critique de droit international privé*, 234. There is a dispute between the writers concerning the extent of the positive function. Some view the matter as a general principle of interpretation which may apply to every domestic law. On this view, there is a large category of laws of "necessary application" which displace foreign law. See G. Sperduti, *Saggi di teoria generale del diritto internazionale privato* (Milan 1967), pp. 175 et seq. and the bibliography there. This approach has been criticised by those writers who argue against recognition of a general principle in addition to the principle of public policy which fills what we have termed a negative function. Foreign law will be rejected only in those cases where the legislator has expressly directed the application of domestic law, even though the case has foreign aspects. See G. Pau, "Limiti di applicazione del diritto

the conflict of laws.[19] We can find a parallel to the distinction between the two functions (particularly developed in German and Swiss Law)[20] in the Israeli Enforcement of Foreign Judgments Law. Section 3(3) of this Law gives two grounds for not enforcing a foreign judgment: that the tenor thereof is repugnant to the laws of the State of Israel or to public policy in Israel. It appears that in specifying the first the legislative intent was directed to the positive function of public policy, to those internal provisions which apply to a matter directly and which, because of their obligatory public character, do not give way to foreign law as formulated in the judgment. The term public policy, on the other hand, expresses the negative function, the rejection of the foreign law because of its content. These two functions (vividly discussed in the literature)[21] may nevertheless serve as a point of departure for examining similar and parallel phenomena in respect of religious law. We are of course aware that the application of religious law in Israeli law differs in many important respects from the application of foreign law under conflict of laws rules. We therefore speak of parallel, not identical, phenomena. But more of this later.

Thus far the public policy of domestic law has been considered in its role in private international law, but a further, if separate, question arises concerning the public policy of foreign law itself. To what extent are we prepared to take it into account when having recourse in principle to foreign law? We follow the common practice of including this question

---

straniero nell'ordinamento italiano," 52 (1969) *Rivista di diritto internazionale,* 477, and the sources there cited.

[19] Neuhaus, *op. cit.,* pp. 49–50, 257–258.

[20] See the sources cited in note 16 above.

[21] Differences of opinion exist over the precise significance of the distinction, particularly in regard to the justification for the positive function of public policy in private international law. To a large extent the various viewpoints are influenced by the general position taken on the significance of the public policy principle as a whole. It is common to identify a Romanist school which postulates the principle of public policy as a rule (the territorial principle) as against another school which conceives of public policy as an exception. See Maury, *op. cit.,* pp. 22 et seq. On the connection between the positive function of the principle and its general significance, see Niederer, *op. cit.,* pp. 5–6, 11 et seq.; Lagarde, *Recherches sur l'ordre public en droit international privé,* (Paris 1959), pp. 94 et seq.; cf. Wiethölter, *Einseitige Kollisionsnormen als Grundlage des internationalen Privatrechts* (Berlin 1956), pp. 61 et seq. See also in general Unger, "Use and Abuse of Statutes in the Conflict of Laws," 83 (1967) *L.Q.R.* 427; Graulich, "Règles de conflit et règles d'application immédiate," *Mélanges Dabin,* II (Paris 1963), 629.

in a general discussion of public policy, and examine the question of the application of religious public policy in Israeli law.

B. The Negative Function of Public Policy: Rejection of Religious Law by Reason of its Content

Reference to religious law in Israeli law is like that to foreign law, general, polyvalent and dynamic.[22] These features characterize the principle of public policy in private international law where it serves as a protective device against the initially unknown content of foreign law.[23] The question is whether the secular courts may reject religious law solution because it appears to be inconsistent with the basic principles of the State of Israel. In its general and principled form, this question was given an unqualifiedly negative answer by Justice Silberg in *Funk-Schlesinger* v. *Minister of Interior*.[24] It was argued that the secular court must ignore religious law insofar as it prohibited mixed marriages between Jews and non-Jews. Justice Silberg rejected this argument outright, distinguishing between the application of foreign law and the application of religious law. In his view, an Israeli judge "cannot say that the laws of the State offend his sense of justice and he is therefore unwilling to uphold them. The law of every state and particularly of every democratic state with a parliamentary legislative body is consonant with—or is deemed to be consonant with—the principles of natural justice accepted in that state. Were it otherwise, laws would not be enacted and once enacted would be set at naught under pressure of public opinion."[25]

The reasoning is not persuasive. Whilst it is true that the Israeli courts cannot invalidate a Knesset law on the grounds that it violates the concept of justice,[26] the question here is the rejection of a rule of religious law,

---

[22] On these concepts, see p. 68 above.
[23] Raape, *op. cit.*, p. 59, notes that "reference to a foreign law is a leap into the dark."
[24] 17 P.D. 225.
[25] At 238.
[26] The Supreme Court returned to this principle of the sovereignty of the legislature in C.A. 450/70, *Rogozinski* v. *State of Israel*, 26 P.D. (1) 129, 134–137: "Since it is clear beyond all doubt that the legislature wished to grant the Jewish religious courts jurisdiction in matters of the marriage and divorce of Jews, when marriage and divorce are carried out in accordance with Jewish law and not any other law, the courts must respect the legislative will and give effect to it, even if it is not consistent with the principle of freedom of conscience in the Declaration of Independence or in Article 83 of the Palestine Order-in-Council." See also C.A. 373/72 *Tepper* v. *State of Israel*, 28 P.D. (2) 7.

as distinct from a Knesset law. The two cannot be equated since the content of religious law was not enacted by the Knesset but the laws of the Knesset receive it by reference. It cannot be urged that the received law is like to domestic legislation, because then how does religious law differ from foreign law which is also received by reference?[27] Properly posed, the question is not whether the court is competent to invalidate a legislative act of the Knesset but whether the legislature itself has restricted the application of another normative system on the basis of the public policy test. In view of the fact that reference to religious law is general and dynamic did the legislator intend to receive it without further examination, or did he wish to restrict its application by the public policy principle?[27a] The problem therefore touches on the quality of the reference: restricted or unrestricted. The court does not raise itself above the legislature. On the contrary, it is concerned to preserve the basic principles of the domestic normative system in accordance with the legislative spirit. By so confining foreign law, precisely those provisions which the legislature has prescribed are protected.

As we have said, restriction on the law of a foreign state has been accepted in Israel within the framework of private international law. However, even if formally no difference exists between reference to foreign law and reference to religious law,[28] it does not follow that the public policy restriction applies to the same extent in both cases. There are still a number of differences, in respect to both background and function.

Historically, the main purpose of reference to religious law was to preserve the autonomy of the religious communities in matters of personal status. The application of religious law was thus from its very inception an *internal* problem of the regime. In view of the fact that generally all

---

[27] In particular, one must emphasize the dynamic nature of the reference in the two instances. In our opinion Rigaux (*Droit international privé* [Brussels 1968], p. 228), was not accurate in writing of the idea of national law being immune from all judicial criticism as to its consistency with public policy. He claims that the absolute immunity of national law is a privilege attaching to the entire *formal system* of domestic law. The term *formal* in this context is not exact, since it is inapt to distinguish between foreign law applying in a state and the domestic law of the state itself; *formally* the foreign law becomes part of the domestic law. See above p. 41. Rigaux, incidentally, is not sure whether public policy is operative with respect to colonial law (*ibid.*, p. 229).

[27a] Cf. Maury, *op. cit.*, pp. 131 et seq.

[28] The reference to "personal law" in Article 47 of the Palestine Order-in-Council includes a reference to both religious law and the national law of the person involved. See p. 26 above.

the parties concerned are local residents of Israel acting within its jurisdiction, we are far from the special problem situation of private international law, where the decisive element is precisely the foreign element which brings the domestic normative system into conflict with foreign law. Moreover, in its reference to religious law, the legislature originally had the intent of *not* itself regulating matters subject to religious law. Even if important changes have subsequently occurred in secular legislation, many areas still remain in which the legislature has not provided any concurrent regulation of its own. In all these cases therefore there is no "competition" between a secular solution and a religious solution in contrast to the conflict of laws situation and the rules of private international law pertaining to it.

This fact assumes great significance with respect to the question of public policy. If there is no alternative secular solution of a particular matter, whence do we derive the basic principles of the legislature for testing the content of the religious solution?[29] Under the British Mandate, a possible solution might have been found since the law was applied by a colonial regime, where the possibility of invalidating local law (largely personal religious or tribal law) was in principle recognized if it appeared to the colonial court to violate certain universal principles[30] drawn from the legal system of the governing power itself. "Colonial" public policy was construed more restrictively than its parallel in the metropolitan country in the context of the conflict of laws.[31] Thus, for example, whilst polygamy was always prohibited there, it was not always so in the colonies.[32] In many colonies, the concept of "colonial" public policy filled two functions. It served as an instrument for directly invalidating local rules par-

---

[29] Similarly Vitta, *Conflict of Laws in Matters of Personal Status in Palestine,* (Tel Aviv 1947); Id., "The Conflict of Personal Laws," 5 (1970) *Is. L. Rev.* 170, 200; Szászy, "Interpersonal Conflicts of Law," *op. cit.,* pp. 812 et seq.

[30] Solus, *Traité sur la condition des indigènes en droit privé* (Paris 1927), pp. 302 et seq.; Vitta, *op. cit.,* p. 200; Id., *Conflitti interni ed internazionali,* Vol. 2 (Torino 1955), pp. 102 et seq.; Szászy, *op. cit.,* pp. 809 et seq.

[31] In the literature it is common to denote the problem arising from the application of religious law to members of the various communities as *inter-personal* or *inter-communal* or *intergentile law,* in contrast to private international law. On the problems of proximity of the two subjects and the possibility of applying legal rules in a parallel manner to both, see Bartholomew, "Private Interpersonal Law," (1952) *Int. & Comp. L.Q.,* 325; Vitta, "The Conflict of Personal Laws," 5 (1970) *Is. L. Rev.* 337, 345 et seq.; Szászy, "Le conflit de lois interpersonnel dans les pays en voie de développement," 138 (1973) I *Recueil des Cours,* pp. 81 et seq.

[32] Vitta, *op. ult. cit.,* p. 201.

ticularly offensive of universal principles; so also local legal institutions frowned upon by the colonial power were abolished. Secondly, the public policy principle served towards a gradual change of local law for bringing it closer to the colonial power's own legal system[33] by rejection of local solution in favour of metropolitan law.[34]

This process was not of equal dimension in all colonial regimes. A correlation exists between it and the general policy of the colonial regime regarding direct interference in the local social order.[35] The English colonial regime was very careful in interfering with local legal systems, in marked contrast to the French.[36] Thus during the British Mandate in Palestine the public policy principle did not play an important role in the invalidation of religious legal rules, or other types of legal rules.[37] Although indeed in their judgments British judges suggested that the secular courts might intervene in the religious system upon a violation of the principles of natural justice, not only in procedural matters[38] but also in substantive matters,[39] these suggestions were never acted upon. The reason is possibly to be found in the general policy of the British as well as in the fact that the religious laws in question were those of the great

---

[33] Vitta, *Conflitti internazionali*, vol. 2, *cit.*, pp. 110 et seq.; Lampué, "Les conflits de lois interrégionaux et interpersonnels dans le système juridique français," 43 (1954) *Rev. crit. dr. int. privé* 249, 290–91.

[34] Lampué properly notes (*op. cit.*, p. 291) that the rejection of the personal law in this case is not a result of conflict rules. That is to say, the question is not one of conflict between *different personal laws* but the general invalidation of a particular personal law. "[Le juge] ne résout pas davantage un conflit interpersonnel, puisque le rapport qui donne lieu au litige se rattache par tous ses éléments au même status. La matière est donc complètement étrangère à la question du conflit des lois."

[35] Vitta, "The Conflict of Personal Laws," p. 201; id., *Conflitti interni*, pp. 106–108.

[36] For the French approach on the primacy of French law, see in general Kollewijn, "Conflicts of Western and Non-Western Law," 4 (1951) *Int. L.Q.*, 307, 311–312; Bartholomew, *op. cit.*, p. 327; Szászy, "Interpersonal Conflicts," *cit.*, p. 796; Batiffol, *op. cit.*, p. 316 n. 31. The last named notes that the idea of the supremacy of the metropolitan law is expressed in practice by the invalidation of local laws by means of public policy. See also the sources there cited.

[37] Vitta, *Conflict of Laws*, pp. 50 et seq., 58 et seq. presents a general review of the Mandatory decisions.

[38] More extensively on this problem, see pp. 161 et seq. below.

[39] H.C. 24/41, *Zaadeh* v. *Chief Execution Officer Jerusalem*, 8 P.L.R. 175, 178; H.C. 103/42, *Abu Khalil* v. *Chief Execution Officer Jerusalem*, 9 P.L.R. 579. The Israeli courts have expressed reservations about this view, see below at note 50.

monotheistic religions which were not so far removed from the cultural conceptions of the Christian British judges.

With the establishment of the State of Israel, the problem changed. The judges were no longer foreigners sitting in judgment on the natives. The Israeli judge regards himself an integral part of the local population in all its variety. The political background also changed. The application of religious law, and above all Jewish law, became involved in the general problem of the relations between religion and state, a matter of political contest and not merely an expression of a "liberal" colonial policy, as it was during the British Mandate.[40]

The domestic nature of the problem brings to the fore its central importance for Israeli law which distinguishes it from the question of the application of the principle in private international law—and thus gives it its unique characteristic. The distinction has two aspects. Some legal systems require as a precondition to the application of the public policy restriction that a dispute be closely connected with the *lex fori*.[41] The rejection of the foreign law is conditional upon solution to the problem having direct effect on the legal situation within the state. This condition is always fulfilled in the case of religious law, where problems generally lack any extra-national element. Although from this aspect one obstacle to the application of public policy to religious law tends to be removed, the political and ideological nature of the problem sets up another serious obstacle. Indeed in *Funk-Schlesinger,* Justice Silberg in excluding the public policy principle did not content himself with the formal argument as above but added a material reason: "In the last analysis, our religious

---

[40] In this respect the problem is similar to the status of the Canon Law in certain Catholic countries, particularly Italy. Vitta rightly observes: "Owing to the homogeneous character of the population in such countries, the existence of two personal sets of rules does not arise from the necessity of facilitating the common life of different groups. The present situation has developed rather out of a complex historical process, namely the agelong clash between Church and State and the subsequent *modus vivendi* reached by these two institutions." "The Conflict of Personal Laws." 5 (1970) *Is. L. Rev.* 350. As to the principle of public policy with respect to the Canon Law, see note 129 below.

[41] In Swiss and German law the terms "Inlandsbeziehung" and "Binnenbeziehung" are employed. See generally Vischer, "Internationales Privatrecht," *op. cit.,* pp. 534–535; Neuhaus, *op. et loc. cit.* For a critical review of the literature in different countries, see Meise, *Zur Relativität der Vorbehaltsklausel im internationalen und interlokalen Privatrecht* (Hamburg 1966) pp. 84–166; Lagarde, *op. cit.,* pp. 44 et seq. On the problem in Anglo-American law, see Paulsen, Sovern, "Public Policy in the Conflict of Laws," (1956) *Col. L. Rev.* 969, 981 et seq.; Dicey & Morris, *Conflict of Laws* (9th ed. London 1973) p. 71.

laws of personal status do not run counter to the views of the Israeli public as a whole."[42] This reason is extremely important, since it exposes the internal ideological differences on the matter. The Jewish *religious* public in Israel, which accepts the precepts of religious law, is not only unable to see any violation of the basic principles of Israeli society in the solutions offered by religious law but regards the latter as the eternal expression of a divinely ordained world order. Any declaration by a secular court that the content of Jewish law violates the public policy of the Jewish State of Israel simply cannot be accepted by the religious public, which constitutes a not insignificant part of the population. The secular judge himself will hesitate long before declaring that a rule of Jewish law, which he views as an important part of Jewish national culture,[43] is contrary to the fundamental principles of society.[44]

In the light of the profound ideological conflict which divides the Israeli public, it is undesirable for religious law to be judicially rejected on the general ground of public policy. That can never persuade the religious public and it would be regarded as a blatant example of the judge's subjective attitude in the ideological dispute.[45] It is better for a question of

---

[42] At p. 328.

[43] As noted at the beginning of this study, the national factor has led a number of judges to the conclusion that religious law is not in the nature of foreign law. See pp. 26, 76, 98 above.

[44] A similar problem exists in Italian law with respect to the Canon Law in matters of marriage. The writers differ as to whether and to what extent it is possible to deny recognition of a marriage under the Canon Law by relying on public policy. Among other things it has even been argued that in view of the universal character of Canon Law and its high morality and legal perfection, no fundamental contradiction between the law of the Church and the law of the State is at all possible. Cf. Spinelli, *La trascrizione del matrimonio canonico* (Milano 1966), p. 101. Although the problem is essentially similar to the one we are considering, there are important differences in the normative background; in particular the concurrent regulation of civil marriage should be noted, which sheds light on the basic viewpoint of the Italian legislature in matters of marriage. Cf. above text at note 29. Among the writers who reject the application of the principle of public policy to Canon Law, see Del Giudice, *Manuale di diritto ecclesiastico* (10th ed. Milano 1964) *passim;* Spinelli, *La trascrizione*, pp. 99 et seq. Of the writers who support its application, see Falco, *Corso di diritto ecclesiastico*, II (Padova 1938) pp. 37, 418; Finocchiaro, *Matrimonio* (Bologna 1971) pp. 257 et seq. See the extensive bibliography in Spinelli, *op. cit.*, and compare Vitta, *op. ult. cit.*, pp. 201–202; Szászy, *op. cit.*, p. 815.

[45] That the judges are hesitant when faced with an ideological question may be learned from the *Shalit* case, H.C.J. 58/68, 23 P.D. (2) 477, English translation S.J.S.C. Special volume, 1971 p. 35, particularly the judgments of Justices Agra-

this nature to be decided directly by the legislature. This conclusion may be supported by an additional empirical argument. Although it is true that formally religious law has been received by a general dynamic reference, the essentials of religious law were nevertheless known to the legislature. The public was equally aware of the religious-prohibitory character of Jewish law and its consequent unchangeability. More particularly, the existence of rules "problematic" from a secular point of view was known and reference to them was made in full knowledge.[46]

In the realities of Israel there is another aspect to the problem—the sustaining of a religious judicial system by the secular courts. Religious law is applied primarily in the religious courts which have exclusive jurisdiction in certain matters. It is axiomatic that for the religious judge the principles of religious law are above all human criticism, and its invalidation for any reason is inconceivable. For them, as for every believer, this law is the perfect expression of public order. But in the contemplation of the State the religious courts are a component part of the domestic judicial system and not considered as foreign tribunals; they are directly subject to the review of the High Court of Justice under section 7 of the Courts Law, 5717–1957. If the principle of public policy indeed constitutes a legal restriction on the application of religious law in the secular courts, logic requires that this restriction apply to the religious courts as well. This conclusion follows from the nature of the principle of public policy. As we have said, the principle operates in situations in which the court finds a serious violation of basic principles of the State. It is not conceivable that religious courts acting within the State should not have to follow these same basic principles, and that the State should execute their judg-

nat, Landau and Witkon. Cf. the reservations of Neuhaus to the use of public policy against foreign law as a weapon in internal political conflict: "Höchst bedenklich ist die Benutzung des ordre public als Waffe im inländischen rechtspolitischen Streit, wenn etwa ein höchstes Gericht die Anwendung eines Satzes der lex fori offenbar gerade deshalb mit Hilfe der Vorbehaltsklausel gegen das abweichende Recht eines Nachbarlandes durchsetzt, um den Wert dieses Satzes gegenüber einer starken Opposition im eigenen Lande hervorzuheben" (*op. cit.,* p. 263). Compare Levontin, *Marriages and Divorces out of the Jurisdiction* (Jerusalem 1957), p. 50 (Hebrew).

[46] We refer to the prohibition of marriage between a *cohen* and a divorcee and the impossibility of mixed marriages. It is interesting that similar reasoning was advanced in Italy also with respect to the recognition of Canon Law. See Finocchiaro, *op. cit.,* pp. 263 et seq. Of course, the normative background is different in Italy. The typical problem regarding the rejection of religious law relates to cases in which Canon Law is prepared to permit marriages which are *prohibited by the secular marriage laws.*

ments which are held to offend against those principles. Invalidation of religious law in the secular courts alone would lead to fragmentation of the concept of public policy, which is intolerable because it would cut the very ground out from under the principle itself.[47]

On the other hand, preservation of the unity of the concept by requiring the religious courts to act in accordance with it, is also problematical, since it means coercing religious judges to diverge from religious law so as to reconcile their decisions with basic principles formulated in the secular courts. As we shall see later, compulsion raises both a moral (requiring the judge to act contrary to his belief) and a practical problem (the effectiveness of compulsion in matters of religious conscience is limited).[48]

We return to our earlier conclusion. Religious law is not to be invalidated by judicial process on the basis of the general and nebulous principle of public policy. As long as religious courts possess judicial powers, it may be assumed that the legislature did not intend to restrict the application of religious law on the basis of a general principle of review, which is not explicit in the legislation, and is left to judicial discretion without clear definition of its content.

The secular courts appear to be aware of the problematic nature of the public policy principle in its application to religious law. In any event, they have not in practice directly employed the principle in order to reject substantive religious law, even when its provisions conflict with their own fundamental outlook.[49] Moreover, on a number of occasions the Supreme Court has expressly dissented from the suggestions in the Mandatory decisions that the secular courts have such a power.[50]

---

[47] To the same effect see Levontin, *op. cit.*, pp. 70–71 n. 89.
[48] Below, text at note 63.
[49] See, for example, the judgments of Justices Sussman and Landau in C.A. 571/69 *Cahana v. Cahana,* 24 P.D. (2) 549, 557. Both judges protested against the results of a religious court judgment which obliged the wife to accept a divorce because of a religious prohibition (the marriage of a *cohen* with a divorcee), but they did not regard themselves competent to invalidate religious law. And see in particular, H.C.J. 10/59, *Vicki Levy v. District Rabbinical Court, Tel Aviv,* 13 P.D. 1182, 1193: "The material content of religious law, to the extent that it is recognized in principle by the laws of the country, need not find favour with the secular judge and he obviously cannot invalidate a judgment which in practice, sustains this material law"; H.C.J. 301/63, *Streit v. Chief Rabbi of Israel,* at 621–622; H.C.J.130–132/66, *Segev v. The Rabbinical Court and the Chief Rabbinate,* 21 P.D. (2) 505, 520–521.
[50] H.C.J. 10/59; H.C.J. 301/63, *ibid.*

It would not be correct to confine ourselves to the formal aspect of the matter. Even if it is formally held that public policy cannot invalidate religious law,[51] the secular courts have found indirect means to limit the actual application of religious law, when they have thought that a religious solution is contrary to public policy. The techniques are many and varied and involve many legal institutions. A few examples will suffice to demonstrate the tendency to use the public policy principle indirectly.

One example is found in the approach of Justice Sussman in *Streit*, which dealt with permission to marry under section 5 of the Penal Law Amendment (Bigamy) Law, 5719–1959.[52] A rabbinical court had granted a man permission to marry a second wife, principally because the first marriage had been celebrated abroad by civil ceremony alone. Justice Sussman assumed that the religious court was competent to decide as it did, even though a secular court, bound by conflict of laws rules, would have decided otherwise. But the man was to be prevented from acting upon the judgment he had obtained. "The religious law which applies to Jews by virtue of section 1 of the [Rabbinical Courts Jurisdiction (Marriage and Divorce) Law, 5713–1953], does not apply only to observant Jews. But the trouble is that after having been married for decades and having had a son, the husband comes to the religious court and obtains a judgment which annuls the marriage on the ground that it was not entered into in a formal religious ceremony. By these means, the husband seeks to renounce a valid marriage ceremony which took place almost 40 years ago, to turn his wife retroactively into his mistress and his son into the offspring of an unmarried woman. *This is unconscionable behaviour which public order does not tolerate.*"[53] Justice Sussman concluded by saying that "the husband's use of the proceedings in the rabbinical court was improper and immoral and *liable to undermine public order*. Accordingly, a court of equity will intervene and prevent the act."[54] (emphasis supplied)

This is indeed the view of a single judge—the other judges ultimately arrived at the same result in other ways—but no reservations to it have been voiced.[55] Whilst assuming that there was no authority directly to invalidate a religious solution, on the ground of public policy, religious

---

[51] See the sources cited above, notes 24 and 49.
[52] H.C.J. 301/63, at 627 et seq.
[53] H.C.J. 301/63, at 629.
[54] *Ibid.*, at 632.
[55] Compare also F.H. 10/69, *Boronovski v. Chief Rabbis of Israel*, 25 P.D. (1) 7, 27.

PUBLIC POLICY

law was rejected indirectly by a personal order aimed at preventing execution of the judgment obtained.[56] No attempt was made to conceal the *consideration* of public policy. This technique of making a personal order is borrowed from English law, going back to a period when the different courts there were waging a battle over jurisdiction. Reliance on this historical precedent seems very strange, in view of the interlocking of the religious court system with the secular, both in respect of the review powers exercised by the High Court of Justice and in respect of the execution of religious court judgments by the secular powers.[57] Years ago Professor Levontin, sensing the parallel between the two situations, commented, "In an earlier period, before the merger of the courts of common law and of equity in England, a critic once scornfully said, 'The English establish one court to do injustice and a second to correct the injustice.' Let us hope that this cutting remark, whose original edge has been dulled in the course of time, will not be sharpened anew—in our country."[58]

This is not the only means adopted by the secular courts to avoid the

---

[56] H.C.J. 301/63, at 630 et seq.

[57] Justice Sussman attempts to demonstrate that in England there is still a possibility of issuing a personal order prohibiting use of a local judgment, despite the unification of the courts of law and equity. But, in our opinion, the cases he cites do not support this view. In the first, *The Teresa* (1894) 71 L.T. 342, the court issued an injunction against a party ordering him to discontinue his action in a lower court. The court's reasons were that the lower court had no jurisdiction to hear the action (salvage of a ship) because of the amount of the claim and that the action there was "exceedingly inconvenient." For reasons of costs the court preferred to issue an injunction, although it was also competent to make prohibition order. This case cannot serve as authority for enjoining for reasons of equity reliance on a local judgment. The same is true of the second case, *McHenry* v. *Lewis* (1883) 47 L.T. 549, which dealt with the rule *lis alibi pendens*. The third case, *Bolton* v. *Bolton* (1891) 65 L.T. 698, is also not in point. The Court of Appeal set aside an injunction in a marital matter, which had been issued in special circumstances (a minor whose property was administered by the court). The decision in Mot. 280/57, *Hachamov* v. *Schmidt*, 12 P.D. 59, 64, dealt with *foreign* judgments obtained by fraud. H.C.J. 91/49, *Frisch* v. *Registrar of Cooperative Societies*, 5 P.D. 287, does not deal with injunctions intended to prevent the continuation of proceedings on equitable grounds, as Justice Sussman argued, but with injunctions as opposed to prohibition orders where the lower court or tribunal "is acting outside the scope of its jurisdiction" (*ibid.*, at 291–292). We have not found any authority which today permits injunctions against the use of local judgments for equitable reasons. Cf. Hanbury, *Modern Equity* (8th ed. London 1962), pp. 13, 20, 566 et seq.

[58] *Marriages and Divorces out of the Jurisdiction*, p. 50 (Hebrew).

151

application of religious law when it appears to violate accepted basic principles. We may mention some of these other means without going into details. There is, first, the view that rabbinical court judgments based on Jewish law are not *res judicata* in the secular courts when the latter would apply foreign law under conflict of laws principles.[59] Another is to extend the jurisdiction of the secular courts at the expense of the religious courts. Such extension may be secured by a restrictive interpretation of the statutory provisions which grant exclusive jurisdiction to the religious courts,[60] or by a broad interpretation of the ancillary powers of the secular courts under section 35 of the Courts Law.[61] Although the main motive for restricting the jurisdiction of the religious courts is often found in general considerations near to the principle of public policy, the latter is never expressly mentioned.

C. The Positive Function of Public Policy: Direct Application of Secular Norms

The similarity of what is called "the positive function of public policy" in private international law and in the application of religious law in Israel is purely formal. In both cases a dispute is settled by reference to the state's own norms. But theoretically a substantial difference exists, springing from the differences in background of the problem. The historical background for the application of religious law is the desire to grant legal autonomy to the religious communities. The secular authorities refrained from independently regulating these matters, and gave them over exclusively to the jurisdiction of the religious-communal system. But as soon as the legislature found it proper to regulate by itself any matter of personal status, religious law became unnecessary. Secular regulation can always in principle replace religious law, which in effect means replacing personal law by a uniform territorial law. Today in Israel the extent to which such a replacement is to be effected is a political and ideo-

---

[59] Cf. H.C.J. 301/63, at 629, in which Justice Sussman leaves the question open for further examination; See H.C.J. 73/66 *Zemulun* v. *Minister of the Interior*, 18 P.D. (4) 645, 667, where Justice Landau expressed the view that a religious court is not competent to give a declaratory judgment for guidance of the Population Registry regarding the validity or invalidity of divorces effected abroad; see in particular C.A. 173/69, *Bakhar* v. *Bakhar*, 23 P.D. (1) 665.

[60] For example, H.C.J. 181/68, *Florsheim* v. *Rabbinical Court, Haifa*, 22 P.D. (2) 723; C.A. 47/62 *Beiter* v. *Beiter* 16 P.D. 154.

[61] See, for example, H.C.J. 51/69, *Rodnitzki* v. *Rabbinical High Court of Appeals*, 24 P.D. (1) 704, 716.

logical question of the highest order, and this is not the place to take up any position in this subsisting dispute. An indication of the associated problems and a short account of existing trends are sufficient.

The main problem stems from the duality of the judicial system, secular and religious. The replacement of religious law by secular law is easy to effect in the secular courts which regard the laws of the State as the only source of their jurisdiction and unreservedly submit to their rule. The situation is otherwise with the religious courts. These consider themselves primarily as an autonomous judicial system and their allegiance is naturally to the religious law by which they adjudicate.[62] The power of the State to force upon religious judges its own laws in divergence from religious law is clearly limited in practice. Professor Tedeschi, in dealing with the possibility of doing so, points out, and with justice, that direct interference by the legislature "would give rise to hatreds, and would ultimately be found to be ineffectual. Hatreds—because everyone has a natural dislike of pressure exerted upon religious conscience; ineffectual— because the religious courts would justifiably rebel against the decree."[63]

Nevertheless, the legislature has on occasion, although not very often, chosen the path of *direct intervention*. In these instances it has placed an express duty on all courts, secular and religious, to act in accordance with the provisions of the law, as in the Women's Equal Rights Law, 5711–1951,[64] the Adoption of Children Law, 5720–1960, the Succession Law, 5725–1965, and the Matrimonial Property Relations Law, 5733–1973.[65] Furthermore the provisions of a Knesset law have been applied to the

---

[62] See on their ambiguous status above pp. 46, 111. On the problem of imposing secular law on religious tribunals in general see Wähler, "Die Bindung religiöser Gerichte an Normen des staatlichen Privat—und Verfahrensrechts", *Multitudo Legum-Ius Unum,* Band II (Berlin 1973), p. 865.

[63] "On the Problem of Marriage in the State of Israel," *Studies in Israel Private Law,* pp. 218, 228 et seq.; Wähler, *op. cit.,* p. 867.

[64] Section 7: "All courts shall act in accordance with this Law; a tribunal competent to deal with matters of personal status shall likewise act in accordance therewith, unless all the parties are eighteen years of age or over and have consented before the tribunal, of their own free will, to have their case tried according to the laws of their community."

[65] Section 24 of the Adoption Law: "The provisions of Sections 1 to 22, 25 and 31 shall apply to a religious court sitting by virtue of this section, and every reference in those sections to a court shall, in that connection be deemed to be a reference to a religious court." Section 148 of the Succession Law: "... this Law alone shall apply to rights of succession and rights of maintenance out of the estate." Section 13(2) of the Matrimonial Property Relations Law.

religious courts under the Marriage Age Law, 5710–1950,[66] and the Religious Courts (Summons) Law, 5716–1956.[67]

It is noteworthy that the introduction of independent, secular regulation by the legislature does not by itself mean that the religious courts are obliged to act in accordance therewith and to forgo the provisions of religious law. There is always the strong presumption that the religious courts are entitled to judge in accordance with religious law. Hence express provision is required to bind the religious courts to decide in accordance with secular law. And indeed the legislature in reality so prescribes.[68] But whenever the duty is imposed on the religious courts, the really difficult problem for the State is how to ensure that the religious courts will apply the secular provisions so that its decree is not a dead letter. The autonomous status of the religious courts, with their separate appeal system, renders it difficult for the High Court of Justice effectively to control the situation. Although it exercises review powers over the religious courts, the general principles guiding its activities do not give it competence to act as a court of appeal with respect to the religious courts nor can it go into the merits of a case. The High Court of Justice has held formally that for a religious court to ignore a binding norm of the State is similar to an excess of jurisdiction and the judgment will not stand.[66]

There is, however, considerable doubt, whether in reality this method of imposing secular norms on the religious courts has proved itself effective, despite the fact that the legislator has been careful to use the method sparingly. On a number of occasions the Supreme Court has complained that the religious courts disregard secular law and the secular courts'

---

[66] Section 3 of the Law, on which see in particular, Tedeschi, "On the Problem of Marriage in the State," *op. cit.*, pp. 220–222.

[67] Section 5 of the Law deals with a person's refusal to comply with the order of a religious court. It provides: "...But the court shall not be competent so to fine or order a person for not answering a question or producing a document which in the opinion of the court he would not be bound to answer or produce in a civil court." See, in particular, E. Harnon, "The Duty to Testify and Privileged Evidence in Rabbinical Courts," 21 (1965) *HaPraklit*, 283.

[68] See the text of the Adoption of Children Law (above, note 65) as compared with the parallel provision of the Capacity and Guardianship Law, 5722–1962, section 79, and in particular the debate in the Knesset on the question whether or not to require the religious courts to act in accordance with the Capacity and Guardianship Law, 34 *Divri HaKnesset*, pp. 3080 et seq.; Shifman, "Child Welfare in the Rabbinical Court," 5 (1974) *Mishpatim* 421.

[69] H.C.J. 202/57, *Sidis v. Rabbinical High Court, Jerusalem*, 12 P.D. 1528, 1539; H.C.J. 187/54, *Barea v. Kadi of the Moslem Shaari Court of Acre*, 9 P.D. 1193, 1199, 1200. Cf. Wähler, *op. cit.* 878 et seq.

interpretation thereof.[70] Both institutions have developed great sensitivity having its origin in the many jurisdictional disputes and in the exercise of review powers by the secular over the religious system which views itself as autonomous.[71]

Apart from direct intervention, the legislature has chosen a middle course. In some cases religious law and religious jurisdiction have been allowed to stand but a criminal sanction is imposed on any juristic act of which the legislature disapproves. For example, a man's bigamous marriage or a divorce against the wife's will may indeed achieve the desired legal result, but a punishable criminal offense has been committed.[72] Another method already mentioned is to deny exclusive jurisdiction to the religious courts, by providing for concurrent jurisdiction in the secular courts where the application of secular norms is assured.[73]

With respect to substantive law a number of solutions have been found. The legislator may prescribe that the provisions of secular law shall apply unless the parties agree that the matter be adjudicated in accordance with religious law.[74] A choice of secular or religious law is

[70] See, for example, F.H. 23/69, *Joseph* v. *Joseph,* 24 P.D. (1) 792, 802: "The rabbinical courts indeed try cases in accordance with Jewish law, with their wide-ranging and profound expertise, but they entirely ignore the laws of the State ... I have searched in vain for any reliance on the laws of the State as such with respect to the matters in dispute. The Women's Equal Rights Law, for example, simply does not exist for them." (Justice Cohn), and see, at 80 (Justice Berinson). See also the stringent remarks of Justice Cohn in his minority opinion in F.H. 10/69, *Boronovski* v. *Chief Rabbis of Israel,* 25 P.D. (1) 7, 15. The judges proceed on the presumption that a decision of the Supreme Court interpreting a law of the Knesset constitutes a precedent binding on the religious courts. As a formal matter, this presumption is not free from doubt. Section 33 of the Courts Law, 5717–1957, which prescribes the rule of binding precedent applies to *secular courts* only. See above p. 134 note 131.

[71] The matter is particularly apparent in the matter of the registration of the marriage of a *cohen* and a *divorcee,* see below at note 149, and particularly H.C.J. 29/71, *Kedar* v. *District Rabbinical Court, Tel Aviv,* 26 P.D. (2) 608.

[72] Penal Law Amendment (Bigamy) Law, 5719–1959. On the question of the validity of the legal result, see below pp. 164 et seq. See also Tedeschi, *ibid.*

[73] In the case of concurrent jurisdiction, a religious court may hear the matter at the choice of one of the parties, as in a wife's claim for maintenance under section 4 of the Rabbinical Courts Jurisdiction (Marriage and Divorce) Law, 5713–1953, or with the consent of the persons interested, as under section 9 of the same law, section 24 of the Adoption of Children Law, 5720–1960, or section 155 of the Succession Law, 5725–1965.

[74] For example, section 7 of the Women's Equal Rights Law (see above note 64) and section 155(b) of the Succession Law. It should be noted that today,

offered.[75] Another solution has been found in the matter of child maintenance. Under section 3(b) of the Family Amendment (Maintenance) Law, 5719–1959, "A person who is not liable for the maintenance of his minor children and the minor children of his spouse under the personal law applying to him ... is liable for the maintenance of his minor children and the minor children of his wife, and the provisions of this law shall apply to that maintenance." The courts have so interpreted this Law that its provisions are in practice treated as a *supplement* to the rights of maintenance under religious law.[76]

Where the secular provisions of state law apply directly and expressly, religious law is not rejected on grounds of public policy. But here as well the influence of the courts' view regarding basic principles appropriate for Israel society is observable. The influence is not exerted within the framework of a formal concept but indirectly through interpretation—*a broad interpretation* of the legislature's secular rules and a *restrictive interpretation* of the provisions which refer us to religious law. Local case law offers examples of both interpretative approaches.

Broad Interpretation: A striking example intended to extend the scope of secular law by rejection of religious law is found in the prohibition of polygamy. Here the fundamental principles of monogamy and of the equal rights of women conflict with certain rules of the *Halakha*. Section 2 of the Penal Law Amendment (Bigamy) Law, 5719–1959, provides a special defence in the form of permission to marry a second wife before the marriage with the first has been legally terminated, which is granted by a final judgment of a rabbinical court with the approval of the two Chief Rabbis of Israel. Section 5 of the Law does not provide any special rule concerning the substantive law under which the rab-

---

apparently, the possibility of statutory choice of material law in matters of personal status exists only in the religious and not in the secular court. From the terms of section 155(b) of the Succession Law it is not clear who has the choice between religious law or the provisions of that Law—the parties or the court. See also sec. 13(2) of the Matrimonial Property Relations Law, 5733–1973.

[75] On this subject, see in general Tedeschi, "On the Choice between Religious and Secular Law in the Legal System of Israel," *Studies in Israel Law* (Jerusalem 1960) pp. 238 et seq.; Wengler, "General Principles of Private International Law," 104 (1961) III *Recueil des Cours* 273, 302–303.

[76] See Shereshevski, *Family Law* (2nd ed. Jerusalem 1967) p. 362 n.1c (Hebrew) and C.A. 508/70, *Natovitz v. Natovitz*, 25 P.D. (1) 603, 609; regarding foreign law, C.A. 240/72, *Peretz v. Peretz*, 26 P.D. (2) 793.

binical court and the Chief Rabbis are to decide whether or not to grant permission. The natural assumption is that "the law follows the judge" and that the rabbinical organs will act exclusively in accordance with Jewish law,[77] but this assumption has been denied by the Supreme Court. It has been held as a matter of principle that section 5 is the creation of the secular legislature and that the Chief Rabbis must act in accordance with and not contrary to the *object of the law*.[78] If the grant of permission is contrary to the object of the secular Law and will lead to its frustration, then the High Court of Justice will intervene to prevent this result. In *Boronovski*[79] the President of the Supreme Court summed up the principle in the following words: "When the Chief Rabbis were given the power of approval for the purpose of the exemption mentioned in section 5, it was contemplated that they would take care that the object of the law—to strengthen the fundamentals of monogamy in social life—would not be stultified by a spate of permissions to marry, and hence that they would be on the alert that permissions are only granted in accordance with the strict rules of the *Halakha* and in exceptional cases where justice requires that the husband be released from his ties, and no injustice is as a result done to the wife." This is a conspicuous instance of religious institutions being placed under an obligation to depart from religious law in order to realize fundamental secular principles. The court reached this result by a broad interpretation of a vague statutory provision. In the concrete case, the Chief Rabbis were required to regard the civil marriage of Jews celebrated abroad as valid and were prohibited, within their powers under section 5 of the Law, from approving a permission to remarry on the sole ground that the first marriage had been celebrated in civil form. The fact that this ground is sufficient in point of religious law is not enough for the purposes of the secular law.

There were very sharp differences of opinion among the judges over the extent to which secular considerations oblige religious institutions, or more precisely over the extent of the obligation to deviate from religious law in order to achieve the "objects of the law." In the minority view of Justice Cohn, the object of the secular law is very wide, since the legislature intended to prevent bigamy in most absolute terms, whatever the provisions of religious law which would or might allow it under appropriate

---

[77] Cf. H.C.J. 143/62, *Funk Schlesinger* v. *Minister of the Interior*, 17 P.D. 225, 250; H.C.J. 450/70, *Rogozinski* v. *State of Israel*, 26 P.D. (1) 129, 134.
[78] H.C.J. 301/63, the *Streit* case.
[79] F.H. 10/69, *Boronovski* v. *Chief Rabbis of Israel*, 25 P.D. (1) 7, 50.

circumstances. Thus, he took the view that only in isolated cases should permission be granted.[80] This approach was indeed rejected in the Further Hearing of the case, but the difference of opinion demonstrates the great possibility latent in the technique of statutory construction for rejecting religious law on the basis of general considerations of public policy. In *Boronovski* we may discern a tendency to impose consideration of secular factors not only upon the Chief Rabbis as administrative organs but equally on the rabbinical courts.[81]

Further examples are to be found in connection with the Women's Equal Rights Law, 5711–1951. The Supreme Court has interpreted one vague general provision of this law[82] as doing away with a form of marital property in which under Jewish law the husband has wide rights.[83] It has also been held that this ruling is of retroactive effect, since the Court regarded the law as a "revolutionary ideological law changing the social order, witness its title and the programmatic nature of its first section.... It is directed at eradicating every thing which, under existing law, consti-

---

[80] Justice Cohn suggested that the authority of the Chief Rabbis to grant permission is limited to cases in which some objective reason exists preventing dissolution of the previous marriage (such as mental illness of the wife which disables her from expressing her will in the divorce proceedings, or her prolonged absence under circumstances which give rise to reasonable doubt as to her being alive). These cases should be distinguished from those in which the cause for non-dissolution of the marriage is the refusal of the woman to receive the deed of divorce from the husband. This viewpoint, which restricts the authority of the Chief Rabbis, was accepted in *Streit*, but the opposite rule prevailed in *Boronovski*.

[81] This was expressly stated by Justice Cohn, in his dissenting judgment in *Boronovski* at 14–15. Agranat P. writing for the majority, does not mention the possibility of intervention with the religious court which grants the permission initially. But a hint to this effect may be found in the view (at 27–28) that it makes no difference to review by the High Court of Justice whether the act of the Chief Rabbis is of an administrative or of a judicial nature. (See another view expressed in *Streit* by Justice Olshan at 636–637, 641). In accordance with this reasoning, it is difficult to understand why the High Court of Justice cannot intervene against the religious court which grants the permission at the first stage.

[82] Section 2 of the Law.

[83] H.C.J. 202/57, *Sidis v. Rabbinical High Court*, 12 P.D. 1528; C.A. 313/59, *Balaban v. Balaban*, 14 P.D. 285. See the criticism of this rule in Shereshevski, *op. cit.*, pp. 216 et seq., but see now section 4 of the Matrimonial Property Relations Law, 5733–1973.

tutes legal discrimination of the woman."[84] This passage indicates that retroactivity is the result of public policy considerations.[85]

A similar attitude is reflected in the treatment of the natural guardianship of parents of their children under section 3(b) of the Women's Equal Rights Law. This section makes the *welfare of the child* the overriding test for determining the rights of custody of his person and property.[86] Certain religious laws happen to contain provisions prescriptive of what is to be viewed as the welfare of the child in given circumstances. Since section 7 of the Women's Equal Rights Law expressly lays down that the religious courts are to act in accordance with its provisions, the Supreme Court has, not surprisingly, declared that the "welfare of the child" test, as a territorial principle, applies to all religious laws, displacing any foreign or religious law to the contrary.[87] Be this, however, as it may, our present concern is to construe the concept of the "welfare of the child" when religious law contains an express definition for a particular set of circumstances. The courts have tended to invest the concept with a secular content. In the words of Justice Goitein: "The test is an objective one and the judges must ignore the theoretical prescriptions of religious law which determine what is the welfare of the child in a specific situation."[88] It is doubtful whether the language of the section requires such a construction; here is but another example of the rejection of religious law by a broad interpretation of a Knesset enactment.

Restrictive Interpretation: As we have noted, a parallel tendency exists regarding state laws which refer us to religious law. Here public policy considerations are apt to lead the judge to a restrictive interpretation aimed at narrowing the scope of religious law. A typical example is the interpre-

---

[84] At 1537.

[85] It is, however, difficult to reconcile the idea that the repeal must be of retroactive effect because of public policy with the provisions of section 7 of the Law, which authorizes the couple to agree to the continued application of Jewish law even after the effective date of the Law. In other words, it is difficult to reconcile the dispositive character of the new law with the retroactive repeal based, as it were, on the necessity of changing the existing system root and branch. On the connection between retroactive repeal and public policy, see in general Savigny, *System des heutigen roemischen Rechts* (Berlin 1849), vol. VIII, pp. 368 et seq.; cf. Broggini, "Intertemporales Privatrecht," *Schweizerisches Privatrecht*, Vol. I (Basel 1969), pp. 353, 405 et seq.

[86] See also sections 17 and 25 of the Capacity and Guardianship Law, 5722–1962.

[87] C.A. 86/63, *Al-Tzafdi v. Benjamin*, 17 P.D. 1419, 1422, 1429.

[88] H.C.J. 187/54, *Barea v. Kadi of the Moslem Shaari Court, Acre*, 9 P.D. 1193, 1198.

tation given to section 2 of the Rabbinical Courts Jurisdiction (Marriage and Divorce) Law, 5713–1953, which provides that "Marriages and divorces of Jews shall be performed in Israel in accordance with Jewish religious law." This section raises inter alia[89] the question whether a general statutory duty to celebrate marriage in accordance with *all* the provisions of religious law is imposed or whether the intention goes only to the validity of the marriage. The answer is important in the not insignificant number of cases in which religious law prohibits celebration of a marriage but nonetheless recognizes its validity after the event.[90] In practice the question has arisen principally in connection with the marriage between a man of priestly descent (a *cohen*) and a divorcee in private ceremony; which whilst forbidden under *Halakha* takes effect when entered into. Are a couple who have celebrated such a marriage guilty of a violation of section 2? In the view of Justice Silberg that section imposes a *civil* prohibition[91] upon celebrating a marriage which is not permitted by Jewish law.[92] Justice Silberg indeed admits that the section does not contain any express sanction, and is therefore in the nature of *lex imperfecta,* but the carrying out of an illegal act is a consideration which may deprive the parties of any relief lying in the discretion of the court, such as a declaratory judgment concerning the validity of the marriage.[93]

This view was rejected by the majority. Justice Landau disagreed[94] on the ground that the control of religious law of the "celebration" of marriage and divorce was not tantamount to the full imposition of the entire religious law dealing with marriage and divorce. Section 2 is not to be interpreted as imposing a prohibition which is religious in source and essence on all Jews in Israel, including those for whom the observance of religious commandment is not a matter of faith. In his view the prohibition of the marriage of a *cohen* and a divorcee is a religious prohibition

---

[89] On the problems of interpreting this section in general, see Silberg, *Personal Status in Israel* (*Jerusalem* 1957), pp. 365 et seq. (in Hebrew).

[90] On the parallel distinction between *impedimentum impediens* and *impedimentum dirimens* see the statement of Justice Kister in *Rodnitzky* at 722–723.

[91] The person who supervises the marriage ceremony, as distinguished from the couple, is subject to criminal prosecution if he does so knowing that it is prohibited *by law;* see section 8 of the Penal Law Amendment (Bigamy) Law, 5719–1959.

[92] H.C.J. 80/63, *Gorfinkel, Chaklai* v. *Minister of the Interior,* at 2062, 2063.

[93] *Ibid.*: "Even if the Law is incomplete, it is a Law, and the citizen may not violate it."

[94] At 2068; and in more detail, H.C.J. 51/69, *Rodnitzky,* 24 P.D. (1) 704, 711–712.

which concerns the relations between a man and his Creator. For the non-believer the prohibition is not only coercion in a matter of conscience but also discrimination between a *cohen* and an ordinary Jew on religious grounds. Justice Landau concludes, "We must adopt an interpretation of the 1953 law which will avoid such a contradiction with the basic principles of the law of the State."[95] The difference of opinion between the judges[96] not only reveals the flexibility of the concept of public policy (as an instrument of interpretation) but also indicates the crucial role which the Supreme Court plays in State-religion relations.

D. Mixed Function of Public Policy: The Principles of Natural Justice

Even under the Mandate the rule had crystallized that a religious court judgment is not to be recognized if it violated the *principles of natural justice*.[97] This concept has its origin in English administrative law and it serves, among other things, as a technical device to set aside judicial decisions of tribunals and other bodies exercising judicial functions. It contemplates the violation of certain basic principles which ensure fair hearing, such as *audi alteram partem*.[98] The idea is close to that of public policy[99] but is more limited in that it goes only to procedural and not to substantive matters. For this reason it lies somewhat outside the area of the present study of the application of religious law in the secular courts. The latter make no recourse to the procedural rules of religious law but always act in accordance with secular procedure. This principle is based, as we shall see, on the distinction between substance and procedure which

---

[95] At 712.
[96] See the contrary view of Justice Kister, at 719 et seq. The approach of the majority, which rejects the "prohibitive" part of Jewish Law in reliance on the basic principles of the law of the State, raises a serious problem. How can the institutions of the Rabbinate act in accordance with the whole body of religious law if the prohibitive part does not apply in the State? On the other hand, it is inconceivable that the rabbis and the religious judges can be forced to act contrary to express prohibitions of Jewish law. It appears that section 8 of the Penal Law Amendment (Bigamy) Law, 5719-1959 (see note 91 above) indicates a legislative intent to receive even the prohibitive part of religious law.
[97] See Silberg, *op. cit.*, pp. 176 et seq. One of the first decisions which recognized this was C.A. 8/32, *Khouri v. Ziadeh*, 5 R. 1673.
[98] Cf. Garner, *Administrative Law* (3rd ed. London 1970) pp. 111 et seq., 167 et seq.
[99] See also generally Wade, *Administrative Law* (3rd ed. Oxford 1971) pp. 171 et seq. In the administrative area a violation of the principles of natural justice is considered an excess of jurisdiction. See note 117 below.

governs all references to religious law. Thus, a secular court as such will not be confronted with the question whether it should follow religious rules of procedure which conflict with fair hearing. The question primarily concerns *decisions* of religious courts taken under defective procedures, or to the *proceeding* itself in a religious court. From the point of view of the secular court what is involved is the recognition of a religious court judgment or the review of the acts of a religious court.

To annul a judgment or a proceeding because of a violation of the principles of natural justice partakes formally of both the positive and the negative functions of the public policy principle.[100] On the one hand, the principles of natural justice are rules according to which all judicial tribunals, secular as well as religious, must *ab initio* act. On the other hand, in any specific instance the manner of conducting a trial in the religious court is examined in accordance with these principles, and it will be invalidated if violative of the basic principles of fair hearing.

As we have said, the problem arises only with respect to those religious courts which act according to religious procedures. The secular court encounters a religious norm effectuated by another judicial institution and finds itself in the position of *reviewing* a decision or judgment rendered by a religious court. In principle, two types of review are possible: direct attack of the decision or judgment, or collateral attack.[101]

Direct attack is carried out by the High Court of Justice, the body authorized to supervise the observance of the principles of natural justice in the religious courts, as in all other tribunals acting on behalf of the state.[102] The scope of the review powers exercised by the High Court of Justice and the principles which guide it are based upon section 7 of the Courts Law, 5717–1957.[103] In the relatively few cases in which the High Court of Justice has intervened since the establishment of the State, it was not at all clear whether indeed there was any substantial conflict between fair hearing, as embodied in the concept of *natural justice,* and religious procedures binding on the religious court in accordance with its own law. It has always been assumed that religious law also requires observance of the same principles. A decision questioned in the High Court

[100] On these concepts generally, see text at note 16 above.
[101] On this distinction, see Rubinstein, *Jurisdiction and Illegality* (Oxford 1965) pp. 35 et seq.
[102] By means of an order in the nature of mandamus or certiorari: section 7 of the Courts Law, 5717–1957.
[103] For the relation between section 7(a) and section 7(b)(4), see H.C.J. 10/59, Levy v. *District Rabbinical Court, Tel Aviv,* 13 P.D. 1182; see also the comments of the judges in *Streit* at 609, 619–620.

of Justice was said to be contrary not only to fundamental "secular" principles, but also to the essence of religious procedure.[104] The intervention of the Court was in the main necessary to enforce basic rules of justice and not necessarily for rejecting religious rules. In this respect the hesitation of the High Court of Justice at intervening in proceedings in religious courts of first instance is understandable.[105] More recently the Court has preferred to direct the complainant to the appellate tribunals of the religious system on the assumption that a violation of the principles of natural justice is also a violation of religious law.[106]

It may also be noted that where religious procedural rules are really contrary to the principles of natural justice, the High Court of Justice will intervene directly in the religious court proceedings by requiring the religious court to act in accordance with secular norms—here, procedural. The religious norms will be rejected for the fundamentals of secular procedure, within the rules of natural justice.[107]

Collateral attack on a religious judgment may be levelled in any secular court where the judgment is relied upon. The court has no direct review authority but it must treat the religious judgment as an element of the hearing before it. The pre-State decision in *Haddad* v. *Haddad*[108] may serve as an example. There the validity of a divorce decree granted *ex parte* by a Greek Orthodox court was in question. The secular court refused to recognize the divorce for two reasons. The first was that even religious law itself does not recognize an *ex parte* dissolution of marriage. This reason does not concern us, since the secular court does not sit in appeal on religious judgments and it is not its function to investigate how far such judgments are in accordance with religious law. (Even the High

---

[104] As to the place of the principle *audi alteram partem* in Jewish law, see the observations of Justice Silberg in *Levy* at 1188; he emphasizes that the rabbis violated the principle of Jewish law.

[105] On this point the judges differed in *Levy*. Justice Silberg in the minority said that it was neither proper nor necessary for the High Court of Justice to intervene in the judgments of a rabbinical court of first instance because of a violation of the principle of natural justice of hearing both sides. This principle is embedded deeply in Jewish Law and it is easy to appeal to the Rabbinical Court of Appeal (at 1133). But see the doubts of Justice Sussman with respect to the effectiveness of the review powers of the Rabbinical Court of Appeal (at 1201).

[106] See H.C.J. 349/65, *Peru* v. *Qadi Madhhab*, 20 P.D. (2) 342, 345.

[107] In *Levy* the result was the setting aside of the religious judgment, but it is clear that its significance was to impose a duty on the religious court to hear the case again in accordance with the rules of natural justice.

[108] C.A. 63/37, *Haddad* v. *Haddad*, 4 P.L.R. 249, 251.

Court of Justice does not regard itself competent in this respect, notwithstanding that it exercises a direct review over religious courts.)[109]

The second reason was that the judgment was contrary to the principles of natural justice of secular law and was therefore deemed entirely null and void. This is an example of a secular court denying legal force to a religious court judgment which it was asked to recognize in the course of maintenance proceedings.[110]

This decision raises a fundamental question. Can a religious judgment which has constitutively changed the personal status of a person (a judgment *in rem*) in fact be denied validity? According to Justice Silberg that is impossible.[111] In his view a secular court cannot disregard a change of status effected by a religious court judgment, even if the latter is tainted by procedural defects which violate the principles of natural justice. Secular court review of religious court judgments is limited to those which are executory (*in personam*). A secular court may refuse to execute the judgment of a religious court in proceedings which violate the principles of natural justice. Justice Silberg finds support for his view in the fact that the Mandatory decision cited gave two reasons for its refusal to recognize the judgment. Since the secular court was not asked to *execute* the defective judgment, it could not ignore the change of status were it not for additional reasons. "Only the cumulative effect of the *two* grounds—(a) that religious law itself does not recognize the judgment as valid and (b) that secular law commands non-recognition of judgments contrary to the principles of natural justice—can defeat the procedural validity of the judgment."[112] Accordingly, therefore, in the event of a violation of the principles of natural justice, we must distinguish between judgments *in personam* and judgments *in rem* particularly those which effect a change in status. The secular court will refuse to assist in the execution of *in personam* judgments but will not withhold recognition from *in rem* judgments, unless they lack validity under religious law itself.

This conclusion is unacceptable. The reaction of the secular court is not determined by the *character of the judgment* (personal or *in rem*) but by the nature of the attack which is directed against it. The solution lies in

---

[109] See H.C.J. 301/63, *Streit* at 608: "But it is an established rule and a firm practice of this court, that we do not sit in appeal on the religious courts."

[110] See Silberg, *op. cit.*, pp. 178 et seq. See also his statement in H.C.J. 10/59 at 1192–1193.

[111] *Op. et loc. cit.*

[112] *Ibid.*, pp. 180–181. He means that the judgment was indeed given contrary to religious law but by a court fully competent to rule on that law.

the distinction between *direct attack* by the High Court of Justice and *collateral attack* in the course of hearings in any other court. When the plea is to the High Court of Justice, it is directed against the religious judgment itself. The Supreme Court, sitting as the High Court of Justice, is responsible for the observance of the principles of natural justice by the religious courts. Direct review of the judgment occurs as a matter of course soon after it has been rendered. If the court is convinced that the violation of natural justice calls for its intervention, it will set aside the judgment without regard to its substance. Even if it effects a change in status, the judgment will be reversed, and this means that the religious judges are in duty bound to rehear the case, this time in accordance with the "secular" rules. (It should incidentally be noted that in Jewish law a judgment in matters of marriage or divorce is as such not constitutive in nature, since both marriage and divorce are legal acts performed wholly by the spouses.)

What is the effect of invalidation when the religious judgment is of a constitutive nature and has in fact brought about a change in status under religious law? Assume that a religious court dissolves a marriage *ex parte* and the result is irreversible under religious law. What is the use of a secular court formally setting aside the religious judgment? Obviously, it cannot change the substantive religious law. The answer is, in our view, that the significance of the annulment of the religious judgment is to deprive it of all legal effect in the *legal system of the State*. The State is not prepared to accept the concrete legal situation created by religious law in consequence of the judgment. The practical significance may be, in a certain sense, a *fragmentation of status,* with religious law recognizing the change of status and the law of the State refusing to do so. Even if, in principle, this is not a desirable situation, it is an inevitable outcome of the review powers of the High Court of Justice and the fact that the religious courts are integrated into the State's legal system. The High Court of Justice has authority to set aside any judicial decision which violates the principles of natural justice. From the point of view of the law of the State, which of course cannot penetrate the religious *normative* system by its own powers,[113] the judgment is with all its consequences annulled.

There remains the question of Justice Silberg: What point is there in differentiating for example, between the divorce of a Moslem woman against her will, the effectiveness of which we recognize, and the *ex parte* divorce of a Greek Orthodox woman, the effect of which we do *not* recognize?

---

[113] See on this subject at length, pp. 43–44 above.

The answer is that in the first case the divorce is a juristic act performed by an individual. Whilst the act is prohibited and its perpetrator liable to severe punishment, the State recognizes its effectiveness under religious law, in the absence of any contrary legal provision. The criminal sanction in itself does not compel non-recognition of the change in status which the prohibited act entails under the religious law. By contrast, in the case of a judgment, violation of the basic principles of the law of the State is committed by an institution which is considered for this purpose an organ of the State. High Court review operates on the judicial body itself and the remedy is directed against the defective judgment. Setting aside the judgment is from the State's viewpoint equivalent to annulment of the *judicial action* in its entirety. No inference can be drawn from the juristic act of an *individual* who may be penalized. It follows that in the case of direct attack, setting aside a judgment by the High Court of Justice amounts to extinction of the legal results in point of state law.[114]

Thus far, direct attack on a judgment. The situation differs in the case of collateral attack. The test for recognition or non-recognition of the religious judgment depends on the nature of the defect affecting it. If the defect goes to the roots of jurisdiction so that it is possible to regard the entire decision as a *nullity,* the secular court before which the judgment is relied upon may deny its validity entirely. For the purpose of the case involved, the whole judgment with all its legal consequences will be considered null and void, including if at all, any change of status. If, however, the defect does not touch the foundations of jurisdiction, the religious decision is valid and will withstand any indirect attack.

Where a religious court violates the principles of natural justice, the decisive question is not whether the judgment is personal or *in rem* but whether the violation of the fundamentals of procedure constitutes a lack of jurisdiction. This question is not limited to religious jurisdiction but affects the judicial decisions of administrative tribunals. In this area the Supreme Court,[115] having due regard to existing differences of opinion on the matter,[116] has decided that a violation of the principles of natural justice is treated as an excess of jurisdiction,[117] and the act of the authority is

---

[114] The idea is that all State institutions must act on the assumption that the religious judgment does not exist and that the prior legal situation still obtains.

[115] C.A. 183/69, *Petach Tiqwa Municipality* v. *Tahan,* 23 P.D. (1) 398.

[116] See the sources cited by Justice Sussman at 403, and particularly Rubinstein, *Jurisdiction, cit.,* pp. 220 et seq.

[117] In Justice Cohn's view a violation of the principles of natural justice is tan-

null and void and no direct attack is needed.[118] But this decision was rendered with respect to an administrative dismissal and its application to the religious courts is still an open question. Doubt stems from the fact that the court arrived at its conclusion not without much hesitation, and that it did not give its mind to the case of a judicial decision. Moreover, section 7(b)(4) of the Courts Law itself evidenced an intent to restrict somewhat the scope of direct review of religious courts in cases of lack of jurisdiction.[119] If that is so with respect to direct attack, should it not also be so with respect to collateral attack? The question of collateral attack on religious judgments which are contrary to the principles of natural justice warrants further consideration. We should strive to encourage the affected party to utilize the liberal opportunity of attacking the judgment directly by a petition to the High Court of Justice.

The existence of this review power of the Supreme Court renders the situation where a court is asked to recognize a foreign judgment significantly different. Here the sole remedy in Israeli law is non-recognition of a foreign judgment which has violated the principles of due process. No analogy can therefore be drawn from the rules relating to recognition of foreign judgments, which may accord wider powers to the local court.[120] It is in the light of this difference that the Mandatory decisions are to be understood, which tended to acknowledge the possibility of non-recognition of religious judgments in violation of the principles of natural justice. These decisions were rendered in the 1930's, before the rule recognizing the possibility of direct attack on religious judgments through the High Court of Justice had crystallized.[121]

To sum up, a violation by a religious court of the principles of natural justice exposes its judgment to direct review by petition to the High Court of Justice which is competent to quash the judgment along with all of its constitutive consequences in the framework of the law of the State. On the other hand, there is some question about the status of a religious judg-

---

tamount to an excess of jurisdiction (at 106). See, on the other hand, the view of Justice Sussman, (at 403–404).
[118] See the comment on the decision by D. Moshewitz, "Violation of the Rules of Natural Justice and its Consequences," 3 (1971) *Mishpatim*, 84 (Hebrew).
[119] The petitioner must raise the question of competence at the first opportunity.
[120] Cf. section 6 of the Foreign Judgments Enforcement Law, 5718–1958.
[121] It appears that the petition to the High Court of Justice became effective at a later stage, and even then, not as a direct attack on the religious court but on the Chief Execution Officer. See H.C.J. 26/51, *Menashe v. Rabbinical Court, Jerusalem*, 5 P.D. 714.

ment in the case of collateral attack; we entertain doubts whether a court is competent to deny recognition.

E. The Public Policy of Religious Law

Public policy appears in another context, although materially different from that which we have been considering up to this point. The situation to which we now turn attention is one in which the legislature has referred to religious law for solution of a particular problem and considerations of public policy attach to that law. Do these considerations constitute an integral part of the religious law to be applied in the law of the State, or can it be said that the secular courts are not obliged to have recourse to this part of the religious law? This is not a question of the public policy of the state rejecting the religious law provision but of internal policy considerations of the religious law affecting the solution in a given dispute.

A similar question arises in private international law with respect to the public policy of foreign law.[122] The situation is that the law of State A makes a general reference to the law of State B. The latter in turn refers to the solution found in the law of State C, but that solution is regarded by State B as contrary to its public policy and is therefore rejected by it. The question in State A is therefore whether this rejection based on public policy (in the international sense) binds it as well. Many writers adopt the view that *in principle* the public policy of another state (in an international sense as distinguished from an internal sense) is not to be recognized.[123] The court of State A must in the ordinary case ignore the provisions of the law of State B which reject the application of the solution of State C.[124] The solution of State C will be rejected only if it also violates the public policy of State A.[125]

The problem differs with respect to religious law in the law of Israel. The *internal public policy* of religious law is here in question. As we have said, religious law does not incline to recognize other legal systems in matters of marriage and divorce. Accordingly, as a matter of course, it

---

[122] Batiffol, *op. cit.*, pp. 417 et seq.; Neuhaus, *op. cit.*, p. 269; Maury, *op. cit.*, pp. 125 et seq.; Wolff, *op. cit.*, p. 184; Raape, *op. cit.*, pp. 63 et seq.; Lagarde, *op. cit.*, pp. 219 et seq.; Meise, *op. cit.*, pp. 11 et seq.; and in particular the sources cited by the last two.

[123] See in particular Lagarde, *op. cit.*, p. 220 n. 2.

[124] See the sources cited in note 122 above.

[125] In the French literature this situation is called "L'effet réflexe de l'ordre public"; Batiffol, *op. cit.*, no. 358, 3°; Lagarde, *op. cit.*, pp. 223 et seq. for further exceptions which are not of concern here.

does not examine foreign law for the extent to which it is consistent with the basic principles of religious law.[126] Religious law is generally lacking in reference to other normative systems. There is therefore no room for the concept of public policy in the sense of private international law.

We return to the basic question. Does *internal* religious public policy bind also the secular courts when these apply religious law? To answer this question one must preface a discussion of the nature of the internal public policy.

It is difficult to find a conceptual common denominator to public policy. Generally in domestic law public policy is taken as a restriction on the free, consensual arrangement of legal relationships between individuals.[127] The concept is, however, not exhausted in the area of agreements. In the present context public policy bears a wider meaning in which the emphasis is on its general objective: the *preservation of the proper functioning of the legal institutions essential to society*.[128]

Under religious law a further important dimension is present. The supreme value is not the existence of society as such but the relationship between society and the Divinity. In terms of Judaism, the purpose of public policy may be said to be the proper functioning of the societal institutions of religious law in society *as an expression of the service of the Lord*. In Canon law the metaphysical dimension appears in the overriding concept of "salvation of the souls" (*salus animarum*).[129]

Public policy in this sense is various. It may affect substantive law at the conscious instigation of the legislative organ. We are not concerned with this aspect, since it is beyond doubt that an express substantive pro-

---

[126] There are some exceptions, in which Moslem law refers us to the personal law of the parties but limits the reference for considerations of public policy or the like. Cf. Vitta, *Conflitti, op. cit.*, pp. 88–89, and the sources there cited at n. 92.

[127] This is the significance of public policy in section 30 of the Law of Contracts (General Part), 5733–1973.

[128] Cf. Malaurie, *L'ordre public et le contract* (Reims 1953), p. 69. This of course is not an exhaustive definition but appropriate for our purpose. See, in general, Simitis, *Gute Sitten und Orde public* (Marburg 1960) pp. 78 et seq.

[129] Malaurie, *op. cit.*, p. 31: "L'ordre public de L'Eglise mêle indissolublement les exigences de la communauté at la fin surnaturelle à laquelle les âmes sont ordonnées." On the distinction between the public policy of the state and of the church, see also D'Avack, *Corso di diritto canonico*, I (Milano 1956) pp. 170 et seq.; Lesage, *La nature du Droit canonique* (Ottawa 1960) pp. 151 et seq.; cf. Fedele, "Natura pubblica del diritto canonico," *Lo spirito del diritto canonico* (Padova 1962), pp. 823 et seq.

vision will bind the secular court, whatever its backgrounds and purpose.[130] Our problem is the use made of public policy by a judicial institution seeking to sustain a *religious* society against a background of religious rules which leave it some discretion. Must the secular courts, when applying the provisions of religious law, take into account the public policy of that law and see to it that the supreme goal mentioned above is achieved wherever religious law applies?

The first argument against such an obligation may be based on the immense psychological difficulty facing the judge. Under the very realistic assumption that the judge is secularly oriented in outlook—he may even be a member of another faith—how can he be required to concern himself in giving reality to metaphysical goals foreign to his mind and philosophy? The difficulty undoubtedly exists and seems decisive when a secular judge is asked himself to define the substance of religious public policy in a specific instance.[131] It is hard to see a secular judge in a creative judicial role at the level of fundamental religious principles. It is, however, possible that a religious organ has already clearly and authoritatively defined the public policy of religious law in a given situation, and then the real question will be whether the secular judge is bound to give it effect when applying the religious law?

There are a number of examples of this kind of situation in Israel, of which the most outstanding concerns private marriage between a *cohen* and divorcee. As we have already noted, such marriages are prohibited although they have ultimate effect. An extended legal struggle has been waged, involving as participants: the couple who have married in a religious but private ceremony, the rabbinical court asked to declare upon the validity of the marriage and thus upon the personal status of the couple and finally the High Court of Justice petitioned to intervene and order the official in charge of the population registry in the Ministry of the Interior to register the couple as married. The question of jurisdiction and other technical matters relating to registration are not our concern here. For the present purpose the interesting feature is the confrontation of the

---

[130] Cf., for example, the rule in Jewish law that a husband is released from maintaining his wife if the marriage was a forbidden one, and he is willing to give her a divorce. See C.A. 571/69, *Cahana* v. *Cahana* 24 P.D. (2) 549, 555.

[131] Compare the similar problem in private international law, when the judge must determine the public policy of foreign law. See Meise, *op. cit.*, pp. 27 et seq.; Vallindas, "Der Vorbehalt des Ordre public im internationalen Privatrecht," 18 (1953) *Rabels Zeitschrift für ausländisches und internationales Privatrecht*, 1, 7.

High Court of Justice and the religious courts, with the registry official between them. It is right to enlarge somewhat upon this situation since it exemplifies the status of religious public policy in the secular courts.

The problem first arose even before the enactment of the Rabbinical Courts Jurisdiction Law. In *Cohen, Buslik*[132] the couple sought a declaration from the secular court that they were married. Justices Silberg and Sussman, in the majority, held that since the marriage has effect under religious law, a declaration concerning the existing situation did not conflict with the "secular" public policy of the State. Justice Cheshin disagreed, describing in trenchant terms the deviant behaviour of the couple in violating a prohibition of religious law and then asking for a declaration of their legal status under that very law.[133] He thought that the declaration should be denied on the ground that the court is not bound to assist those who break the law to benefit from their deeds.[134] All three judges assumed it as self-evident that had the matter come before a religious court, that court would have declared the marriage of effect, as the matter is viewed by religious law in point of substance. In this regard Justice Cheshin commented that the considerations which guide the secular courts are not decisive for the religious courts.[135] Thus, the difference of opinion between the judges revolved around the State's approach to secular public policy.

In the later case of *Gorfinkel*,[136] the problem was discussed in the light of the Rabbinical Courts Jurisdiction Law. The respondent was the Minister of the Interior as the person responsible for the registration. All the judges assumed that a rabbinical court would not hesitate to declare upon the effect of the marriage, despite the initial prohibition thereof (*impedimentum impediens*). Once again, the judges differed as to the final outcome. The majority[137] referred the couple to the rabbinical court for the desired declaration. The minority[138] argued that the reference was unnecessary and that the High Court of Justice must itself declare the marriage valid and order the couple's registration as married.

Justice Silberg dissented vigorously from the view which regards with

---

[132] C.A. 238/53, *Cohen, Buslik* v. *A.G.*, 8 P.D. 4 (English translation 2 S.J.S.C. 239).
[133] At 55–56 (306–307).
[134] At 56 (306).
[135] At 57 (308).
[136] H.C.J. 80/63, 17 P.D. 2048.
[137] Justices Silberg, Landau and Berinson.
[138] Justices Witkon and Manny.

sympathy and understanding the petitioners' use of the provisions of religious law itself in order to evade the prohibition on their marriage. In fact, he adopted a position similar to that of Justice Cheshin in *Cohen, Buslik*, with which he had then differed.[139] It should be noted that in the instant case the petition was treated by all the judges as a matter of secular public policy, that is, the policy of the Israeli legislature. By the time that the third case, *Rodnitzki* v. *The Rabbinical Court of Appeal*,[140] was heard the background had changed. It had become clear that the rabbinical courts were not prepared to declare that the marriage existed, either directly or indirectly.[141] It had thus become apparent that for reasons of religious public policy, the rabbinical court would reject the petition of the couple on the explicit ground that no assistance should be given to wrongdoers.[142] The rabbinical court was trying in this way to prevent registration of the couple in the population registry. For the first time the Supreme Court was faced with an express proclamation of the religious judicial institutions concerning religious public policy in this specific case. The rabbinical court saw in a declaration of validity an encouragement of the celebration of marriages prohibited by Jewish law. Under that law, although the marriage has effect, the couple are forbidden to cohabit and are under a duty to divorce.

Rabbinical court opposition to registration of couples as married was expressed even more explicitly in another case, *Cohen* v. *The Rabbinical District Court, Tel Aviv-Jaffo*.[143] Here, the rabbinical court first pointed out that the couple were forbidden to marry anyone else, that they were forbidden to continue to live together and that they were required to divorce. It added, however, "The prohibition against either of the petitioners marrying another is not intended to confer any status of marriage upon the petitioners and they are therefore *not to be registered* as married."[144]

---

[139] Justice Silberg explains the difference between the two decisions by the terms of the Rabbinical Courts Jurisdiction Law which became effective after the decision in *Cohen, Buslik*. See H.C.J. 80/63, at 2064–2066.
[140] H.C.J. 51/69, 24 P.D. (1) 704.
[141] In view of the fact that even the indirect declaration that neither could lawfully marry another without a divorce was sufficient for their being registered as married, the court refused to make such a declaration.
[142] See the text of the decision in H.C.J. 51/69 at 721.
[143] H.C.J. 275/71 and 330/71, 26 P.D. (1) 227.
[144] The negative attitude of the rabbinical courts has been expressed in the most recent case, which dealt with the marriage between a *cohen* and a childless widow who had received *Halitza* from her deceased husband's brother (in

We cannot doubt that theoretically religious public policy constitutes an integral part of religious law. Where the legislator refers to the religious system, the assumption is that the entire complex of religious rules found therein are meant to be included.[145] Why indeed should religious public policy be excluded, particularly as it concerns the basic principles of the entire system? Even in references to the law of foreign states under private international law, the national public policy of the foreign state is not ignored.[146]

The Supreme Court, however, did not see the matter in this light but decided by a decisive majority that the couple should be registered as married.[147] The Court was not willing to heed the demands of religious public policy, aimed at rendering the prohibition of marriage between a *cohen* and a divorcee fully effective. It did not hide its ideological reasons —the prohibition of such a marriage is unreasonable in the eyes of the non-believer; therefore the severity of the law should be relaxed and couples who have resorted to the manoeuvre of a private marriage ceremony are to be enabled to obtain formal confirmation of the validity of their marriage by means of official registration. This path is, however, only open to those who cannot marry in an official religious ceremony; a couple able to be married by the Rabbinate but does not desire a religious ceremony for reasons of conscience is not entitled to the assistance of the court.[148] These rules were laid down by a secular court for reasons of public interest, which in principle negates private marriages except where a purely religious obstacle to marriage exists.

When the stand of the religious court in interpreting religious public policy was raised before the civil court, it said (per Justice Landau):

> such an instance the woman is treated as a divorcee under Jewish law): H.C.J. 29/71 (*Kedar, Cohen* v. *District Rabbinical Court, Tel Aviv*) 26 P.D. (2) 608, where the religious court said: "this court is forbidden... to give official effect to a marriage which is an offence in law, and thereby render it valid when under the law it is forbidden for persons involved in such a marriage to continue to cohabit."

[145] Cf. the remarks of Justice Agranat in *Segev Reichert*, 21 P.D. (2) 505, 526, on the Jerusalem Ban: "By virtue of section 2 of the Rabbinical Courts Jurisdiction (Marriage and Divorce) Law, 5713–1953, these regulations became, insofar as they concern the performance of marriages between Jews in Israel, a part of the law of the State and as a result they reflect the *policy* of the secular legislature in this field."

[146] Cf. note 123 above.

[147] Justices Landau, Sussman, Berinson and Witkon in *Rodnitzki;* Justices Manny and Etzioni joined this position in *Cohen*.

[148] The majority opinion in *Segev, Reichert*.

"That is the view of the rabbinical court on the public interest, a view which is nourished by its religious convictions. This Court takes a different view of what the public interest requires in this matter, as has been explained in the *Haklai* and *Segev* cases. Our view rests on the law of the State which was enacted by representatives of the public as a whole, both believers and non-believers, for the public as a whole."[149]

Whilst the ideological foundation of this decision is clear, its formal reasoning is more problematic. First of all, it does not say that as a matter of principle recourse is not to be had to religious public policy; it was held that religious public policy is contrary to the public policy of the State and therefore cannot be accepted. But if religious public policy forms an integral part of the religious law to which the legislature has referred us without qualification, the concept of the public policy of the State should not be utilized to reject the provisions of the religious law. So at least it follows from our analysis of the concept of public policy.[150] One possible answer is that the public policy of the State overrides religious *public policy,* as distinct from other provisions of religious law. But that also is not free from doubt. Considerations of State public policy should bind the entire judicial system, religious as well as secular. It appears, however, that the courts tend to the conclusion that the religious court will and indeed may act in accordance with the considerations of religious public interest, whilst the secular courts will act in accordance with those of the State.[151] As we have said, it is hard to see how two judicial institutions acting within and on behalf of the State can do so according to conflicting considerations of the public interest. The fact is that the patent ideological nature of the entire subject impedes legal analysis. The judges of the Supreme Court do not hide their awareness that they are sidestepping religious law the content of which seems unreasonable to them (the prohibition of marriage between a *cohen* and a divorcee). The conflict with religious public policy is only collateral to a prior value judgment, the rejection of the prohibitory part of religious law as explained above in

---

[149] *Rodnitzki,* at 715.
[150] Above at note 49.
[151] See *Rodnitzki* (Justice Landau): "So also in this case the rabbinical court regarded itself barred from dealing with the petitioner's second petition on the merits, but we must view the matter in a different light." See in particular *Kedar, Cohen*: "I have no complaint against the Rabbinical Court of Appeal for attempting to delay the hearing and final decision in such a matter, which is repugnant to it, and I can understand why it was not willing to assist in an act which is a violation of religious commandment."

the discussion of section 2 of the Rabbinical Courts Jurisdiction Law.[152] Registration of a couple in the population registry is no more than final confirmation of the rejection of religious law on this subject. This aspect of the matter is particularly emphasized in the minority opinion of Justice Kister.[153] It is our feeling that the value judgment here is altogether too manifest and detached as it is from legal reasoning and too closely connected with the personal outlook of the judges. As a result, it is difficult to draw from this area alone any conclusions about the status of religious public policy.

Disregard of religious public policy when it does not fit in with a secular outlook is also discernible in other areas, for example, where the issue is a promise to marry between persons prohibited from marrying under religious law, or agreements to cohabit between such persons. In contrast to the celebration of a prohibited marriage, there is here no reference to religious law. The validity of the agreement is decided in accordance with the ordinary contract law of the State. The connection with religious public policy is indirect. Under religious law such agreements are clearly illegal; under contract law they are invalid if contrary to public policy or to morality. The question is therefore whether the secular court is willing to be guided in determining the *content* of public policy or moral values by the position taken by religious law in matters of marriage. It is not surprising that in view of the flexibility of the concepts of "public policy" and of "morality", the judges have here also not been at one. In *Badash v. Badash*,[154] Justice Kister was of the opinion that a marriage agreement between a woman and the man she was living with, the marriage being prohibited under religious law, is an illegal agreement. The other judges refrained from expressing any view on the matter. On the other hand, in *Yeger v. Pelvitz*,[155] the Supreme Court decided that a maintenance agreement between a married woman and another man is neither illegal nor immoral although under religious law the relationship was without doubt a most serious offence.[156] In this context it is worth recalling Justice Wit-

---

[152] Above at pp. 160–161.
[153] In *Rodnitzki* at 719, 722: "Since the laws of marriage of Jews in Israel are the religious laws, I do not think that any court may treat certain prohibitions as less binding than others."
[154] C.A. 174/65, 20 P.D. (1) 617, 627.
[155] C.A. 563/65, 20 P.D. (3) 224.
[156] The reasoning of Justice Berinson is based on the existence of the institution of "the reputed spouse": "Is it possible that there are two classes of morality and public interest, one in legislation and the other in the cases?"

kon's approach to an agreement between a married man and his mistress. He said: "Indeed it may be asked whether the agreement on the basis of which the property was registered in the name of (the woman) was immoral and contrary to public policy because one of the parties thereto was a married man when the agreement was made. To this question my colleague Justice Silberg says yes, and my colleague Justice Cohn, no. Both of them from their extensive knowledge cite chapter and verse from Jewish law. I take no part in this debate on Jewish law... because I cannot believe that public opinion is reflected in laws dealing with conditional marriages, *halitza* and conversion. Not in these laws will the vast majority of our public find inspiration on the problem which faces us here."[157] Finally, we mention a further example from another context illustrating an approach which gives preference to considerations based on liberal secular outlook over religious consideration. According to Jewish religious law, mixed marriages between Jews and Gentiles are forbidden and do not take effect (*impedimentum dirimens*). In *Funk Schlesinger* v. *the Minister of the Interior*,[158] Justice Sussman examined the status of such marriages entered into abroad, in the light of the test of public policy in the private international law sense. In his view the general provision of section 2 of the Rabbinical Court Jurisdiction Law which applies Jewish law to marriages between Jews in Israel is, at the most, an expression of domestic public policy. The fact that Jewish religious law invalidates mixed marriages does not necessarily require such marriages to be invalidated when entered into in accordance with foreign law. "The invalidation of the marriage under religious law is a weighty consideration but it need not be the only one. The Israeli public is today divided into two camps. The one observant of the commandments, or most of them. The other camp emphasizes the difference between a state based on secular law and based on *Halakha*. The outlook of the members of each of these camps is diametrically at variance. Public order in Israel does not mean that the judge should impose the viewpoint of one camp upon the other. Life requires tolerance of one's fellow man and regard for his differing outlook. The judge's measuring rod should therefore be to achieve a balancing of *all* the views prevalent in the public."[159]

---

[157] C.A. 337/62, *Riesenfeld* v. *Jacobson*, 17 P.D. 1009, 1025.
[158] H.C.J. 143/62, 17 P.D. 225, 241.
[159] At 257. The other judges took no position on this subject.

We doubt greatly whether this measuring rod is meaningful when it comes to deciding between conflicting values. The central question is whether to content ourselves with the decision of the legislature and, for better or worse, leave to it the initiation to make changes. In other words, the real question touches the role which the court should play in the sharp ideological debate on the question of religion in the state. This question in turn is a question of values, the answer to which necessarily lies beyond the sphere of legal analysis.

3. *Substantive Law and Procedure*

A. Introduction

The accepted rule in all secular case law is that in applying religious law a distinction must be drawn between substance and procedure. As with foreign law applied under private international law, the secular court will have no resort to religious procedural law. This is a conscious limitation officially acknowledged to affect the application of religious law, which has served as a foundation for the well-known dictum of Justice Silberg: "Jewish law as applied by a civil court is different from Jewish Law as applied by a religious court. There is a difference in approach, in method, and sometimes also in the actual content of the judgment."[1]

In what follows we shall first examine the formal and substantive grounds advanced for the distinction and then review its operation in local case law by a critical analysis of the characteristic situations in which it is met.

B. Formal Grounds for the Distinction

The leading judgment—and indeed the only one in which the question of the formal basis for the prevailing principle was canvassed—was delivered by Justice Silberg in *Kotik* v. *Wolfson*,[2] in which he rested the distinction upon the phrase "personal law" which figures in Art. 47 of the Palestine Order in Council and serves as the source for applying religious law to matters of personal status in the secular courts. The Article states broadly that in matters of personal status the civil courts must exercise jurisdiction in conformity with the appropriate personal law. The court explained the limitation in the application of religious law in the following

---

[1] C.A. 238/55 *Cohen, Buslik* v. *A.G.* 8 P.D. 4, 19 (English translation 2 S.J.S.C. 239, 254).
[2] 5 P.D. 1341.

manner. "The expression itself—personal law—which in regard to an Israeli national means the religious law of the party concerned, in regard to a foreigner means his national law (Art. 64 of the Order in Council), since Art. 47 is a general provision embracing the two. Hence the ambit of the noun 'law' here cannot be wider in respect of a national than it is in respect of a foreigner. And just as the civil courts employ only the substantive law appertaining to him and not the procedural law or the rules of evidence thereof when dealing with matters affecting the personal position of a *foreigner*—and about that there is certainly no dispute... so also when dealing with the personal status of an Israeli national they proceed in the same manner, for it is inconceivable to attach different meanings to the very same word."

This formal ground is not very persuasive. The simple expression "personal law" is not potent enough to create absolute symmetry in the application of both foreign law and religious law. The pre-supposition that to attach different meanings to the very same word is inconceivable has been controverted by the legislature itself treating religious law as "law" within the meaning of the Interpretation Ordinance in contrast to foreign law which is still held to be a question of fact with all that follows therefrom.[3] Furthermore, Justice Silberg himself has on other occasions come out against attempts to identify the status of religious law with that of foreign law and has defended with much ideological fervour the singular status of religious law in the State of Israel.[4] This singularity is not exhausted in his particular ideological appraisal thereof nor in the consequences which follow upon its inclusion under "law", but it is of significance for our present purpose. The public policy rule is expressly excluded in respect of religious law in striking contrast to the situation with foreign law.[5] The latter, as we have learned, is always applied subject to the public policy criterion to which every conflicting foreign provision must yield. Thus in any event the assumption of Justice Silberg in this particular case is unsustainable. The effect of excluding public policy from the area of Jewish law is that the area of its application is more extensive than that of foreign law under conflicts rules.

The formal reason based on a strict interpretation of the statutory terms therefore falls away. But what then is the basis for the distinction between

---

[3] See p. 84 above.
[4] See the remarks of Justice Silberg in *Yosifof* (5 P.D. 481, 501) cited at p. 76 above, and more particularly in *Funk Schlesinger* 17 P.D. 225, 235 cited at p. 146 above.
[5] P. 142 above.

substance and procedure? The question in truth calls first for answer in private international law from which it is taken. There the distinction has been received in our law by way of Art. 46 of the Palestine Order in Council which refers us to English Common law for completing the local legal order. The distinction is one of the many principles which has been received from English private international law.[6] Art. 47 of the Order in Council refers very generally to personal law for matters of personal status, and to apprehend the details the only course is to go to the rules of choice-of-law in English Common law. The Supreme Court took this course in the leading case of *Skornik* v. *Skornik*[7] where it resolved the conflict between local religious and foreign law by English tests. In the same spirit and on a matter immediately relevant to the present purpose, it was held in *Wandel-Hirshberg* v. *Yakobsfeld-Yakurska*[8] that the question of applying any foreign law of evidence must be answered negatively according to the rules of English private international law.

Thus a formal basis has been found in local private international law for distinguishing between substantive and procedural law in all its details, but that basis is insufficient for the application of the distinction in the case of religious law. The operation of the latter in respect of matters of personal status is, as we know, not bound up with the existence of a foreign element, and therefore no question of choice-of-law in the strict sense arises. It is therefore not possible to resort to English private international law for supplying the *lacuna* within the meaning of Art. 46. Reliance upon English choice-of-law rules for applying the substance-procedure distinction to religious law can only be made by way of analogy and not by process of filling a gap concerning a like topic. We could perhaps speak of filling a gap if recourse were had to English rules regarding the application of ecclesiastical law in the Common law system. (It is extremely doubtful whether a like distinction can be found there in view of the fact that the foundations of the system are completely different.)[9]

Hence we may infer that the strict adherence of the courts to English private international law rules lacks any formal basis so far as concerns

---

[6] Generally see Levontin and Goldwater, *Conflict of Law Rules in Israel and Art. 46 of the Palestine Order in Council* (Jerusalem 1974) (Hebrew).
[7] C.A. 191/51, 8 P.D. 141, 159 et seq., 180.
[8] 12 P.D. 1896, 1901.
[9] According to the English view, Ecclesiastical Law is part of the Common Law, and no distinction is made between substance and procedure. Cf. *Bishop of Exeter* v. *Marshall* (1868) L.R. 3 H.L. 17, 52–53. *Caudrey's Case* (1591) 5 Co.Rep la; 77 E.R.1.

the application of religious law. Nevertheless, before attempting to offer a different formal solution to the problem of religious rules of procedure, we must examine the material grounds suggested by the courts to support the distinction between substance and procedure.

C. Material Grounds for the Distinction

In *Kotik* v. *Wolfson*[10] the court was not satisfied with a formal reason for reference to English law but sought to found the limitation of application of religious law on rational grounds. It suggested first a practical reason relating to the composition of the court. The submission that religious law must be applied as it is, with nothing left out, including the law of evidence, could not, it said, be accepted because it was impossible to expect a secular court to be composed of judges fully competent under Jewish law when hearing matters involving the personal status of a Jew.

A further material reason was found in the very nature of procedure. Substantive law, it was suggested, can be applied "relatively" and variably but "it was inconceivable to introduce any such discrimination in respect of the form of trial and *a fortiori* in respect of finding the facts. If a given muster of evidence is considered by the legislature as valid and persuasive in the case of A, it could not possibly be treated as inadmissible and unpersuasive in the case of B".[11] The court thought that a possible difference in substantive law applied to matters of personal status might be justified because "a thread of life and tradition is intricately woven into these matters and they vary with differences in philosophical outlook—religion, ethics, culture, tradition, custom and so on—of those concerned. On the other hand, this concept has no place at all when what is involved are not the rights and duties of the parties but the duties and functions which the court must perform and exercise according to a firmly prescribed design in the trial of every person".[12]

This argument as postulated by the court is manifestly weak. The fact that not all the religious rules of procedure can be applied does not compel the conclusion that they must be rejected in all instances. Clearly, a special

---

[10] Note 2 above.
[11] *Ibid.* at p. 224. There is reason for thinking that the Court was influenced by the grounds mentioned by M. Wolff, *Private International Law* (2nd ed. Oxford 1950) p. 230. For a comprehensive survey of the reasons for rejecting foreign procedural rules in private international law and criticism thereof, see I. Szászy, *International Civil Procedure, A Comparative Study* (Budapest 1967), pp. 203 et seq.
[12] Cf. Wolff, *op. cit.,* p. 229.

court cannot be constituted in accordance with religious rules determinative of the composition of the religious courts and of the qualifications of the judges. Upon entrusting the administration of Jewish law to the secular courts, the legislature assumed the existence of the secular courts and bestowed jurisdiction upon them. The courts exist by virtue of the law of the State which exclusively regulates their establishment and their composition. *These courts* are commanded to apply religious law and obviously they are not to be replaced or varied. Religious law cannot apply to the structure of the judicial organ itself. Hence, the question of applying religious procedure is likely to arise only in respect of the *form* of the hearing of a matter of personal status.

Again the distinction between a party's rights and duties and the court's duties is not tenable.[13] In *Kotik* Justice Silberg coupled procedure in the narrow sense with the law of evidence, and treated both as *ius cogens* beyond the governance of the parties, in contrast to substantive law. So to perceive the situation is not correct. The parties may exert considerable influence both on the mode of trial and on the manner of determining the facts. They may, for instance, agree to special modes of proof divergent from the usual rules.[14] It is also very possible that a particular body of evidence, considered by the legislature to be valid and persuasive in the case of A, is not so in the case of B if the parties have consented thereto before or during trial. Nothing therefore in the nature of civil procedure as such bars the application of other rules of procedure,[15] in this instance religious.

The idea of uniformity in procedure, for all its importance in principle, is not enough on which to base the absolute rejection of all the rules of procedure and evidence of religious law. Whilst in *Kotik* the court rightly laid great stress on the variability of substantive law, it did not inquire whether in practice a rigid insistence upon the distinction between procedure and substance does not in fact hinder the achievement of the main

---

[13] See the criticism mentioned by Wolff himself *op. et loc. cit.*
[14] E. Harnon, *The Law of Evidence,* Part I (Jerusalem 1970) pp. 36, 37 (Hebrew): "The parties may agree to a variation of the law of evidence, both in the course of the hearings and prior thereto. The agreement can render faulty evidence valid, such as hearsay or oral evidence against a document. The agreement can also disqualify evidence otherwise valid, such as that contractual terms which normally may be proved orally should only be proved in writing." See also Huet, *Les conflits de lois en matière de preuve* (Paris 1965) nos. 30 et seq.
[15] See generally Szászy, *ibid.*

purpose of preserving the material difference in matters of philosophical outlook, as defined by the court itself.

The English approach, which over-extends the notion of procedure in choice-of-law, has earned strong criticism, especially as regards questions of evidence.[16] Many have challenged the broad rejection of foreign law based on a technical classification of substance and procedure.[17] It seems that in recent years English case law has itself moderated its stand and is no longer persuaded of the accuracy of the sharp and unequivocal division between procedural rules and substantive law.[18] Against procedural uniformity and efficacy, the no lesser good of uniformity of solution has been posed. Ultimately the application of foreign law under choice-of-law betokens a desire to arrive at a solution identical as far as possible for all jurisdictions. The application of local procedure does not have to be an end in itself. The circumstances may sometimes require it for reasons of efficacy or convenience or for reasons of public policy, but in the absence of these it is widely held that regard should properly be had to those foreign procedural provisions which are so intimately bound up with substantive law that to overlook them would directly affect the outcome of the case.[19]

If these considerations obtain in choice-of-law, they are all the more deserving of attention in the application of religious law. The application of religious law by the secular courts parallels its application in the religious courts, and accordingly there is no place for the territorial principle which, in the view of some, supports the uniform operation of domestic procedure in private international law.[20] By accord of the legislature, religious procedure fully prevails in the religious courts.[21] Religious jurisdic-

---

[16] Cheshire, *Private International Law* (8th ed. London 1970), pp. 661, 664 et seq.; Dicey & Morris, *Conflict of Laws* (9th ed. London 1973) pp. 1099 et seq.; Graveson, *Conflict of Laws* (6th ed. London 1969) pp. 632–33.

[17] Cook, "Substance and 'Procedure'", *Logical and Legal Bases of Conflict of Law* (Cambridge Mass. 1942) p. 154; Cavers, "Procedure for—and in—the Choice of Law Process", *The Choice-of-Law Process* (Ann Arbor 1965) p. 268; cf. A. Shapira, *The Interest Approach to Choice of Law* (The Hague 1970) pp. 170 et seq.

[18] Cf. *Mahadervan* v. *Mahadervan* [1964] P. 233, 243.

[19] See the sources mentioned in nn. 15, 16 and 17 above; and also Morgan, "Choice-of-Law Governing Proof", 58 *Harv. L. R.* 153, 194–195. By contrast cf. the rigid approach of Justice Cohn in C.A. 99/63 *Peleg* v. *A.G.* 17 P.D. 1122, 1128.

[20] Riezler, *Internationales Zivilprozessrecht* (Tübingen 1949) p. 94.

[21] Subject to the principles of natural justice, see pp. 161 et seq. above.

tion is taken by the State to belong integrally to its own legal system. Thus religious procedural rules will obviously apply within the State and the idea of territorial uniformity of procedure is not of great weight.

The general conclusion from the foregoing is that rejection of religious procedural law (in the wide sense) on the basis of the English differentiation between substance and procedure lacks any formal-legal foundation. Even the material reasons advanced by the Supreme Court are not convincing. Nevertheless no one will dispute that not all religious procedure can be applied in the secular courts. We shall try in the sequel to suggest a solution of this problem on a different formal and material basis. Thereafter local case law will be examined in greater detail in a critical review of the solutions offered.

D. The Proposed Solution: Direct Application of Civil Procedure for Reasons of Efficacy and Public Policy

The rigid distinction between substance and procedure, as it is understood in English law, should, it is suggested, be abandoned. The starting point must be that procedural religious law is not to be rejected *a priori* but as a result of the binding nature of secular procedure and law of evidence. What is in mind here is the "positive" role of public policy on which we have already dwelt.[22] Secular, as opposed to religious, procedure takes effect in the secular courts by "direct application". That means that the formal ground for limiting religious law does not actually lie in a technical distinction between substance and procedure but in the legislative intention to have secular procedural law apply in the civil court even when dealing with personal status. The test is therefore to be found not in the character of the religious provisions alone but in that of the secular provisions as well. The initial presumption is that the legislature, including the secondary-law-maker, has set up a procedural structure for the courts which is to apply in all cases without distinction as to the cause in issue or the nature of the substantive law involved. In some sense this approach can in principle be adopted equally in private international law, as a number of writers suggest,[23] but we shall content ourselves in confining it to religious law. (There, one has freedom of action since, as we have said, no formal ground exists for employing the narrow test of English Common law which prevails in choice-of-law.) But the foregoing presumption is rebuttable. The decision depends on the general nature of religious pro-

---

[22] P. 152 above.
[23] Cf. Battifol, *Droit international privé* (5e éd., Paris 1970–71) nos. 249, 697.

cedure. Opposed to the interests of procedural efficacy, uniformity and public policy stands the nature of the final solution in the secular and religious jurisdictions.

The question of the application of religious procedure can, it is suggested, be answered by the following test—the more general a religious procedural provision and the less specific it is to the matter in issue, the more will a secular procedural provision tend to take precedence. On the other hand, where the former is *specific* to the matter in dispute, it is not to be rejected without further examining the degree of its compatibility with the principles of equitable and effective procedure. In other words, where the religious rule is expressive of generalized trial principles, priority will be given to the secular principles fashioning legal procedure, but where a specific religious rule of procedure (in the broad sense which embraces evidence) has taken shape in immediate and intimate relation to a matter of personal status in dispute, the secular procedural rule should give place to it.

The specific and limited character of a procedural rule is sometimes indicative of a close connection between the rule and the substantive law, most prominently in the case of legal presumptions.[24] Clearly secular law which leaves certain topics to exclusive regulation by religious law does not comprehend all the special procedural rules appertaining to such topics. If the special religious procedural rules are dismissed simply because of their procedural character, the secular courts can only rely on general rules of procedure and evidence and that may yield undesirable results in point of substantive solution.

We now proceed to examine various aspects of the problem in the light of Israel case law and to compare the operation of the traditional test distinguishing between substance and procedure with the test proposed here to replace it.

E. Substance and Procedure in Case Law

The matters dealt with by the secular courts in accordance with religious law are restricted in number and extent. The status of religious procedural law only arises in actuality in relatively few instances as compared with the corresponding situation in private international law. Moreover, the fact that religious law in general is not practised and enforced as an independent positive system is of decisive effect. In the absence of independent institutions for the execution of judgments the law relies for its im-

---

[24] See pp. 190 et seq. infra.

plementation upon the secular authorities, with the result that many procedural matters are naturally regulated by state law and no question of ignoring religious law will arise.

Competence of Witnesses and Modes of Proof

Jewish law relating to testimony is noted for its many restrictions in respect of the competence of witnesses. Among others, close relatives, wives, interested parties, persons guilty of religious transgression are disqualified.[25] Such disqualification is not admitted in secular law which conspicuously allows a latitude that is only to be restricted in exceptional cases.[26] On the basis of the English distinction between substantive and procedural law, the secular courts have rejected the restrictive provisions of religious law. This result seems justified in principle even according to the approach here proposed; it is reasonable to assume that the legislative intention was that state law relating to testimony should apply in preference to any conflicting rule of religious law to all litigation in the secular courts, even where such litigation concerns matters of personal status. If, however, the disqualification of a witness under religious law is not the outcome of some general principle—such as that of the incompetence of the persons mentioned above—but is a rule specific to a particular matter of personal status, it is not to be set aside without close examination. Perhaps it is difficult to find in Jewish law any specific disqualification in matters of marriage and divorce, beyond the many general restrictions, but such disqualification is not entirely impossible in the religious law of some other community.

A kindred, but not quite identical, problem confronted the court in *Feldman* v. *Feldman*.[27] Before the enactment of the Succession Law of 1965 a will could be made in accordance with either religious law or secular law. Under the latter a will had always to be in writing; under the former a death-bed could be made orally in the presence of two witnesses. In the instant case, a death-bed will was made in the presence of two relatives who are disqualified as witnesses under the general principles of Jewish law. Under section 13 of the then applicable Succession Ordinance as well, no person was entitled to take any interest under a will in civil form if he was one of the attesting witnesses, so that the two relatives would have in any event lost such legacies as they might have been entitled

---

[25] Maimonides, *Hilkhot Edut* IX, 1; *Tur Hoshen Mishpat* 35.
[26] See C.A. 238/53, 8 P.D. 4, 19 (2 S.J.S.C. 239, 254–255).
[27] C.A. 423/64 *Feldman* v. *Feldman* 19 P.D. (2) 197.

to. The Supreme Court, however, upheld the will by a dual classification. The *secular* provision denying the right of legacy to a witness, it argued, is a matter of substantive law and therefore does not apply to a will made under religious law. The religious provision regarding witness disqualification is a matter of procedure and does not take effect in hearings before a secular court. In the result the will was admitted to probate by a combination of substantive religious law (oral will) and a secular rule of evidence (competence of witnesses). The final outcome would seem contrary in spirit to both systems of law.

A different result could have been reached if the religious restriction had been treated as specific to wills. Assuming that to be the case, the argument might have been that there was occasion to apply the religious provision, notwithstanding its procedural character. But the disqualification of relatives is a general provision of religious law and was therefore properly disregarded by the secular court. There is, however, some warrant for the view that the evidence of relatives in this instance suffers from the additional disability both in religious and in secular law of their being interested parties. Accordingly the religious disqualification might inferentially be seemed specific to the will. Avoidance of the will in this instance would, it seems, have been more consonant with the spirit of the two systems.[28]

In essence, rejection of religious law relating to witness disqualification is without doubt not merely a matter of convenience or of procedural uniformity. *Halakhic* disqualification is not compatible with the basic outlook of secular judges who in particular find it difficult to disqualify people who have transgressed religious precept. As one judge has said, "witnesses qualified in accordance with Jewish law are almost no longer to be found amongst us, and in any event we cannot inquire into their religious conformity in order to decide whether or not they are competent."[29] Justice Landau put it more sharply in *Rodnitzki*[30]: "The last judgment of the Rabbinical High Court disqualifying as witnesses people who desecrate the Sabbath creates a most difficult situation in which a religious court, having exclusive jurisdiction over Jews in this country in the most vital of matters, disqualifies all that section of the public who do not observe the Sabbath in all its details—and I do not err in saying that it comprises

---

[28] The solution proposed here is actually an adaptation process later to be explained; see pp. 199 et seq.
[29] C.A. 99/63 at 1128 (per Justice Cohn).
[30] H.C.J. 51/69, *Rodnitzki v. Rabbinical Court of Appeal* 24 P.D. (1) 704, 718.

the majority of the Jewish population in the entire country—from testifying before us in those vital matters. This court must clearly disgregard such wholesale disqualification, if only because under sections 2 and 3 of the Evidence Ordinance all persons are competent to give evidence in all cases in a secular court." [31]

When, however, disqualification affects not only the modes of proof but the substance of the matter, the validity of the entire act, the application of the religious law in every particular cannot be avoided by the secular court. That will be the case where under religious law *constitutive* witnesses are required for an act in law which has been wholly received into the law of the State.

In a line of cases, the courts have been called upon to decide whether some religious provision goes to substance or only to proof; in the case of witness disqualification, whether the witnesses are necessary *ad probationem* or *ad substantiam*. The answer has on occasion called for inquiry into the recesses of religious law, where systematic classification is largely absent or at least classification of the law in accordance with secular concepts is not usual. The Supreme Court has not overlooked the problem: "So long as the civil courts bear the task of adjudicating according to religious law, this 'artificiality' and dreary necessity cannot be escaped". [32] The Court went on to indicate clearly its own view that the application of the modes of secular procedure is to be preferred: "every act of choice-of-law yields a hybrid but in our own situation this hybrid is the lesser of two evils, *verbum sapienti*." [33]

It would appear, however, that Justice Landau's severely expressed opposition to religious rules concerning witness disqualification, mentioned above,[34] was not soundly based in law.[35] In *Rodnitzki*, the question was the validity of a marriage where witnesses are *constitutive* and their disqualification leads to the avoidance of the act itself. Thus in deciding whe-

---

[31] For a criticism of these observations in their concrete context, see text at n. 35 *infra*. Justice Landau's formulation, however, embodies the idea of *direct application* of the Evidence Ordinance, which accords with the view taken here of the problem of religious procedure, as explained in the text above.

[32] C.A. 99/63 *Peleg* v. *A.G.* at 1128 (per Justice Cohn).

[33] *Ibid*. The Court also found that according to *Halakha* witnesses of a deathbed will are probative as against constitutive and their competence may be inquired into in accordance with secular law.

[34] See text at n. 30 above.

[35] The observations of Justice Landau are meant, *ibid.*, at 718; "in the view of this Court witnesses who attested to the marriage are not considered to be thereby disqualified."

ther the marriage is of effect, the court must have regard to the witness disqualification rules figuring as part of the substantive law.[36]

Turning to the modes of proof under religious law, a distinction must be drawn between those cases where religious law recognizes additional special forms and those where it restricts the common modes. As for the former, we must regard the recognized modes of proof in secular procedure as a closed list not to be added to. The different types of oath and sanctions peculiar to any religious law are not to be received. The presumption is that the legislature wished the secular courts to proceed in every instance according to accepted procedural fundamentals and not to act beyond their defined tasks, even where a special mode of proof is in principle available to religious courts.[37] The Court[38] was right in denying the possibility of dealing with a "rebellious wife" according to the special procedure of the *Halakha*—threat of excommunication as a means of ascertaining the truth. These modes conflict with the adversary system practised in the secular courts. Excommunication is also repugnant to the secular outlook and it may not be presumed that the legislature empowered the secular court to implement this religious act even if specific to the issue being heard by it. In the same case the Supreme Court explained that "today when we no longer excommunicate ... we permit each of the couple to come and testify, even though a party to the proceedings, and his or her testimony may serve as evidence provided it is credible." [39]

The problem is different in the reverse case where religious law limits the admission of ordinary testimony by requiring for instance written or other proof which is recognized by secular law but not as being exclusive. Here the question is whether to accept a limitation on the liberal approach to evidence in *the particular instance,* in contrast to a repugnant general principle. As for the last, for instance a prescribed requirement to prove a matter by two witnesses, there can be no doubt that it is to be rejected. The secular principle of free admissibility of evidence must clearly prevail in accordance with the outlook referred to above. But the matter is not so clear when religious law requires, for reasons going materially to the matter in issue, a specific mode of proof. The problem has in practice arisen in paternity actions,[40] before it was finally decided that these do not come

[36] Justice Kister, *ibid.,* at 727–728.

[37] The truth is that the rabbinical court as well encounters the difficulty of how to implement today the special provisions of *Halakha;* see App. 112/5725, 6 *Law Reports of the Rabbinical Courts,* 54.

[38] C.A. 151/60, *Avdan* v. *Avdan,* 14 P.D. 1828.

[39] *Ibid.* at 1931.

[40] C.A. 26/51, *Kotik* v. *Wolfson,* 5 P.D. 1341; C.A. 275/61, *A* v. *B,* 15 P.D. 2300.

under personal status within the meaning of Article 51.[41] Jewish law possesses detailed provisions regarding the modes of proving paternity and considerable legal importance attaches to the attitude of the father.[42] The secular courts have held that the religious law of evidence is not to be resorted to and a liberal principle must be followed, so that all the modes of proof recognized in secular law are valid, admissible and effective in this area.[43] Apparently the secular courts have also been influenced by their liberal approach to the rights of "natural" children, which has over the years received conspicuous expression in Israeli legislation which accords "natural" children all rights against the biological parents.[44] The practical outcome of dismissing the religious law of evidence is that the question of substantive law becomes to a large extent theoretical, because the main problem is the proof of paternity.

It seems that there was no occasion for rejecting in its entirety the religious law of evidence, assuming obviously that substantive religious law was applicable. Limitation on the modes of proof is here an expression of a specific policy on the matter, and according to the approach adopted in this study the special rules of evidence of Jewish law are to be applied. Even today the question is not devoid of all practical importance since possibly paternity may arise in an area still regulated by substantive religious law, such as capacity to marry.[45]

To set aside all religious limitation on proof of paternity and to replace them by a liberal view as to evidence may indeed lead to results contrary to the liberal policy of the secular courts. Where a man claims paternity of a child born to a woman married to another, the easing of the burden of proving paternity may well affect the social status of the child. Not surprisingly therefore the courts,[46] faced with a case of this kind, need to rely on a presumption of religious law that a child born in wedlock is the legitimate offspring of the husband.[47] To rely on this presumption goes against the

---

[41] It was held in H.C.J. 283/72, *Boaron v. Rabbinical Court, Tel Aviv*, 26 P.D. (2) 727 that paternity is not a matter of personal status. See P. Shifman, "Jurisdiction and Law in Paternity Matters," 4 *Mishpatim* 664.

[42] Shereshevski, *Family Law* (2nd ed. Jerusalem 1967), pp. 352 et seq., (Hebrew).

[43] See the sources cited in nn. 40 and 41.

[44] Shifman, *op. cit.*, p. 665; Family Law Amendment (Maintenance) Law, 5719–1959, (secs. 1(a) and 3); Succession Law, 5725–1965, secs. 3(c) and 10(2).

[45] Shifman, *op. cit.*, pp. 665–666.

[46] C.A. 231/61 *Chesam v. Gershel* 15 P.D. 2087, 2094.

[47] Shereshevski, *op. et loc. cit.;* Shifman, *op. cit.* n. 14. Cf. C.A. 447/58, *A. v. B.,*

principled statement that religious law of evidence never has application. As we have already said, that principle is erroneous and the courts have indeed been compelled to depart from it.

In summing up the discussion we may emphasize again that the limitations of religious law regarding requirements of proof specific to the matter in issue are not to be dismissed in advance. They are to be implemented unless they conflict with the fundamental understanding of the court of proper and effective procedure.

Burden of Proof, Presumptions and Weight of Evidence

In the traditional English view all these interrelated matters are part of procedural law.[48] Notwithstanding their kinship to substantive law, they have been caught by the rigid classification operative in choice-of-law.[49] The English approach has, however, received trenchant criticism.[50] Even English case law contains certain deviations in respect of presumptions,[51] which are echoed in Israeli decisions.[52]

Consistently with the approach taken here, there is no reason or necessity to resolve the problem by adopting another classification. Not only are these subjects closely allied with substantive law,[53] but they constitute provisions specific to the particular point in issue. The decision who is to bear the burden of proof generally involves the entire given set of facts. In contrast to rules of procedure in the narrow sense the legislature is not to be assumed to have specifically desired to apply to it secular provisions. There are a number of grounds for this conclusion. First, in many topics dealt with by religious law, there are no independent "competing" provisions in state law.[54] Hence also no parallel evidentiary provisions exist to replace those of religious law. For example, the rejection *ab initio* of the special legal presumptions of religious law in respect of marriage and divorce because of their procedural character would create a vacuum which could only be filled by general (civil) rules of evidence, the suitability of

---

13 P.D. 903, where the court refused to give a declaratory judgment in a paternity case instituted by a man other than the husband of the married mother.

[48] Harnon, *op. cit.*, para. 1.3.

[49] Cf. Cheshire, *op. cit.*, pp. 668 et seq.

[50] See p. 182 above.

[51] See n. 18 above and *Re Cohn* [1945] 1 Ch. 5, cf. Cheshire, *op. et loc. cit.*; Wolff, *op. et loc. cit.*

[52] C.A. 179/54 *Provalski v. Silber* 11 P.D. 626, 630–631; C.A. 70/49 *Borstein v. Yudelevitz* 5 P.D. 858.

[53] Cf. Szászy, *op. cit.*, pp. 247 et seq.; 285 et seq. See Shaki, *op. cit.*, p. 43.

[54] Cf. pp. 90 et seq. above.

which in the situation is doubtful.[55] It is possible that had the legislature put its mind to the specific topic, it also would have adopted the same religious legal presumption.

Secondly, no special difficulty is faced in applying religious evidentiary rules, such as those which determine upon whom the burden of proof lies. The efficacy test is thus no obstacle to applying religious law.[56] When there is nothing in the religious law of evidence repugnant to the understanding of the secular courts with regard to due process, the latter must resort to that law.

The courts have been exercised with the problem of the burden of proof and weight of evidence, at first in connection with a claim for maintenance by a woman who had left the matrimonial home. Under Jewish law, the woman forfeits her right to maintenance unless she is justified in leaving. The question which troubled the court was who bore the burden of proving that the woman had reason to refuse to cohabit. In *Mekitan* v. *Mekitan*[57] Justice Cohn held (without citing any authority) that the burden was always upon the husband to show that the wife had no justification for leaving him and so long as he did not discharge that burden the woman was entitled to maintenance by virtue of the marriage. This view did not meet the approval of the other judges who inferred from Jewish law that the burden was upon the woman to show justification. "A woman living apart from her husband cannot under Jewish law claim maintenance from him unless she shows or explains to the court that there was no blame on her side in leaving her husband or in refusing to return to him."[58]

On the question of the weight of evidence the court in the same case came to the conclusion, on an analysis of Jewish law, that it bears lightly on the woman. As Justice Kister put it, "if the material law prescribes that the obligation of proving a party's case is less onerous than usual, there is no need under the rules of evidence operative in the District Court for evidence corraborative of the woman's submissions but it is enough for the judge to be satisfied on the evidence before him."[59] We can see

---

[55] The possibility under Art. 46 of the Palestine Order in Council of a reference to the English law of evidence for the purpose of personal status does not recommend itself. As regards divorce cf. Silberg, *Personal Status in Israel*, (Jerusalem 1957), p. 260 (Hebrew).

[56] Cf. Shaki, *op. cit.;* Levontin, *ibid.*

[57] C.A. 634/61, 16 P.D. 945, 951.

[58] C.A. 256/65, *Miller* v. *Miller* 19 P.D. (3) 171, 177 and in the same spirit C.A. 353/65 *Haham* v. *Haham,* 20 P.D. (2) 199, 204. Cf. C.A. 460/67, *A.* v. *B.*, 22 P.D. (1) 157, 160 and C.A. 8/66 *Dana* v. *Dana,* 20 P.D. (3) 110.

[59] C.A. 256/65 at 180. See also C.A. 460/67.

therefore that in this case the court applied religious evidence law despite the court's conflicting statements of principle. In our view, the court acted properly.

Burden of proof is also involved in a further context specific to Jewish law. There opinion is divided on how to treat the "surplus" personal earnings of a wife.[60] Does her earned income belong to the husband? The question has not received any final answer in Jewish law and accordingly the rabbinical principle of *non liquet* applies; each party may submit that the law is according to those authorities which are in his favour.[61] The result is that the party in possession will always succeed since the other party is treated as a plaintiff upon whom the onus of proof lies. In Jewish law the rule as to burden of proof also applies in respect of a question of law to which no answer is forthcoming. Hence any person claiming from another in a *non liquet* situation carries an onus which he is unable *ab initio* to discharge.[62] The matter does not, however, rest here. When a woman who retains her personal earnings sues for maintenance the husband may plead that he has met his obligations to pay maintenance on the basis of the above *non liquet* submission, reasoning that the wife retains what belongs to him and he has designated that to meet his obligation to maintain. The practical significance is that he may refuse maintenance as long as the woman has sufficient personal earnings for that purpose.[63] The *non liquet* argument as such is taken to fall under the law of evidence since it prescribes the primary burden of proof, that is, which of the parties is making the positive claim, and in the instant case it is a procedural rule although closely linked to the substantive law.[64] In *Joseph v. Joseph*[65] the Supreme Court did not hesitate to apply in its entirety religious law and a woman's claim for maintenance was dismissed on the above *halakhic* grounds.

It is to be observed that the equal treatment of a doubt as to the law

---

[60] Shereshevski, *op. cit.*, pp. 177 et seq.
[61] *Ibid.* and the sources cited there.
[62] Generally see P. Shifman, *Doubtful Marriage in Israeli Law* (Doctoral Thesis, Jerusalem 1972), pp. 16 et seq., 120 (Hebrew); Id., "The Status of Doubt," 33 (1967) *De'ot* 153 (Hebrew).
[63] Shereshevski, *op. cit.*, p. 178.
[64] Cf. Shifman, "The Status of Doubt", *cit.*, nn. 13 and 15; but of Id. *Doubtful Marriage, cit.*, p. 120 n. 72, where it is rightly questioned whether one should not regard an undischargeable burden of proof as a substantive provision according to traditional English classification.
[65] F.H. 23/69, 24 P.D. (1) 792.

and as to fact, in respect of burden of proof, is peculiar to Jewish law.[66] In secular law a question of law can never be the subject of proof and the judge must decide it.[67]

Again we may note that in the approach adopted here no great importance attaches to whether a religious provision is classified under substance or procedure. If it is specific to the matter in dispute it is proper to be applied on the presumption that the legislature did not intend to replace it by a secular provision of its own. The *non liquet* argument, notwithstanding its generalized nature in religious law, is peculiar because its application is conditional upon the existence of a doubt as to the law.

On the face of it, where the doubt goes to the facts and not to the law, there need be no difference between religious and secular law. Both proclaim in principle the view that a claimant must always prove his case. Yet in *Bassan* v. *Bassan*[68] a District Court arrived at a different result. A woman whose Jewishness was in doubt in point of fact sued her Jewish husband for maintenance. The doubt obviously affected the status and validity of the marriage, since disparity of religion entails nullity of the marriage. According to religious law the woman had the onus of proving her Jewishness and thus the validity of her marriage so as to support her claim, since so long as the doubt was not removed the husband might not be found liable. But the court did not accept this: "The rule in the Jewish law of evidence that a claimant must prove his case would in the present instance lead to the woman, deemed to be the claimant, failing in her claim for maintenance. For this court which is not bound by this rule within the meaning of Jewish law, the situation is different. Those considerations which induced the Rabbinical High Court to regard the woman as Jewish for the purpose of having to accept a bill of divorce are sufficient for this court to make the husband liable for maintenance." [69] According to the court, a marriage subsists so long as it is not annulled and along with it the property rights that stem therefrom also continue to subsist.

The reasoning and conclusions of the court may be criticized. The argument that a secular court is not bound by the rule that a claimant

---

[66] See generally Shifman, *Doubtful Marriage cit.*, pp. 20 et seq., and A. M. Rabello, "Non Liquet: From Modern Law to Roman Law", 9 (1974) *Is. L. R.* 63 and the authorities cited there.

[67] Under sec. 33 of the Interpretation Ordinance judicial notice is taken thereof. Cf. p. 93 above.

[68] 315/65, 57 P.M. 63.

[69] *Ibid.* at 68.

must prove his case cannot be correct. This rule, as we have said, is common to all legal systems (*probandi necessitas incumbit illi qui agit*). Even if we were always to apply the procedural rules of the State (according to our approach that is not necessary) the conclusion is the same, a claimant must prove his case.[70]

Obviously the truth of the matter is that what was involved was not rejection of a rule of evidence but of the whole doubt about the right to maintenance. The obligation of a woman to accept a divorce under religious law (by reason of doubt as to the validity of the marriage) was in the opinion of the court enough for charging the husband with maintenance. It follows that on the argument of the court a doubtful marriage is identical with an incontestable marriage in respect of all ensuing property rights. That means that when under religious law a divorce is required because of doubt as to the facts, there is a legal presumption that the marriage subsists so long as the contrary is not proved.[71] A legal presumption of this kind is a creature of the court itself and lacks all legal foundation.[72] As long as maintenance is regulated according to Jewish law (by way of "law reference"),[73] the claimant wife has the burden of proving that the marriage is of effect.[74] Doubts on this point operate to her disadvantage. The fact itself that she is required to obtain a divorce if she wishes

---

[70] See also Shifman, *op. cit.*, p. 120.

[71] Logically, when doubt is as to the law, which cannot be resolved, the presumption is absolute and irrebuttable.

[72] See also Shifman, *op. cit.*, pp. 120, 123–124, who notes the inconsistency of the Court over the question of jurisdiction. In H.C.J. 214/64, *Bassan v. Rabbinical Court of Appeal,* 18 P.D. (4) 309, 317, it held that "the marriage of a doubtfully Jewish woman does not fall within the jurisdiction of the rabbinical court either as regards the woman or as regards the husband since as a consequence of the doubt the phrase "marriage of Jews", upon which rabbinical jurisdiction depends under section 1 of the Law, cannot attach." If the test is the woman's need of a divorce, then she is to be deemed closer to being a Jewess and the rabbinical court should have jurisdiction. Cf. H.C.J. 359/66, *Gitea v. Chief Rabbinate,* 22 P.D. (1) 290, 295.

[73] That is, reference to the legal result of religious law. As to the concept of law reference, see pp. 58, 61 et seq. above.

[74] The situation may be different when a fact reference (see pp. 58 et seq. above) is concerned. There the application of religious law is limited to determining the factual basis of the legal norm. Thus the court is freer in drawing the secular legal consequence. For instance in C.A. 603/65, *Feldman v. Feldman,* 20 P.D. (2) 465; F.H. 14/66, 20 P.D. (4) 693, the court held that the woman, who was doubtfully married because of the *levirate* rules, was entitled to succeed to her husband's estate. This result could be based on the ground that the phrase "spouse of the deceased" in the Succession Law can be construed as

to wed another cannot affect her right to maintenance, which is entirely laid down by reference to religious law.[75]

We may conclude this survey with an authentic legal presumption of Jewish law, that a man does not cohabit for illicit fornication.[76] The courts have more than once dealt with this presumption.[77] Although in certain instances, it is paralleled by like presumptions in most legal systems, such as *semper praesumitur pro matrimonio*,[78] its religious character has left its mark, and its definition and scope are prescribed by religious law.[79] Accordingly, in view of the approach adopted here this special presumption must be applied in its entirety notwithstanding its procedural evidentiary nature.[80]

Quantum of Maintenance

This topic has received special consideration in the case law. The problem here springs from the rule of English private international law that the "remedy" is always a matter of the *lex fori*.[81] In reliance on this rule, the Supreme Court held in *Skornik* v. *Skornik*[82] that the quantum of main-

> pertaining to a person who in religious law is doubtfully married. Clearly, the court must bear in mind the purpose of the Law when it decides upon the meaning of terms in the context of religious law. Possibly a doubt as to the law may here be distinguished from a doubt as to the facts. See generally Shifman, "Status of Doubt", *cit.*, pp. 119 et seq.

[75] Religious law does not accord a doubtfully married woman any maintenance rights, irrespective of whether the doubt is as to the law or as to the facts. If, however, the man refuses to deliver a *get*, the woman may become entitled under religious law to maintenance because of the impediment she thereby suffers. See Shereshevski, *op. cit.*, pp. 93 and 342, who notes that the authorities are not agreed on the point. It may be observed that if the civil court were to accord maintenance in every instance of a doubtful marriage, that would mean a "fictitious" application of religious law, *i.e.*, of the religious legal result in respect of facts not covered by the religious norm.

[76] On the nature of this presumption, see Shereshevski, *op. cit.*, pp. 35, 85, 341.

[77] 1542/59 *Zarfati* v. *Zarfati*, 23 P.M. 240, 244; 799/59 *Yatom* v. *Yatom*, 6 P.M. 473, 476; C.A. 79/52, *Porter* v. *Sufrin*, 8 P.D. 1430. Cf. H.C. 46/46, *Pollak* v. *Pollak*, 13 P.L.R. 390.

[78] C.A. 191/51, *Skornik* v. *Skornik*, 8 P.D. 141, 148 (English translation 2 S.J.S.C. 327, 334).

[79] C.A. 79/52, *cit.*, C.A. 238/53 *Cohen, Buslik* v. *A.G.* 8 P.D. 4, 24 (2 S.J.S.C. 239, 261–262).

[80] It is interesting that the courts which at first explicitly denied recourse to religious rules of evidence have unhesitatingly relied on the presumption mentioned; see, *e.g.*, 1542/59, *cit.*, at 243–244.

[81] Cheshire, *op. cit.*, pp. 678 et seq.; Dicey & Morris, *op. cit.*, p. 1101.

[82] C.A. 191/51, *cit.*

tenance must be decided according to local law and not the *lex celebrationis*. The Court so held by way of analogy from the English rule as it operates in claims for compensation. In English law it is usual to distinguish between the right to receive compensation and its amount.[83] The Court thought that the question of the amount of compensation is comparable with that of the quantum of maintenance. Both are a matter of remedy subject to the *lex fori*. In *Skornik*, however, the Court did not lay down any hard and fast rule as regards the substance of local law but mentioned in one breath religious personal law and "those rules according to which the civil courts in this country act." If we are to follow the case law which adopts the distinction between substance and procedure, then the conclusion must be to reject religious law regarding quantum, since that is a matter of remedy, *i.e.*, of procedure. If we are to transplant the substance-procedure distinction, as it is understood in choice-of-laws, to the matter of applying religious law, then the quantum of maintenance must be determined not according to religious law but according to "civil principles." [84]

In *Skornik*, the Court alluded to such secular principles in reliance upon the judgment in *Levin*,[85] but in truth the distinction itself between a right to maintenance and its amount is not clear. It is difficult to see how the latter can be determined without falling back on the substantive provisions.[86] Furthermore, whence does the court arrive at the rules affecting quantum if not from religious law? In *Levin* the court proposed certain

---

[83] Cheshire, *op. cit.*, pp. 683 et seq.; Dicey & Morris, *op. cit.*, p. 1103; cf. *Boys v. Chaplin* [1971] A.C. 356, 394.

[84] C.A. 191/51, *cit.* at 172, 174 (2 S.J.S.C. 368, 370): "Everything relating to the determination of the amount of maintenance is nothing more than a matter of the procedure for giving effect to the substantive right of a married woman to recover maintenance from her husband, and the obligation of the husband to pay such maintenance; in other words it is a matter of remedy and nothing more."

[85] *Ibid.* at 174 (370). See next note.

[86] It is easy to argue that the amount of the obligation is simply its extent, and according to Justice Agranat, *ibid.* at 172–173 (368–369) the extent of the right is part of the substantive problem of the existence of the obligation. The difficulty can be illustrated by the following. A woman who enjoys income from her own property claims maintenance from her husband. The question whether her income must be deducted from the maintenance due from the husband certainly touches on the amount thereof but is also inextricably bound up with the substantive law. The distinction proposed by Justice Agranat between the extent of the right and its realization is a difficult one.

tests for this purpose [87] but they seem to be an independent creation of its own and their foundation in law is very doubtful.[88]

A summary provision regarding the extent of maintenance is found in section 6 of the Family Law Amendment (Maintenance) Law 5719–1959 [89] but section 2 expressly prescribes that "a person is liable for the maintenance of his spouse in accordance with the provisions of the personal law applying to him, and the provisions of this Law shall not apply to that maintenance." [90] The simple meaning of this section is that the legislature intended to apply religious law in the spouse relationship, excluding the application of section 6, otherwise it would have qualified section 2. Hence, also formally there is no foundation for the distinction between the right to and the amount of maintenance. In both cases, religious law is to be applied.[91] There is no point to detail again our grounds for the

---

[87] C.A. 84/49, *Levin* v. *Levin*, 5 P.D. 921, 936. The considerations mentioned in this case for calculating the amount of maintenance are inter alia (a) that the husband has lost the wife's company without being alone the guilty party; (b) that the woman has income from property of her own and the husband has no large income; (c) that it is desirable for the woman to know that she must seek a permanent arrangement by accepting a divorce. Both at first instance and on appeal the court rejected the third of these considerations but relied on the other two. It is suggested that all are of a substantive character and therefore lack legal foundation.

[88] Taking account of the woman's private income patently conflicts with a later decision (C.A. 61/71, 25 P.D. (2) 372) in which the court, on substantive grounds founded in religious law, refused to make any deduction in respect thereof.

[89] "The extent, measure and modes of provision of maintenance shall, in the absence of agreement between the parties, be prescribed by the Court, having regard to the circumstances and, except in the case of maintenance under section 3, according to the need of the person entitled and the ability of the person liable."

[90] A similar provision is contained in sec. 3 in respect of child maintenance.

[91] See, however, M. Shawa, "The Mode of the Application of the Family Law Amendment (Maintenance) Law, 5719–1959, to Spouse and Child Maintenance" 3 (1973) *Iyune Mishpat* 337, who proposes to interpret the limiting sections 2 and 3 as going only to substantive provisions. In his view, the special procedural provisions of the Law apply in every case, even when substantive religious law operates. This interpretation is quite unacceptable. It is contrary to the unambiguous language of the sections which do not distinguish between provisions. Again, if it were correct that procedure is always determined according to secular law, the "competition" is at the outset not between the Law and religious law but between the general law of procedure prevailing prior to the Law and the special rules of procedure the Law introduced. In view

application of the special provisions of religious law, even if according to English classification they come under procedure in point of private international law.

The fact is that in all the case law after *Skornik* no attempt appears to be made to apply any secular provisions to the amount of maintenance. In a series of judgments the provisions of religious law have been applied as self understood.[92] Furthermore the court has rejected the plea made in a maintenance claim about the woman's income that the obligation to pay should be distinguished from the amount, and has applied religious law in full.[93]

---

of the explicit terms of secs. 2 and 3, the *lex specialis* cannot displace the earlier secular *lex generalis*.

[92] See, *e.g.*, C.A. 328/72, *Langel v. Langel*, 27 P.D. (2) 470; C.A. 206/60, *Derham v. Derham*, 14 P.D. 1726; C.A. 426/65, *Rinat v. Rinat*, 20 P.D. (2) 21; C.A. 72/62, *Zukerman v. Zukerman*, 16 P.D. 1781. Cf. Shawa *op. cit.*, n. 15.

[93] C.A. 426/65, *cit. at* 24–25. The question was the wife's income. At first instance, it was thought to be relevant for determining the amount of maintenance, as distinct from the existence of the obligation as such. The Supreme Court, *per* Justice Silberg, said "what is the difference between the obligation to pay and the amount of maintenance? As to both, the rights pertaining to the husband prior to the enactment of the Women's Equal Rights Law cannot be taken into account."

Chapter V

THE GRAFTING OF RELIGIOUS LAW UPON SECULAR LAW AND THE PROCESS OF ADAPTATION

The combined operation of rules from different legal systems will, failing a special effort in that regard, sometimes lead to difficulties of coordination.[1] The problem of adaptation (*Anpassung*) is characteristic of private international law and many writers have dwelt upon it.[2] The more the legal systems involved differ in nature, the greater is the friction generated. This is especially true when religious and secular law with their considerable differences come together.[3] Attempts have been made to classify and characterize the cases in which this problem of adaptation arises[4] and it would appear with some success, at least with more success than the parallel attempts to find agreed solutions to the problems created by the absence of harmony.

In principle, two modes of proceeding to this end in private international law can be distinguished,[5] one by a change of the choice-of-law rule and one by a change of the substance of the material norm. These alternatives can be illustrated by an example which, as we shall see, is related to the theme of this study.

A couple get married in country X, the law of which gives a widow rights of succession in her husband's estate but no other rights in his property by virtue of marriage. The couple then become nationals of country

---

[1] Cf. Neuhaus, *Die Grundbegriffe des internationalen Privatrechts* (Berlin-Tübingen 1962), p. 250.
[2] Continental writers have in particular dealt with the subject. In English, see K. Lipstein, "The General Principles of Private International Law", 135 (1972) I *Recueil des Cours* 97, 207 et seq.; Wengler, "The General Principles of Private International Law," 104 (1961) III *Recueil des Cours*, 273, 405 et seq.
[3] J. Schröder, *Die Anpassung von Kollisions-und Sachnormen* (Berlin 1961), pp. 20, 32.
[4] Lewald, "Règles générales des conflits de lois", 69 (1939) III *Recueil des Cours* 1, 126 et seq.; Cansacchi, "Le choix et l'adaptation de la règle étrangère dans les conflits de lois", 83 (1953) II *Recueil des Cours*, 79, 111 et seq.; Schröder, *op. cit.*, passim.
[5] Kegel, *Internationales Privatrecht* (3. Aufl. München 1971), § 8, III.

Y where a widow enjoys no succession rights as such but property rights in the estate by virtue of marriage. According to the choice-of-law rules of the court hearing the matter it is possible for the *lex celebrationis* of country X to apply to the rights deriving from the marriage and the law of country Y to the succession rights, with the result that the widow will be entitled to nothing, a situation which is unacceptable. The result necessarily follows from the conjunction of conflicting norms but the consequence is repugnant to the spirit of both legal systems. The law of X denies the widow any rights under the marriage because it gives her a right of succession. The law of Y denies her a right of succession because it gives her other property rights in her husband's estate. The loss of all rights is not consonant with the intention of the law of either country and if the position of X and Y are interchanged, the result is again unreasonable, for then the widow will enjoy double rights, that of succession and that of property.[6]

Applying the alternatives mentioned above we will find that under the first the choice-of-law rule, under which the rights are split because of reference to two legal systems, would be replaced by a rule that both kinds of rights are to be dealt with in accordance with one system alone, either that of X or that of Y. This solution succeeds in avoiding *ab initio* the problem of disharmony since the court will at once resort to a single legal system. Under the second alternative a satisfactory conclusion would be reached by changing the substantive law of either system. Where denial of all rights to a widow is to be anticipated, the court would, for instance, vary the law of X with the aim of according her succession rights, by holding that a widow not entitled to other rights in the estate shall be deemed to have a succession right.[7] In the reverse case the court would introduce a change in the law of Y, by which a widow's marriage rights in X would be set off against her succession right in Y.

Clearly, the process of adaptation as above patently and consciously embodies a significant instance of judicial law-making, the court interfering with the material law of another country.[8] Sometimes, however, the court's intervention is not so substantive and the adaptation consists mostly of applying the law "with necessary modification."[9]

---

[6] Lipstein, *op. et loc. cit.*, p. 209; Lewald, *op. et loc. cit.*, pp. 144–145.

[7] Cf. Lewald, *ibid.*

[8] Raape, "Les rapports juridiques entre parents et enfants", 50 (1934), *Recueil des Cours* 403, 497 et seq.

[9] Cansacchi, *op. et loc. cit.*, p. 120 et seq. See generally Barak, "On the Codification of Law", 3 (1973) *Iyune Mishpat*, 5, 15 n. 65.

For our purpose here, the problem of adaptation—the application of religious law in a secular system—calls for emphasis of a number of special features which distinguish it from that occurring in "ordinary" choice-of-law. First, religious law, and particularly Jewish law, is not unknown to the legislature. The reception of religious law in matters of personal status is a familiar process. Thus the legislature has reasonable opportunity to reconcile any disharmony by rules of its own. Again, the secular law is not entirely hidden from religious law and the latter may fashion its own rules of adaptation where concord with secular law is absent. The problem will then obviously be whether the religious rules of adaptation are binding on the civil court.

Secondly, as regards characterizing the cases in which disharmony occurs, the disharmony is possibly the outcome of a partial application of religious law and combining it with secular law in a given factual situation. The combination will largely be the result of a limitation on the application of religious law, which has already been discussed in the previous chapter. The three main instances in which lack of concord may be created as a consequence of compounding one system with another are where religious law is partially rejected by foreign law under the rules of private international law, where it is partially rejected on the basis of the distinction between substance and procedure, and where it is partially rejected by the direct application of substantive secular law.

As for the first, it was held in *Skornik v. Skornik*[10] that marriage status acquired abroad in the past must be recognized even if the present personal law does not. The combination of religious law (which applies thenceforth) with the foreign law creates serious discord.[11] The problems this situation can entail were demonstrated in *Skornik* itself. The wife claimed maintenance but the applicable religious law did not recognize the foreign marriage. For the court the solution was a simple and easy one:[12] "I have no hesitation therefore in activating the right to maintenance of a wife under Jewish law in favour of a wife whose marriage is based upon foreign law but is recognized by the law of this country."[13]

---

[10] C.A. 191/51, 8 P.D. 141 (English translation 2 S.J.S.C. 327). The judgment is subjected to critical comment by Levontin, *Marriages and Divorces out of the Jurisdiction* (Jerusalem 1957) (Hebrew).
[11] The situation has been dubbed "hinkendes Rechtsverhältnis" (a limping legal relationship) according to the old concept of *matrimonium claudicans*: see Neuhaus, *op. cit.*, p. 253.
[12] At 180, (2 S.J.S.C. 379) per Justice Witkon.
[13] According to Justice Olshan also (at 161) (353–354) religious law applies.

Actually, the court carried out a process of adaptation, finding a solution by a fictitious operation of religious law.[14] It gave effect under religious law to a set of facts which was entirely non-existent under that law. It assumed the existence of a legal situation within the framework of religious law and attached to it the legal result flowing from that law but the assumption was itself fictitious. Thus what we have here is a judicial variation of a hypothetical set of facts constituting part of a religious norm and the attribution of the legal result of religious law to a concrete situation which is wholly foreign to it.

Both formally and materially the matter belongs to the sphere of private international law and it appears that in principle another solution presents itself. Instead of a fictitious application of religious law, the scope of the application of the two legal systems can be altered by changing the choice-of-law rule. In this manner, it can be established that foreign law applies not only to the determination of status but also to the ensuing legal result. Thus discord is avoided because it becomes unnecessary to combine foreign and religious law.[15] It is nevertheless extremely doubtful whether this last solution can be adopted without express legislature intervention.[16]

The "fictitious application" of religious law is not as simple as it was assumed to be in *Skornik*.[17] It is not always easy to attach the results of religious law to a status acquired under foreign law. For instance, in the case of a *cohen* and a divorcee, both residents of Israel but married abroad civilly, such marriage, as explained above, is prohibited under religious law but once celebrated takes effect. Thus even if the marriage is recognized by virtue of foreign law, it remains doubtful whether any right of maintenance enures in view of the nature of the initial prohibition. Under Jewish law notwithstanding the partial effect of the marriage, the woman is not entitled to maintenance since the husband is under a con-

---

Justice Agranat, on the other hand, distinguishes between the existence of the right and the amount of maintenance, as explained at p. 196 above.

[14] Neuhaus, *op. cit.*, p. 256.

[15] The contrary solution which also avoids the problem of disharmony is to apply religious law retrospectively beyond the borders of the State. Cf. Levontin, *op. cit.*, p. 33, for still another solution.

[16] This would create serious problems because of the jurisdiction given to the religious court. Cf. Levontin, *op. cit.*, p. 28.

[17] We pass over the other problems of principle dealt with by Levontin, *op. cit.* See in this regard, the differing views of Tedeschi, "Transition from Secular to Religious Matrimonial Status and the Retroactive Application of the Latter", *Studies in Israel Private Law* (Jerusalem 1966), pp. 212, 216 n. 4.

tinuing obligation to divorce her.[18] Assuming this sanction is operative in respect of a prohibited marriage as aforesaid effected in Israel,[19] the question is whether it should not also attach to a foreign marriage of this kind. It can be urged that in view of the celebration abroad of the marriage one must completely disregard the prohibition under local religious law. As against that, it would be difficult to justify the difference in legal result had the marriage been celebrated in Israel.

As to the second of the above instances of disharmony, the distinction between substance and procedure in religious law will naturally yield that result. To join secular procedure with substantive religious law necessitates a process of adaptation, although the "depth" thereof is not a predetermined matter. Sometimes adaptation may be a minor matter, sometimes it may require significant changes. It will be important, for instance, in the field of evidence when religious law is applied to a set of facts the existence of which is proved by secular rules. A conspicuous example of the consequent disharmony is provided by *Feldman* v. *Feldman*,[20] referred to at length in the previous chapter. There a mechanical juncture of secular and religious law yielded a conclusion contrary to the spirit of both systems. In the view taken here, which advocates tempering the traditional distinction between substance and procedure, the more extreme cases of discord can be avoided by applying Jewish law.

Thirdly, the most important instance of the adaptation problem occurs when substantive secular law is conjoined with substantive religious law. At times lack of harmony will here manifest itself as a consequence of the

---

[18] Shereshevski, *Family Law* (2nd ed., Jerusalem 1967) pp. 203-204. The denial of maintenance is intended to "encourage" the couple to get divorced so as to put an end to a relationship forbidden by religious law.

[19] It is doubtful whether the courts will deny the wife of such a doubtful marriage maintenance despite the express provision of religious law. The court will possibly regard the denial of maintenance as a consequence of religious law, which is not part of Israeli law. This was the approach in *Rodnitzki* (H.C.J. 51/69, 24 P.D. (1) 704, 711-712) considered above pp. 160-161. In view, however, of the fact that in matters of maintenance reference to religious law partakes of a "law reference" and the court must apply the legal result of religious law, it is difficult to see how the husband can be charged with payment when he is expressly exempted under religious law. Cf. C.A. 571/69, *Cahana* v. *Cahana*, 24 P.D. (2) 549, where maintenance was denied but on the ground that the wife was required by a previous rabbinical judgment to accept a *get;* see especially the judgment of Justice Kister (at 553) from which it would emerge that in his opinion a woman, the validity of whose marriage is doubtful, is not entitled to maintenance.

[20] C.A. 423/64, 19 P.D. (2) 197; pp. 185-186 above.

APPLICATION OF RELIGIOUS LAW

inner balance of the religious or secular system being upset. That will be particularly evident when in one of the systems a correlated link exists between different legal institutions and the exclusion or replacement of one of them by the other (different) system completely disturbs the equilibrium of the first system.[21]

In contrast to private international law, a solution, it seems, can only be found in an adaptative process. The court cannot change the scope of application of religious law. It must accept the legislative prescript explicitly fixing the boundaries thereof. To move the boundary marks in two directions is in the nature of trespass. In principle therefore the court cannot *ab initio* avoid disharmony. It must either reconcile itself to the unreasonable consequences or try to repair the situation by a process of adaptation. In reality two main matters give rise to the problem of adaptation, and these merit separate treatment.

The first which has so disturbed the courts that it has evoked legislative intervention concerns the relationship between secular succession law and the widow's rights under religious law. The *Halakha* does not recognise any right in the widow of succession to her husband's estate; instead it confers other rights having their source in the marriage relationship—the *Ketubah* and maintenance. Since matters of marriage are subject to religious law whereas a deceased's estate is distributed according to secular law, the question is whether the two groups of rights are cumulative in favour of a widow.[22] As we saw at the beginning of the present chapter a similar problem can arise in private international law.[23]

The secular courts have recognized the widow's right to her *Ketubah* in addition to a succession right. Two main grounds were given for this in *Skindar* v. *Schwartz*:[24] since neither secular nor religious law contains any provisions coordinating the two rights, the court may not change the law and can only recognize the existence of both rights. On maintenance, however, the court expressed a different view,[25] holding that whilst a succession right under secular law does not affect the widow's right as such

---

[21] Schröder, *op. cit.*, no. 17, 46 et seq., terms these cases "transverse" (*Ueberkreuzung*) situations on the basis of the analysis in Wengler, "Die Qualifikation der materiellen Rechtssätze im internationalen Privatrecht", *Festschrift Wolff* (Tübingen 1952), pp. 337, 368.

[22] Shereshevski, *op. cit.*, pp. 267–270.

[23] Above pp. 199–200.

[24] C.A. 95/54, *Skinder* v. *Schwarz*, 9 P.D. 931, 935.

[25] In C.A. 186/60, *Levitzki* v. *Levitzki*, 15 P.D. 2027 opinion was divided between Justice Cohn (at 2033) and Justice Silberg (at 2035). The latter thought the widow entitled to both rights. Justice Cohn reiterated his view that the suc-

to maintenance out of the estate under religious law, the succession right must be taken into account in determining the amount of maintenance.[26] The principal reason was that religious law itself [27] so prescribes and the religious courts in fact act in this manner.[28] This reason therefore rests on a rule of coordination in religious law.[29] The question remains whether the court may have recourse to any such rule found in religious law,[30] whether reference to religious law includes its adaptation provisions. We incline to the view that the court must indeed apply religious law along with its adaptation provisions and decide as it did in the instant case.[31]

In the absence of a rule of coordination, the court may, on this view, effect a process of adaptation on its own motion. But we need not lay down any firm rule in the matter since the problem has been resolved in general by express statutory provision. Section 11 (e) of the Succession Law, 5725–1965, provides that "there shall be deducted from the spouse's share in the estate anything due to a spouse on a claim which arises out of the

cession right is deductible from the amount of maintenance (C.A. 447/61, *Perez v. Director of Estate Duty*, 16 P.D. 85). See particularly 1181/51, *Wolf v. Land Registrar*, 7 P.M. 327, 336 (Justice Kister).

[26] See C.A. 447/61, at 88 and cf. 67/55, *Re Estate Ahmar*, 20 P.M. 302.

[27] Shereshevski, *op. cit.*, p. 269: "Were the widow to succeed under Jewish law, she would not be entitled to maintenance out of the estate." The author thinks that the same is true in respect of the *Ketuba* rights, contrary to the distinction drawn in C.A. 95/54 above.

[28] 1181/51, *Wolf v. Land Registrar*, at 336.

[29] In the Supreme Court judgments mentioned (n. 25 above) there is no express or uniform reason given. Justice Cohn who advocates deduction of succession rights from maintenance does not rely on religious law (in contrast to Justice Kister in 1181/51). Justice Silberg on the other hand, who expressed the view that the widow has both rights, relies on the concept of "gift" under religious law (C.A. 186/60 at 2035).

[30] What is intended here is a religious rule prescribing how to act in face of the existence of a secular provision.

[31] A similar though not identical question may arise in private international and inter-religious law. Assuming that under choice-of-law rules (or some other rules) the court is referred to religious law and examination reveals that that law contains no substantive provision but a *renvoi* to secular law, must we accept such *renvoi*? The question arose in Germany regarding the applicability of Canon law in Israel in a maintenance case and the court received an affirmative opinion of the Max Planck Institute of Hamburg. According to that opinion, the foreign reference was of a comprehensive character and the Israeli choice-of-law rules must be applied (in this instance sec. 17 of the Family Law Amendment (Maintenance) Law, 5719–1959): *Gutachten zum internationalen und ausländischen Privatrecht 1970*, Tübingen 1971, p. 125, cf. Szászy, "Interpersonal Conflicts of Laws," *op. cit.*, at 805 et seq.

marital bound, including anything which the wife receives under the *Ketubah."* Thus the legislature has chosen to introduce a form of statutory adaptation of the two groups of rights. As for a widow's maintenance out of her husband's estate, the Law provides an arrangement of its own [32] which includes a rule of coordination.[33] The secular court is no longer referred to religious law in this respect [34] and so all possibility of discord is obviated.

But another matter in which discord occurs still continues to cause difficulty. Here the lack of adaptation is created as a result of legislative intervention in abolishing the application of part of religious law regarding matrimonial property rights—the right of the husband to the income of the *melug* property of the wife which he enjoys under Jewish law.[35] When a wife sues for maintenance, her husband may plead that the avoidance of his *melug* rights under Jewish law entails the denial of the wife's right to maintenance.

To understand the problem fully we must first enquire into the internal system of Jewish law. According to that law a link exists between the husband's right in the wife's property and his obligations towards her. As against his duty to provide for her, he has the right to her personal earnings. As against his right to income, he has the duty to ransom her, when necessary.[36] But in Jewish law, the fact that the wife owns property does not release the husband from his duty of support. When, however, she is seized of money due to him, he may set off the amount against the maintenance due from him. In consequence of this last rule, the secular courts have decided that the husband may set off *the personal earnings of the wife* from any maintenance due by him.[37] This solution accords in principle with the modern notion of equality between spouses, which lies

---

[32] Part Four of the Law, secs. 56–65.

[33] Sec. 59.

[34] Sec. 148. A certain connection with religious law is maintained by sec. 57(b) of the law which makes the widow's right to maintenance from the estate conditional upon the existence of her right to maintenance during her husband's life.

[35] The Supreme Court decided on the avoidance of the husband's right in *Sidis* (H.C.J. 202/57, 12 P.D. 1528) in reliance upon its interpretation of sec. 2 of the Women's Equal Rights Law, 5711–1951, an interpretation criticized by Shereshevski, *op. cit.,* pp. 216 et seq. The courts have, however, continued to follow *Sidis.* See now sec. 4 of the Matrimonial Property Relations Law, 5733–1973, which expressly provides that contracting a marriage does not itself vest in any one of the parties rights in the property of the other.

[36] Shereshevski, *op. cit.*, pp. 162, 171 et seq.

[37] F.H. 23/69, *Josef* v. *Josef,* 24 P.D. (1) 792 and see the authorities cited.

behind the abrogation of the husband's right to the wife's income. In the present day perception of equality between the sexes, it is not justifiable for a propertied wife to retain the income of her property and at the same time require to have the household expenses paid in full by the husband. In point of law, however, the courts could find no way to arrive at the desired result of taking account of *the wife's property* (as distinct from her earnings) when determining the amount of maintenance which the husband has to pay her.[38] The mechanical linking of secular and religious law prevents that being achieved for the following reason. Whilst secular law has abolished the husband's income rights, religious law obliges him in principle to pay maintenance even if the wife has property of her own. If the two systems are linked, the wife's property must be treated as being released from the husband's income rights, a situation possible under religious law as well,[39] although the existence of property in the wife does not release him from the duty to maintain.[40]

This unreasonable result is contrary to the spirit of both systems. It creates a distinction between a woman with personal earnings (which are deductible from the amount of maintenance) and one with property (which is not so deductible).[41] It is opposed to the spirit of secular law because the principle of equality of spouses is invaded;[42] and it is opposed to the spirit of religious law because in the complex of that law's provisions the internal balance between the husband's rights and obligations is disturbed by the unilateral abolition of the *melug* income right.

We are faced with a characteristic instance of lack of accord resulting from a bringing together of systems. The question is whether legislative

---

[38] C.A. 61/71, *Cohen v. Cohen*, 25 P.D. (2) 327 and particularly at 335.

[39] For instance, property given to the wife as a gift on the condition that the husband does not receive the income thereof. See Shereshevski, *op. cit.*, p. 156. The legislative prescript may therefore be understood as treating all the wife's property as property which is neither *nikhse zon barzel* nor *nikhse melug*, that is, as property which is under the wife's control.

[40] C.A. 426/65, *Rinui v. Rinui*, 20 P.D. (2) 21, 25, 27, C.A. 61/71 where the court, in our view rightly, rejected the submission resting on the possibility in religious law to debit *nikhse melug* income against maintenance owed by the husband. That is only possible because in Jewish law the property income belongs to the husband. If it does not (as under enactment) the husband must pay the entire maintenance. See C.A. 61/71 at 334; Shereshevski, *op. cit.*, p. 124 n. 30.

[41] As was submitted for the wife in C.A. 61/71 at 331: "it follows that the Women's Equal Rights Law confers 'equality' upon rich women alone, whilst abandons those wives who toil hard to the good grace of their husbands."

[42] C.A. 61/71 at 332, 335.

intervention is the only means of remedying the situation, as the Supreme Court urged in *Cohen* v. *Cohen*.[43] In the view of the present writer the course open to the court is judicial adaptation. Since a mechanical joinder yields a result repugnant to the spirit of both systems, the court may vary the substantive law and in determining the amount of maintenance take into account the wife's property income.

The process of adaptation is frequently pursued in practice, although not consciously. Awareness of the process may enable its scope to be defined and the conditions for its operation determined. The courts, it is hoped, will use this technique notwithstanding they have despaired of finding an independent solution of the matter and have thrust the burden upon the legislature.

---

[43] *Ibid.* at 333 (Justice Etzioni); 335 (President Agranat). Actually, a Bill amending the Law has been presented to the Knesset: *Hatza'ot-Hok*, 1975, No. 1168.

[44] It seems that in fact the Supreme Court has so acted in the past regarding the juncture of succession rights and maintenance of the estate. Cf. pp. 204–205 above.

ADDENDUM

Pp. 139 n. 15, 141: sec. 3(3) of the Foreign Judgment Enforcement Law, 5718–1958, was amended in December 1974 to read as follows: "A court in Israel may declare a foreign judgment enforceable if it finds that— ... (3) the obligation under the judgment is enforceable according to the laws relating to the enforcement of judgments in Israel and the tenor of the judgment is not repugnant to public policy."

The former provision as cited in the text created considerable difficulties of interpretation. In the course of negotiations of reciprocal agreements with other countries it also encountered objections.

BIBLIOGRAPHY AND INDEXES

BIBLIOGRAPHY

ABBO, HANNAN, *The Sacred Canons*, Vol. I (St. Louis, Mo. 1952)   125
AGO, "Positive Law and International Law", 51 (1957) *A.J.I.L.* 691   19, 28
— "Règles générales des conflits de lois", 58 (1936) *Recueil des Cours*, IV, 247   35
— *Scienza giuridica e diritto internazionale* (Milano 1950)   19
— *Teoria del diritto internazionale privato* (Padova 1934)   35
ALLEN, *Law in the Making* (7th ed., Oxford 1964)   134
ANZILOTTI, *Corso di diritto internazionale*, I (Padova 1955)   60, 65
— *Corso di diritto internazionale* (Roma 1928)   35, 74
AUSTIN, *Lectures on Jurisprudence* (5th ed., London 1885)   19

BACCARI, R., "Il sentimento religioso nell'interpretazione del Diritto Canonico", *Studi in Onore di Vicenzo Del Giudice*, I (Milano 1952)   107, 108
BALLADORE-PALLIERI, G., *Diritto internazionale privato* (Milano 1946)   57, 66
— "Le dottrine di Hans Kelsen e il problema dei rapporti fra diritto interno e diritto internazionale", 14 (1935) *Riv. dir. intern.* 24   40
BARAK, "On the Codification of Law", 3 (1973) *Iyune Mishpat* 5   200
BARTH, K., *Die Ordnung der Gemeinde* (München 1955)   22
BARTHOLOMEW, "Private Interpersonal Law", (1952) *Int. & Comp. L. Q.* 325   144, 145
BATIFFOL, *Aspects philosophiques du droit international privé* (Paris 1956)   33, 35, 41, 85
— *Droit international privé* (5e éd., Paris 1970)   35, 36, 41, 66, 85, 90, 91, 100, 127, 140, 145, 168, 183
BAUMLIN, "Staatslehre und Kirchenrechtslehre, über gemeinsame Fragen ihrer Grundproblematik", *Staatsverfassung und Kirchenordnung, Festgabe für Rudolf Smend* (Tübingen 1962), 3   22
BELGESAY, "La reception des lois étrangères en Turquie", (1956) *Annales de la Faculté de Droit d'Istanbul* 93   53
BELLINI, "Osservazioni sulla completezza dell'ordinamento giuridico canonico", (1957) *Il diritto ecclesiastico* 121   37
— "Per una sistemazione canonistica delle relazioni fra diritto della Chiesa e diritto dello Stato", 30 (1955) *Annuario di diritto comparato et di studi legislativi* 338   34, 35, 36, 41, 42, 45, 50, 59, 60
BERNARDINI, *Produzione di norme giuridiche mediante rinvio* (Milano 1966)   35, 36, 41, 50, 57, 58, 60, 63, 64, 65, 66, 67, 68, 69, 72, 81
BETTI, E., "Grundprobleme des internationalen Privatrechts", *Jus et Lex, Festschrift Max Gutzwiller* (Basel 1959)   40

BIBLIOGRAPHY

— *Problematica del diritto internazionale* (Milano 1956)   40, 41, 66, 68, 140
BOBBIO, N., "Antinomia", *Novissimo Digesto Italiano*, Vol. 1, 667   33
— "Sanzione", *Novissimo Digesto Italiano*, Vol. 16, 530   31
BOUSQUET, *Précis de Droit musulman* (3e éd., Alger)   24
BROGGINI, "Intertemporales Privatrecht", *Schweizerisches Privatrecht*, Vol. I (Basel 1969), 353   159

CAMMARATA, *Il concetto del diritto e la pluralità degli ordinamenti giuridici* (Catania 1926)   36
CANSACCHI, "Le choix et l'adaptation de la règle étrangère dans les conflits de lois", 83 (1953) II *Recueil des Cours* 79   199, 200
CAPPELLETTI, "Jura novit curia", *Scritti in memoria di Antonio Giuffrè*, II(Milano 1967), 143   91, 100
CAPUTO, G., *Il problema della qualificazione giuridica dello Stato in materia religiosa* (Milano 1967)   51
CARBONNIER, "Loi étrangère et jurisprudence étrangère", 62 (1935) *Clunet* 473   109
CARNELUTTI, *Teoria generale del diritto* (Roma 1940)   21
CAVERS, "Procedure for—and in—the Choice of Law Process", *The Choice-of-Law Process* (Ann Arbor 1965), 268   182
CHEATHAM, "American Theories of Conflict of Laws: Their Role and Utility", 58 (1944–45) *Harv. L. R.* 361   67
CHECCHINI, "Introduzione dommatica al diritto ecclesiastico italiano", *Scritti giuridici e storico-giuridici*, vol. III (Padova 1958), 11   51, 65
— "L'ordinamento canonico nel diritto italiano", *Scritti giuridici e storico-giuridici* (vol. III, Padova 1958), 67   51, 71, 72, 73
CHESHIRE, *Private International Law* (8th ed., London 1970)   89, 101, 182, 190, 195, 196
CIPROTTI, *Contributo alla teoria della canonizzazione delle leggi civili* (Roma 1941)   45
COHN, H., "On Those Who Immerse Themselves in the Halakha", *Mishpat Wekalkala* (*Law and Economics*), vol. 3, 129 (in Hebrew)   116, 117
COLOMER, A., "A propos du lien entre le droit et le religion dans les systèmes juridiques orientaux, le droit musulman existe-il?", *Etudes de droit contemporain* (*nouvelle série*) (Paris 1966), 67   24
CONTE, "Ordinamento giuridico", *Novissimo Digesto Italiano*, Vol. 12, 53   37
COOK, "Substance and 'Procedure'", *Logical and Legal Bases of Conflict of Law* (Cambridge Mass. 1942), 154   182
CRISAFULLI, V., "Fonti del diritto", *Enciclopedia del diritto*, vol. 17 (1968)   43
CROSS & WILKINS, *An Outline of the Law of Evidence* (3rd ed., London 1971)   99
CURRIE, "On the Displacement of the Law of the Forum", 58 (1958) *Col. L.R.* 964   91
— *Selected Essays on the Conflict of Laws* (Durham 1963)   91

D'AVACK, *Corso di Diritto canonico*, Vol. I, *Introduzione sistematica al diritto della Chiesa* (Milano 1956)   21, 22, 23, 32, 45, 107, 169

- "La posizione giuridica del diritto canonico nell'ordinamento italiano", (1939) *Archivio di diritto ecclesiastico* 205   50, 70, 72
- *Lezioni di diritto ecclesiastico italiano,* I (Milano 1963)   43
- *Trattato di diritto ecclesiastico italiano* (Milano 1964)   50, 70, 72

DAVID, C., *La loi étrangère devant de judge du fond* (Paris 1965)   36, 83, 90, 91, 99, 100, 101, 103, 109, 110

DE LUCA, *Diritto ecclesiastico ed esperienza giuridica* (Milano 1969)   19, 20, 21
- *Il concetto del diritto ecclesiastico nel suo sviluppo storico* (Padova 1946)   20
- *Rilevanza dell'ordinamento canonico nel diritto italiano* (Padova 1943)   20, 34, 35, 36, 38, 39, 42, 43, 57, 59, 63, 64, 65, 66, 67, 70, 71, 72, 73

DE NOVA, "New Trends in Italian Private International Law", 28 (1963) *Law & Contemp. Problems* 808   66

DEL GIUDICE, *Manuale di diritto ecclesiastico* (10a ed., Milano 1964)   71, 124, 147
- "Note conclusive circa la questione del metodo nello studio del diritto canonico", (1940) *Arch. di dir. eccl.* 3   107
- *Nozioni di diritto canonico* (11a ed., Milano 1962)   45, 107, 116

DEL VECCHIO, "A propos de la conception étatique du droit", *Justice-Droit-Etat* (Paris 1938), 282   22

DERRETT, "Statutory Amendments of Personal Law of Hindus since Indian Independence", *Rapports généraux au Ve. Congrès international de droit comparé,* I (Brussels 1960), 101   95
- "Statutory Amendments of the Personal Law of Hindus since Indian Independence", 7 (1958) *A.J.C.L.* 380   95

DICEY & MORRIS, *Conflict of Laws* (9th ed., London 1973)   89, 91, 101, 146, 182, 195, 196

DICKSTEIN (Dykan), "Jewish Law in the Framework of the Law of Palestine", 2 (1945) *HaPraklit* 291   93
- *Law of Marriage and Divorce* (Tel Aviv 1957) (in Hebrew)   27

DÖLLE, H., "De l'application du droit étranger par le juge interne", 44 (1955) *Rev. crit. dr. int. pr.* 233   41

EHRENZWEIG, *Conflict of Laws* (St. Paul 1962)   91, 92, 101, 105

EICHMANN & MÖRSDORF, *Lehrbuch des Kirchenrechts*, 1. Band (11. Aufl., Paderborn 1964)   21, 45, 108

ELGEDDAWY, *Relations entre systèmes confessionnel et laïque en droit international privé* (Paris 1971)   140

ELON, M., "Jewish Law in the Law of the State", 25 (1969) *HaPraklit* 27   28, 54, 96
- *Jewish Law—History, Sources, Principles,* vol. 3 (Jerusalem 1973) (in Hebrew)   54, 116, 117
- *Religious Legislation* (1968) (in Hebrew)   54, 62

ENGISCH, *Die Einheit der Rechtsordnung* (Heidelberg 1935)   34, 35
- *Einführung in das juristische Denken* (5. Aufl., Stuttgart 1971)   34, 58, 103

ENGLARD, "Il diritto ecclesiastico italiano visto da un giurista straniero", (1968) *Il diritto ecclesiastico* 22   51
- "The Problem of Jewish Law in a Jewish State", 3 (1968) *Isr. L. Rev.* 254   27, 54, 94, 105, 108

— "The Relationship between Religion and State in Israel", *Scripta Hierosolymitana* (Jerusalem 1965), vol. 16, 254   30, 45
— "The Status of the Council of the Chief Rabbinate and the Review Authority of the High Court of Justice", 22 (1965) *HaPraklit* 68   30, 122, 123, 124
— "The Witness' Oath—A Requirement of the Torah?" 21 (1965) *HaPraklit* 435   128
ENNECCERUS-NIPPERDEY, *Allgemeiner Teil des bürgerlichen Rechts* (14. Aufl., Tübingen 1955)   58
ESSER, *Grundsatz und Norm in der richterlichen Fortbildung des Privatrechts* (Tübingen 1956)   104
— *Vorverständnis und Methodenwahl in der Rechtsfindung* (Frankfurt/M 1970)   104
ETTER, K.H., *Vom Einfluss des Souveränitätsgedankens auf das Internationale Privatrecht* (Zürich 1959)   65, 66

FALCO, *Corso di diritto ecclesiastico*, II (Padova 1938)   147
FEDELE, "Certezza del diritto ed aequitas canonica", *Lo spirito del diritto canonico* (Padova 1962) 197   108
— "Diritto canonico", *Enciclopedia del diritto*, Vol. XII (1964), 871   21, 22, 23, 24, 107
— *Discorsi sul diritto canonico* (Roma 1973)   22, 108
— "Il problema del metodo nello studio del diritto canonico", *Lo spirito del diritto canonico* (Padova 1962), 35   107
— "L'equità canonica", *Discorsi sul diritto canonico* (Roma 1973), 59   108
— *Lo Spirito del diritto canonico* (Padova 1962)   23, 169
— "Natura pubblica del diritto canonico", *Lo spirito del diritto canonico* (Padova 1962), 823   169
FEINBERG, "'Obiter Dictum' which Calls for Interpretation (People and Nation, Religious Law and National Law)", 10 (1954) *HaPraklit* 289   27, 74
FELLER, "Reference and Reception Provisions", 25 (1969) *HaPraklit* 320   69
FINOCCHIARO, *Matrimonio* (Bologna 1971)   147, 148
FLEINER, "Geistliches Weltrecht und weltliches Staatsrecht", *Ausgewählte Schriften und Reden* (Zürich 1941)   32
FLEINER & GIACOMETTI, *Schweizerisches Bundesstaatsrecht* (Zürich 1949)   43
FORCHIELLI, "La giuridicità del diritto canonico al vaglio della dottrina contemporanea", *Studi in onore di V. Del Giudice*, Vol. 2 (Milano 1953), 471   21, 23
FRANCESCAKIS, "Sulla funzione delle norme di diritto internazionale privato", 45 (1956) *Revue critique de droit international privé* 603   65
FRIEDRICH, O., *Einführung in das Kirchenrecht* (Göttingen 1961)   21, 22
FREIMAN, "Maintenance of the Child Born out of Wedlock Under the Religious Law of Israel", 2 (1945) *HaPraklit* 163   93

GARNER, *Administrative Law* (3rd ed., London 1970)   161
GARAZZI, *Delle Antinomie* (1959)   33
GENY, *Science et technique en droit privé positif*, vol. 1 (Paris 1913)   31

GERMANN, *Grundlagen der Rechtswissenschaft* (Bern 1950) 32
GHIRARDINI, C., "La comunità internazionale e il suo diritto", 13 (1919) *Riv. dir. intern.* 3 35, 66
GIACCHI, *La giurisdizione ecclesiastica nel diritto italiano* (2a ed., Milano 1970) 70
— L'ordinamento della Chiesa nel diritto italiano attuale", *Chiesa e Stato* (Milano 1939), vol. II., 345 50, 51, 70, 72
GINZBURG, Y.M., *Law for Israel* (Jerusalem 1956) (in Hebrew) 115
GISMONDI, *Il potere di certificazione della Chiesa nel diritto italiano* (Milano 1943) 49, 50
GIULIANO, M., "Le traitement du droit étranger dans le procès civil dans les systèmes juridiques continentaux", 14 (1962) *Rev. int. de droit comparé* 5 83, 100
GLOBUS, "Responsa Concerning Family Law and Personal Status (Who is a Jew Under Existing Law)", 10 (1954) *HaPraklit* 225 59
— "Responsa in Matters of Family Law and Personal Status", 10 (1954) *HaPraklit* 225 73
GOADBY, *International and Interreligious Private Law in Palestine* (Jerusalem 1926) 125, 126
GOLDMAN, E., *Religious Issues in Israel's Political Life* (Jerusalem 1964) 30
GOLDSCHMIDT, "Jacques Maury et les aspects philosophiques du droit international privé", *Mélanges Maury*, t. 1., 152 36, 41, 84
— "Système et philosophie du droit international privé", 45 (1956) *Revue critique de droit international privé* 234 140
GRAULICH, "Règles de conflit et règles d'application immédiate", *Mélanges Dabin*, II (Paris 1963), 629 141
GRAVESON, *Conflict of Laws* (6th ed., London 1969) 182
GULAK, *The Foundations of Jewish Law,* vol. 4 (in Hebrew) 115, 117, 119

HANBURY, *Modern Equity* (9th ed., London 1969) 151
HARNON, E., "The Duty to Testify and Privileged Evidence in Rabbinical Courts", 21 (1965) *HaPraklit* 283 154
— "The Judge's Initiative in Calling Witnesses", 19 (1953) *HaPraklit* 246 100
— *The Law of Evidence*, Part I (Jerusalem 1970) (in Hebrew) 181, 190
HART, *The Concept of Law* (Oxford 1961) 34, 35, 37, 40, 42, 103, 104
HAUSER, *Norm, Recht und Staat* (Wien 1968) 20, 21, 38, 39, 43
HERZOG, I., *The Main Institutions of Jewish Law* Vol. 1 (2nd ed., London 1965) 117
HOOPER, C.A., *The Civil Law of Palestine and Trans-Jordan* (London 1934) 55
HUET, *Les conflits de lois en matière de preuve* (Paris 1965) 181
HURGRONJE SNOUCK, C., De la nature du 'droit' musulman", *Oeuvres choisis* (Leiden 1957), 256 24

ISRAELI, *Amud HaJemini (The Right-Hand Pillar)* (Tel Aviv 1966) (in Hebrew) 117, 121

JEMOLO, "Ancora sui concetti giuridici", *Pagine sparse di diritto e storiografia* (Milano 1957), 117 51

- "I concetti giuridici", *Pagine sparse di diritto e storiografia* (Milano 1957), 100 — 51
- "Il valore del diritto della Chiesa nell'ordinamento giuridico italiano", 90 (1923) *Archivio giuridico* 3 — 71
- "La Chiesa e il suo diritto", 39 (1925) *Archivio giuridico* 245 — 71
- "La classifica dei rapporti fra Stato e Chiesa", *Pagine sparse di diritto e storiografia* (Milano 1957), 69 — 46, 50, 51
- *Lezioni di diritto ecclesiastico* (2a ed., Milano 1957) — 29, 50, 71
- *Premesse ai rapporti tra Chiesa e Stato,* (Milano 1965) — 29
- "Un caso di abuso di astrattismo giuridico", *Pagine sparse di diritto e storiografia* (Milano 1957), 265 — 108, 116

JHERING VON, *Der Zweck im Recht,* 1. Band, (2. Aufl. Leipzig 1884) — 19

JENKS, C.W., "The Authority in English Courts of Decisions of the Permanent Court of International Justice", 20 (1939) *B.Y.I.L.* 1 — 130, 131, 134
- "The Interpretation and Application of Municipal Law by the Permanent Court of International Justice", 19 (1938) *B.Y.I.L.* 67 — 110

KAUFMANN, E., "Kritik der neukantianischen Rechtsphilosophie", *Gesammelte Schriften* vol. 3 (Göttingen 1960), 193 — 37

KEGEL, *Internationales Privatrecht* (3. Aufl. München 1971) — 85, 91, 100, 109, 111, 127, 199

KELSEN, "Allgemeine Staatslehre", *Enzyklopädie der Rechts und Staatswissenschaft*, Abt. Rechtswissenschaft, XXIII, (Berlin 1925), 133 — 20, 43
- *Das Problem der Souveränität und die Theorie des Völkerrechts* (Tübingen 1920) — 35, 37, 39, 40, 45
- *General Theory of Law and State* (New York 1961) — 34, 36, 37, 38, 39, 41
- *Hauptprobleme der Staatsrechtslehre* (2. Aufl., Tübingen 1923) — 37
- *Pure Theory of Law* (Berkeley 1970) — 20, 23, 31, 33, 34, 36, 37, 38, 58, 66, 104
- *Reine Rechtslehre* (2. Aufl., Wien 1960) — 35

KELSEN & TUCKER, *Principles of International Law* (2nd ed., New York 1967) — 36, 38, 39, 40

KLUG, "Note", 2 (1945) *HaPraklit* 209 — 93

KOLLEWIJN, "Conflicts of Western and Non-Western Law", 4 (1951) *Int. L.Q.* 307 — 145

LAGARDE, *Recherches sur l'ordre public en droit international privé* (Paris 1959) — 141, 146, 168

LAMPUE, "Les conflits de lois interrégionaux et interpersonnels dans le système juridique français", 43 (1954) *Rev. crit. dr. int. privé* 249 — 145

LARENZ, *Methodenlehre der Rechtswissenschaft* (2. Aufl. Berlin 1969) — 34, 37, 39, 51, 58, 59, 82, 104

LASSON, *System der Rechtsphilosophie* (Berlin 1882) — 19, 20

LATHAM, *The Law and the Commonwealth* (London 1949) — 35

LECHLEITNER, *Der Mensh zwischen Staat und Kirche* (Zürich 1957) — 19, 32, 36, 44

LESAGE, *La nature du droit canonique* (Ottawa 1960) — 21, 22, 23, 24, 32, 108, 169

LEVINGER, "Will Civil Marriages Split the Nation?," (1966) *Ovnaim* 65 (in Hebrew) — 106

LEVONTIN, "Book review", (1962) *HaPraklit* 182 25
— *Marriages and Divorces out of the Jurisdiction* (Jerusalem 1957) (in
   Hebrew) 137, 138, 148, 149, 151, 191, 201, 202
— *The Myth of International Security* (Jerusalem 1958) 20
LEVONTIN & GOLDWATER, *Conflict of Law in Israel and Art. 46 of the
   Palestine Order in Council* (Jerusalem 1974) (in Hebrew) 179
LEWALD, "Règles générales des conflits de lois", 69 (1939) III *Recueil des
   Cours* 1 199
— *Règles générales des conflits de lois* (1941) 59, 200
LINANT DE BELLEFONDS, Y., *Rev. int. dr. comp.* (1964) 644 24
LIPSTEIN, K., "The General Principles of Private International Law", 135
   (1972) I *Recueil des Cours* 97 199, 200

MAGNI, *Teoria del diritto ecclesiastico civile*, I (2a ed., Padova 1952) 55, 56, 74
MALAURIE, *L'ordre public et le contract* (Reims 1953) 169
MANTEL, *Studies in the History of the Sanhedrin* (Tel Aviv 1969) (in Hebrew) 115
MARGIOTTA BROGLIO, F., La qualificazione giuridica delle relazioni fra lo
   Stato Italiano e la Chiesa Cattolica", 165 (1963) *Archivio Giuridico*
   53 36, 50, 70, 72
MAURY, "Aspects philosophiques du droit international privé", 46 (1957)
   Rev. crit. du dr. int. privé 229 41
— *L'éviction de la loi normalement competente: l'ordre public et la fraude
   à la loi* (Valladolid 1952) 140, 141, 143, 168
— "Règles des conflits de lois", (1936) III *Recueil des Cours* 329 41
MCCORMICK, T., "Judicial Notice", 5 (1951–52) *Vanderbilt L.R.* 296 99
MECHLOWITCH, A., "Finality of Judgments in Jewish Law", *Dine Israel,
   an Annual of Jewish Law and Israeli Family Law,* vol. 1 (Jerusalem
   1969) (in Hebrew) 7 115, 117
MEISE, *Zur Relativität der Vorbehaltsklausel im internationalen und
   interlokalen Privatrecht* (Hamburg 1966) 140, 146, 168, 170
MERON, S., "Jewish Law in the Law Reports of 1968–1969", *Dine Israel,
   an Annual of Jewish Law and Israeli Family Law* (Z. Falk, ed.) vol.
   1 (Jerusalem 1969) (in Hebrew) 101 96
MILLER, "Federal Rule 44.1 and the 'Fact' Approach to Determining
   Foreign Law: Death knell for a Die-Hard Doctrine", 65 (1966–1967)
   Michigan L. R. 615 89, 129
MILLIOT, *Introduction à l'étude du droit musulman* (Paris 1952) 24
MOORE, *Federal Practice*, (2d ed., New York 1965) 110
MORELLI, "Limiti dell'ordinamento statuale e limiti della giurisdizione",
   (1933) *Riv. Dir. Int.* 391 67
— *Nozioni di diritto internazionale* (5a ed., Padova 1958) 42, 43
MORGAN, "Choice-of-Law Governing Proof", 58 *Harv. L.R.* 153 182
MORGENSTERN, F., "Judicial Practice and the Supremacy of International
   Law", 27 (1950) *B.Y.I.L.* 42 131
MOSHEWITZ, D., "Violation of the Rules of Natural Justice and its Consequences",
   3 (1971) *Mishpatim* 84 167
MOTULSKI, "L'office du juge et la loi étrangère", *Mélanges Maury* 337 100

NEUHAUS, P.H., *Die Grundbegriffe des internationalen Privatrechts* (Berlin-Tübingen 1962) 40, 140, 141,146, 148, 168, 199, 201, 202

NIBOYET, "Qu'est-ce que la loi étrangère aux yeux des juges d'un pays déterminé", (1928) *Revue de droit international et de législation camparée* 753 109, 110, 114, 132

NIEDERER, W., *Einführung in die allgemeinen Lehren des internationalen Privatrechts* (3. Aufl., Zürich 1961) 66, 110

— "Ordre Public in der neueren Rechtssprechung des Bundesgerichts", 62 (1943) *ZSR* 1 140, 141

NUSSBAUM, A., "The Problem of Proving Foreign Law", 50 (1940–41) *Yale L.J.*, 1018 83, 91, 92, 109, 110, 127, 129

O'CONNELL, *International Law*, Vol. I, (London 1965) 131

OMAR, "La codification d'une partie du droit musulman dans l'empire ottoman", 4 (1954) *Annales de la Faculté de droit d'Istanbul* 90 55

OPPENHEIM, LAUTERPACHT, *International Law* (8th ed., London 1955) 36

PARESCE, E., "Dogmatica giuridica", *Enciclopedia del diritto*, vol. 13, 699 34

PATON, *Jurisprudence* (4th ed., Oxford 1972) 19, 20, 31, 83

PAU, *Caratteri del riconoscimento di situazioni giuridiche straniere nell'ordinamento italiano* (Milano 1958) 63

— "Limiti di applicazione del diritto straniero nell'ordinamento italiano", 52 (1969) *Rivista di diritto internazionale* 477 140

PAULSEN, SOVERN, "Public Policy in the Conflict of Laws", (1956) *Col. L. Rev.* 969 146

PERASSI, *Lezioni di diritto internazionale*, vol. II (Padova 1952) 35, 49, 55, 57, 60, 67, 68

— "Teoria dommatica delle fonti di norme giuridiche in diritto internazionale" 6 (1971) *Riv. dir. int.* 195 34

PERELMAN (ed.), *Le fait et le droit, Etudes de logique juridique* (Brussels 1961) 83

PERLES, S., "Rabbinical Courts Jurisdiction (Marriage and Divorce) Law, 5713–1953, and its Relationship to Earlier Laws", 10 (1954) *HaPraklit* 272 59

PESCATORE, *Introduction à la science du droit* (Louxembourg 1960) 58

PETRONCELLI, *Manuale di diritto ecclesiastico* (Napoli 1961) 72

PHIPSON, *Evidence* (11th ed., London 1970) 99

PRIVAT, G., "Des Patriarcats catholiques d'Orient et de la juridiction suprême de la sainte Cour de Rome en pays Ottoman pour les procès matrimoniaux", 22 (1895) *Clunet* 994 125, 126

RAAPE, *Deutsches Internationales Privatrecht*, I (Berlin 1938) 140, 142, 168

— "Les rapports juridiques entre parents et enfants", 50 (1934) *Recueil des Cours* 403 200

RABEL, E., *The Conflict of Laws* (Ann Arbor 1958), Vol. I 65, 67

RABELLO, "Non Liquet: From Modern Law to Roman Law", 9 (1974) *Is. L.R.* 63 193

RAKOVER, N., *The Jewish Law of Agency in Legal Proceedings* (Jerusalem 1972) (in Hebrew)   54
— "The Principles of Hebrew Law in the Gift Law, 5728–1968" 24 (1969) *HaPraklit* 496   54
RAZ, *The Concept of Legal System* (Oxford 1970)   35
RHEINSTEIN, M., "Types of Reception", 6 (1956) *Annales de la Faculté de Droit d'Istanbul* 33   49, 53
RIEZLER, *Internationales Zivilprozessrecht* (Tübingen 1949)   182
RIGAUX, F., *Droit international privé* (Brussels 1968)   81, 100, 143
ROMANO, S., *Corso di diritto costituzionale* (6a ed., Padova 1941)   71
— *L'ordinamento giuridico* (Pisa 1918)   20, 41
ROSETTI, "L'autorité judiciare du Pape dans L'Empire Ottoman", *L'Egypte Contemporaine* (1912), 371   125
RUBINSTEIN, A., *Jurisdiction and Illegality* (Oxford 1965)   162, 166
— *The Constitutional Law of the State of Israel* (2nd ed., Tel Aviv 1974) (in Hebrew)   122

SALANT, A., *The Law of Evidence* (Tel Aviv 1963) (1969 Supplement) (in Hebrew)   84
SAPIENZA, "Il principio 'iura novit curia' e il problema della prova delle leggi straniere", 1961) *Riv. trim. dir. proc. civile* 41   100
SASS, S.L., "Foreign Law in Civil Litigation, a Comparative Survey", 16 (1968) *A.J.C.L.* 332   83, 89, 100
SAVIGNY, *System des heutigen roemischen Rechts* (Berlin 1849), vol. VIII   149
SCADUTO, F., *Diritto ecclesiastico vigente in Italia*, (2a ed., Torino 1892, 1894), Vol. I, Vol. II   20
SCHIAPPOLI, D., *Manuale di diritto ecclesiastico* (Napoli 1913)   20
SCHREY, V.V., *Die Generation der Entscheidung* (München 1955)   22
SCHRÖDER, J., *Die Anpassung von Kollisions—und Sachnormen* (Berlin 1961)   199, 204
SEIDMAN, "The Judicial Process Reconsidered in the Light of Role-Theory", 32 (1969) *M.L.R.* 516   104
SFORZA, W.C., Il diritto dei privati", (1929) *Riv. it. per le scienze giuridiche*, fasc. I–II   36
SHAKI, "Civil Marriage contracted between Jews outside Israel—A Cause for Granting a 'Permit to Marry' to the Husband", 22 (1966) *HaPraklit* 347   137
— "Effect of Civil Marriages between Jews contracted outside Israel—in Rabbinical Courts in Israel", 20 (1964) *HaPraklit* 385   137, 138
— "The Confusion of Spheres and the Restriction of the Religious Jurisdiction", 21–22 (1965) *Gevilin* 38 (in Hebrew)   84, 129, 134, 135, 190, 191
— "The Criterion 'Domicile' and its Preference over the Criterion of Nationality in Israel Private International Law", *Scripta Hierosolymitana*, Vol. XVI (Jerusalem 1966), 163   88
SHAPIRA, A., *The Interest Approach to Choice of Law* (The Hague 1970)   182
SHAWA, M., "Error in the Determination of Jewishness which Denies Jurisdiction", 25 (1970) *HaPraklit* 617   84, 112, 113, 116, 117, 123, 134

BIBLIOGRAPHY

- "The Mode of the Application of the Family Law Amendment (Maintenance) Law, 5719–1959, to Spouse and Child Maintenance", 3 (1973) *Iyune Mishpat* 337   197, 198
- "The Nature and Manner of Proving Foreign Law in Anglo-American Law and in Israeli Law", 3 (1974) *Iyune Mishpat* 725   92, 97

SHERESHEVSKI, *Family Law* (2nd ed., Jerusalem 1967) (in Hebrew)   105, 106, 156, 158, 189, 192, 195, 202, 204, 205, 206, 207

SHIFMAN, P., "Child Welfare in the Rabbinical Court", 5 (1974) *Mishpatim* 421   106, 154
- *Doubtful Marriage in Israeli Law* (Doctoral Thesis, Jerusalem 1972) (in Hebrew)   192, 193, 194
- "Jurisdiction and Law in Paternity Matters", 4 *Mishpatim* 664   189
- "The Status of Doubt", 33 (1967) *De'ot* 153 (in Hebrew)   192, 195

SHILO, S., *Dina De-Malkhuta Dina, The Law of the State is Law* (Jerusalem 1974)   45

SIDAROUSS, S., *Des Patriarcats* (Paris 1907)   13, 125

SILBERG, *Personal Status in Israel* (Jerusalem 1957) (in Hebrew)   27, 59, 62, 76, 88, 91, 136, 160, 161, 164, 191
- *Talmudic Law and the Modern State* (New York 1973)   24, 69

SIMITIS, *Gute Sitten und Ordre public* (Marburg 1960)   169

SOHM, RUDOLPH, *Kirchenrecht*, I (Leipzig 1892)   21

SOLOVEICHIK, JOSEPH, RABBI, "The Man of *Halakha*", (1944) *Talpioth* 65 (in Hebrew)   25

SOLUS, *Traité sur la condition des indigènes en droit privé* (Paris 1927)   144

SOMLÓ, *Juristische Grundlehre* (Leipzig 1917)   19

SPERDUTI, G., *Saggi di teoria generale del diritto internazionale privato* (Milano 1967)   140

SPINELLI, *La trascrizione del matrimonio canonico* (Milano 1966)   147

STERNBERG, M., "The Basic Norm of the Law in Israel", 9 (1953) *HaPraklit* 129   43

STONE, *Legal System and Lawyers' Reasoning* (London 1964)   104, 134
- "Two Theories of 'The Institution' ", *Essays in Jurisprudence in Honour of Roscoe Pound* (1962), 296   20, 33, 35

SZASZY, I., *International Civil Procedure, A Comparative Study* (Budapest 1967)   180, 181, 190
- "Interpersonal Conflicts of Laws", *Multitudo Legum-Ius Unum* (Berlin 1973) Band 2, 793   50, 66, 137, 144, 145, 147, 205
- "Le conflit de lois interpersonnel dans les pays en voie de développement", 138 (1973) I *Recueil des Cours* 81   144

TEDESCHI, "Note di diritto matrimoniale israeliano (in margine a una polemica altrui)", *Raccolta di scritti in onore di A.C. Jemolo*, Vol. IV, 629   75
- "On Reception and on the Legislative Policy of Israel", *Scripta Hierosolymitana*, Vol. XVI (Jerusalem 1966), 11   49, 53, 54, 61
- "On the Choice Between Religious and Secular Law in the Legal System of Israel", *Studies in Israel Law* (Jerusalem 1960), 238   69, 75, 77, 90, 156
- "On the Inductive Study of Law", *Studies in Israel Law* (Jerusalem 1960), 1   28

— "On the Principle of *Stare Decisis*", *Studies in Israel Law* (Jerusalem 1960), 114　　　　　　　　　　　　　　　　　　　　　　　　　111, 132
— "On the Problem of Marriage in the State of Israel", *Studies in Israel Private Law* (Jerusalem 1966) 218　　　　　　　　　　　153, 154, 155
— "One Hundred Years of the Mejelle", 25 (1969) *HaPraklit* 312　　　55
— "Paralipomena on *Stare Decisis*", 17 (1961) *HaPraklit* 244　　108, 131, 132, 134
— "Recent Trends in *Stare Decisis*", 22 (1966) *HaPraklit* 320　　　133, 135
— "The Problem of Lacunae in the Law and Article 46 of Palestine Order in Council, 1922", *Studies in Israel Law* (Jerusalem 1960), 166　　69, 111
— "Transition from Secular to Religious Matrimonial Status, and the Retroactive Application of the Latter", *Studies in Israel Private Law* (Jerusalem 1966), 212　　　　　　　　　　　　　　　　27, 138, 202
— "Volontà privata autonoma", (1929) *Riv. int. di filosofia del diritto*, fasc. VI　36
TRIEPEL, "Les rapports entre le droit interne et le droit international", (1923) *Recueil des Cours* 77　　　　　　　　　　　　　　　　54, 60, 64
— *Völkerrecht und Landesrecht* (Leipzig 1899)　　　54, 60, 61, 63, 64, 68, 69, 71

UNGER, "Use and Abuse of Statutes in the Conflict of Laws", 83 (1967) *L.Q.R.* 427　　　　　　　　　　　　　　　　　　　　　　　　　　141

VALLINDAS, "Der Vorbehalt des Ordre public im internationalen Privatrecht", 18 (1953) *Rabels Zeitschrift für ausländisches und internationales Privatrecht* 1　　　　　　　　　　　　　　　　　　　170
VISCHER, "Internationales Privatrecht", *Schweizerisches Privatrecht* I (Basel-Stuttgart 1969), 509　　　　　　　　　　　　　　　　140, 146
VITTA, E., "Religious Courts and their Jurisdiction in Palestine and Their Legal Nature", 3 (1946) *HaPraklit* 70, reprinted, 65 (1969) *HaPraklit* 174　　　　　　　　　　　　　　　　　　　　　　　　　　　77, 84
— *Conflict of Laws in Matters of Personal Status in Palestine*, (Tel Aviv 1947)　　　　　　　　　　　　　　　　　　60, 84, 125, 126, 144, 145
— *Conflitti interni ed internazionali*, vol. I, II (Torino 1954, 1955)　　46, 137, 144, 145, 169
— "The Conflict of Personal Laws", 5 (1970) *Is. L. Rev.* 170, 337　　144, 145, 146, 147

WADE, *Administrative Law* (3rd ed., Oxford 1971)　　　　　　　　161
WAHLER, "Die Bindung religiöser Gerichte an Normen des staatlichen Privat-und Verfahrensrechts", *Multitudo Legum—Ius Unum*, Band II (Berlin 1973), 865　　　　　　　　　　　　　　　　　　　153, 154
WAHRHAFTIG, Z., *Rabbinical Jurisdiction in Israel* (Tel Aviv 1955) (in Hebrew)　　　　　　　　　　　　　　　　　　　　　　　　　46
WALKER, *The Law of Evidence in Scotland* (Edinburgh and Glasgow 1964)　　　　　　　　　　　　　　　　　　　　　　　　　99, 100
WALZ, *Völkerrecht und staatliches Recht* (Stuttgart 1933)　　　　68, 69
WIETHÖLTER, *Einseitige Kollisionsnormen als Grundlage des internationalen Privatrechts* (Berlin 1956)　　　　　　　　　　　　　　　141
WENGLER, "Betrachtungen über den Zusammenhang der Rechtsnormen in der Rechtsordnung und die Verschiedenheit der Rechtsordnungen," *Festschrift Laun* (Hamburg 1953), 719　　　　　　　　　　　35

— "Die Qualifikation der materiellen Rechtssätze im internationalen
Privatrecht", *Festschrift Wolff* (Tübingen 1952), 337 204
— "General Principles of Private International Law", 104 (1961) III
Recueil des Cours 273 156
— "Grundprobleme des interreligiösen Kollisionsrechts", *Aphieroma eis
Charalampon N. Phragkistan* (Thessaloniki 1967), 483 138
— *Völkerrecht*, Band 1 (Berlin 1964) 61, 66, 68, 69
WOLF, ERIK, *Ordnung der Kirche* (Frankfurt a/M 1961) 22
WOLF, ERNST, "Sinn und Grenze der Anwendung der Zwei-Reiche-Lehre
auf das Kirchenrecht", *Staatsverfassung und Kirchenordnung, Festgabe
für Rudolf Smend* (Tübingen 1962), 443 22
WOLFF, M., *Private International Law* (2nd ed., Oxford 1950) 97, 109, 110,
127, 140, 168, 180, 181, 190

YOUNG, *Corps de droit ottoman* (Oxford 1905) Vol. II 13, 30

ZAJTAY, "The Application of Foreign Law", *International Encyclopedia of
Comparative Law*, vol. III, ch. 14. (1972) 83, 86, 89, 90, 91, 100, 110, 127
— Zur Stellung des ausländischen Rechts im französischen internationalen
Privatrecht (Berlin 1963) 83, 86, 127, 134
ZANCHINI, F., *La Chiesa come ordinamento sacramentale* (Milano 1968) 23, 24
ZITELMANN, *Internationales Privatrecht*, I (München 1914) (1. Aufl., 1897) 59, 63

NOTES

"Authority in State Courts of Lower Federal Court Decisions on National
Law", 48 (1948) *Col. L.R.* 943 110
"How a Federal Court Determines State Law", 59 (1946) *Harv. L.R.* 1299 110
"Proof of the Law of Foreign Countries; Appellate Review and Subsequent Litigation", 72 (1958–59) *Harv. L. Rev.* 318 127, 129, 130, 133

TABLE OF LEGISLATION

Adoption of Children Law, 5720–1960
   section 24   153, 154, 155
Agency Law, 5725–1965
   section 2   54
Anatomy and Pathology Law, 5713–1953
   In general   54
Bailment Law, 5727–1967
   In general   54
Bankruptcy Ordinance, 1936
   In general   53
Bills of Exchange Ordinance, 1929
   In general   53
British Law Ascertainment Act, 1859
   In general   89
Capacity and Guardianship Law, 5722–1962
   section 17   159
   section 25   159
   section 79   154
Carriage of Goods by Sea Ordinance, 1926
   In general   57
Civil Procedure Rules, 5723–1963
   Rule 182(a)   127
   Rule 192   59
Civil Wrongs Ordinance, 1944
   In general   53, 95
Company Ordinance, 1929
   In general   53
Courts Law, 5717–1957
   section 7   113, 148, 162
     "   7(a)   162
     "   7(b)   162
     "   7(b)(4)   167
     "   33   127, 128, 129, 131, 134, 155
     "   33(b)   128
     "   35   134, 152
     "   48(8)   88, 102

TABLE OF LEGISLATION

Criminal Law Ordinance, 1936
In general 53, 95
section 146 60

Dayanim Law, 5716–1955
section 4 118
" 8(a) 118
" 8(c) 118

Evidence Ordinance [New Version], 5731–1971
section 2 187

Family Law Amendment (Maintenance) Law, 5719–1959
section 1(a) 189
" 2 . . . . 63, 197, 198
" 3 . . . . 63, 189, 197, 198
" 3(b) 68, 156
" 6 197
" 17 205

Foreign Judgments Enforcement Law, 5718–1958
In general 126
section 3(3) 139, 141
" 4(a) 67
" 6 167

Foreign Law Ascertainment Act, 1861
In general 89

Interpretation Ordinance, 1945 (New Version, 1954)
In general 53, 84, 93, 99, 101, 102, 126, 127, 128, 178
section 1 . . . . 114, 130, 131
" 33 . . . . 85, 93, 94, 96, 97, 98, 127, 193

Knesset Israel Regulations, 1928
In general 122

Law of Contracts (General Part), 5733–1973
section 30 . . . . 28, 169

Law of Return, 5710–1950
In general 61, 62

Law of Return (Amendment No. 2), 5730–1970
Section 4B 62

Local Authorities (Special Enablement) Law, 5717–1956
In general 82

Marriage Age Law, 5710–1950
section 3 154

Matrimonial Property Relations Law, 5733–1973
section 4 . . . . 158, 206
" 13(2) 153, 156

Mejelle
In general 55

Palestine Order in Council, 1922
In general 126

Article 35	57, 89
" 46	69, 91, 95, 111, 179, 191
" 47	26, 102, 143, 177, 178, 179
" 51	63, 96, 189
" 51(ii)(b)	73
" 54	60
" 55	89
" 64	26, 88, 178
" 64(ii)	27
" 64(iii)	89, 92, 94, 96
" 83	142

Palestine Order in Council (Holy Places), 1924
  In general   60

Penal Law Amendment (Bigamy) Law, 5719–1959
In general	96, 155
section 2	156
" 4	27
" 5	70, 150, 156, 157
" 6	70
" 8	160, 161

Procedural Rules of Rabbinical Courts in Israel, 5720–1960
In general	118
rule 116	117, 120
" 117	117

Prohibiting of Pig Raising Law, 5723–1963
  In general   54

Prohibition of Defamation Law, 5725–1965
  In general   54

Protection of Holy Places (The Tomb of Rabbi Shimon Bar Yohai in Meron) Regulations, 5728–1968
  In general   60

Protection of Holy Places Law, 5727–1967
  In general   60

Rabbinical Courts Jurisdiction (Marriage and Divorce) Law, 5713–1953
In general	70, 73, 88
section 1	59, 150
" 2	68, 160, 173, 175, 176
" 4	155
" 9	155

Religious Courts (Summons) Law, 5716–1956
  section 5   154

State Education Law, 5713–1953
In general	60
section 18	60

Succession Law, 5725–1965
section 3(c)	189
" 10(2)	189

227

TABLE OF LEGISLATION

section 11(2)	205
" 56–65	206
" 57(b)	206
" 59	206
" 148	153, 206
" 155	155
" 155(b)	155, 156
Succession Ordinance (1923)	
section 13	185
Women's Equal Rights Law, 5711–1951	
In general	44, 155, 198, 207
section 2	158, 206
" 3(b)	159
" 7	153, 155, 159

RELIGIOUS LEGAL SOURCES

JEWISH

Babylonian Talmud	
Gittin, 36 b	116
Shabbat, 31a	108, 116
Yebamoth, 13–14	121
Maimonides	
Hilkhot Avodat Kokhavim, XII, 14	121
Hilkhot Edut, IX, 1	185
Hilkhot Mamrim, I, 1	115, 116
Hilkhot Sanhedrin, XXIV, 4	115
Mishna	
Eduyot, I, 5	116
Shulhan Arukh	
Hoshen Mishpat, 35	185
Yoreh Deah, 245, 22	118

CATHOLIC

Codex Juris Canonici	
can. 17	124
cann. 1597–1605	125

TABLE OF CASES

1. Israel and Palestine Cases (according to the Parties) *

A. v. B. (C.A. 447/58, 13 P.D. 903)	189
A. v. B. (C.A. 275/61, 15 P.D. 2300)	189
A. v. B. (C.A. 460/67, 22 P.D. (1) 157)	191
Abu Chorash v. Sharia Court of Acco (H.C.J. 111/63, 18 P.D. (1) 589)	87
Abu Khalil v. C.E.O. Jerusalem (H.C. 11/43, 1943 A.L.R. 143)	126
A.G. v. Avraham (C.A. 164/67, 220/67, 22 P.D. (1) 29)	86
A.G. v. Matana (F.H. 13/60, 16 P.D. 430)	133
A.G. v. Melnik (Cr. A. 85/38, (1939) 1 S.C.J. 15)	92, 94
A.G. v. Yagoda (Cr. A. 141/60, 14 P.D. 1355)	**92**
Al-Tzafdi v. Benjamin (C.A. 86/63, 17 P.D. 1419)	159
Altgar v. Municipality of Ramat-Gan (H.C.J. 290/65, 20 P.D. (1) 29)	96
Amash v. Att'y. General (Cr. A. 485/65, 20 P.D. (1) 378)	96
Arshid v. Arshid (99/66, 58 P.M. 331)	87, 99, 101, 104
Artan v. "The Four Carpenters" (216/65, 50 P.M. 352)	96, 98, 127
Avdan v. Avdan (C.A. 151/60, 14 P.D. 1828)	188
Badash v. Badash (C.A. 174/65, 20 P.D. (1) 617)	175
Bakhar v. Bakhar (C.A. 173/69, 23 P.D. (1) 665)	152
Balaban v. Balaban (C.A. 313/59, 14 P.D. 285)	44, 158
Barea v. Kadi of the Moslem Shaaria Court of Acre (H.C.J. 187/54, 9 P.D. 1193)	154, 159
Bassan v. Rabbinical Court of Appeal (H.C.J. 214/64, 18 P.D. (4) 309)	118, 194
Bassan v. Bassan (315/65, 57 P.M. 63)	193
Baum v. Nathanson (C.C. 38/44, 1946 S.J.D.C. 41)	97
Beiter v. Beiter (C.A. 47/62, 16 P.D. 154)	152
Bloom, In re, deceased (377/56, 12 P.M. 154)	117
Boaron v. Rabbinical Court, Tel Aviv (H.C.J. 283/72, 26 P.D. (2) 727)	189
Boronovski v. Chief Rabbis of Israel (F.H. 10/69, 25 P.D. (1) 7)	150, 155, 157, 158
Borstein v. Yudelevitz (C.A. 70/49, 5 P.D. 858)	190

* The names of the parties of the Israel cases are given in transliteration from the Hebrew. This presents many difficulties since very often the Hebrew is itself a transliteration from some other language and may take on varying forms. In addition modern Hebrew lacks vowel signs. As a result, the names as they appear in this Table may be wide of the mark. The author asks for the indulgence of the persons concerned.

TABLE OF CASES

Cahana v. Cahana (C.A. 571/69, 24 P.D. (2) 549)   149, 170, 203
Chesam v. Gershel (C.A. 231/61, 15 P.D. 2087)   189
Cohen v. Cohen (C.A. 61/71, 25 P.D. (2) 327)   44, 120, 197, 207, 208
Cohen v. The Rabbinical District Court, Tel Aviv-Jaffo (H.C.J. 275/71, 330/71, 26 P.D. (1) 227)   172
Cohen-Buslik v. A.G. (C.A. 238/53, 8 P.D. 4 (English translation in 2 S.J.S.C. 239)   76, 123, 136, 137, 171, 172, 177, 185, 195
Craig v. Corbett (C.C. 41/45, (1946) S.J.D.C. 105)   91

Dana v. Dana (C.A. 8/66, 20 P.D. (3) 110)   191
Davis v. Woodall (77/66, 59 P.M. 151)   95
Derham v. Derham (C.A. 206/60, 14 P.D. 1726)   198

Estate Ahmar, *In re* (67/55, 20 P.M. 302)   205

Federman v. Governor of the Southern District (H.C.J. 69/25, 1 P.L.R. 57)   122
Feldman v. Feldman (C.A. 603/65, 20 P.D. (2) 465; F.H. 14/66, 20 P.D. (4) 693   194
Florsheim v. Rabbinical Court, Haifa (H.C.J. 181/68, 22 P.D. (2) 723)   152
Frankenthal v. Leibel (C.A. 51/30, 1 P.L.R. 639)   93
Frisch v. Registrar of Cooperative Societies (H.C.J. 91/49, 5 P.D. 287)   151
Funk-Schlesinger v. Minister of the Interior (H.C.J. 143/62, 17 P.D. 222)   86, 139, 142, 146, 157, 176, 178

Gitea v. The Chief Rabbinate (H.C.J. 359/66, 22 P.D. (1) 290)   100, 112, 113, 119, 123, 194
Goldman v. Goldman (C.A. 166/66, 20 P.D. (2) 533)   120
Gorfinkel, Chaklai v. Minister of the Interior (H.C.J. 80/63, 17 P.D. 2048)   107, 115, 160, 171, 174
Grenzburg v. Bulein (115/54, 12 P.M. 129)   89, 97, 98, 101, 102
Gutman v. Shen (C.A. 446/63, 18 P.D. (1) 371)   133

Hachamov v. Schmidt (Mo. 280/57, 12 P.D. 59)   151
Haddad v. Haddad (C.A. 63/37, 4 P.L.R. 243)   163
Haham v. Haham (C.A. 353/65, 20 P.D. (2) 199)   114, 191
Hakhari v. Hakhari (C.A. 231/66, 20 P.D. (2) 685)   120
Hanzalis v. Ecclesiastical Tribunal of the Greek Orthodox Patriarchate (H.C.J. 171/68, 23 P.D. (1) 260)   126
Hassan v. Benjamin (2542/62/8, 35 P.M. 243)   98, 101
Havra v. Havra (839/67, 73 P.M. 183)   87

Jacobs v. Kartuz (C.A. 110/53, 9 P.D. 1401)   96
Joseph v. Joseph (C.A. 63/69, 23 P.D. (1) 804)   99, 120
— (F.H. 23/69, 24 P.D. (1) 792)   114, 120, 155, 192, 206

Karam v. C.E.O. Jerusalem (H.C. 36/37, (1937) S.C.J. 302)   126

Karnovsky v. Reichman (C.A. 20/29, 1 P.L.R. 420)	92
Kedar, Cohen v. District Rabbinical Court, Tel Aviv (H.C.J. 29/71. 26 P.D. (2) 608)	155, 173, 174
Kerz v. Estate of Kerz (779/59, 21 P.M. 400)	117, 130
Khouri v. Ziadeh (C.A. 8/32, 5 R. 1673)	161
Korlandski v. Zioni (60/64, 49 P.M. 13)	98
Kotik v. Wolfson (C.A. 26/51, 5 P.D. 1341)	26, 177, 180, 181, 188
Kurz v. Kirshen (C.A. 65/67, 21 P.D. 20)	27
Langel v. Langel (C.A. 328/72, 27 P.D. (2) 470)	198
Levin v. Levin (C.A. 84/49, 5 P.D. 921)	197
Levitzki v. Levitzki (C.A. 186/60, 15 P.D. 2027)	204
Levy, N. v. Levy (C.A. 267/64, 18 P.D. (4) 119)	98
Levy, V. v. District Rabbinical Court, Tel Aviv (H.C.J. 10/59, 13 P.D. 1182)	149, 162, 163, 164
Lubin v. Municipality of Tel Aviv-Jaffo (H.C.J. 163/57, 12 P.D. 1041)	82
Marashli v. A.G. (Cr. A. 11/40, 7 Ct. L.R. 118)	92
Martsefot P.P., B.M. v. Alfasi (C.A. 269/64, 18 P.D. (4) 63)	128
Mekitan v. Mekitan (C.A. 634/61, 16 P.D. 945)	114, 191
— (C.A. 54/65, 19 P.D. (2) 651)	114, 115
Menashe v. Rabbinical Court, Jerusalem (H.C.J. 26/51, 5 P.D. 714)	167
Mendelovitz v. Porath (C.A. 160/58, 14 P.D. 666)	131
Miller v. Miller (C.A. 256/65, 19 P.D. (3) 171)	191
Mitova B.M. v. Kazam (Mo. 98/51, 6 P.D. 4)	83
Moror v. Zordick (C.A. 109/56, 11 P.D. 904)	91
Natovitz v. Natovitz (C.A. 508/70, 25 P.D. (1) 603)	156
New Zealand Insurance Co. Ltd. v. Youval (C.A. 118/51, 7 P.D. 518) (English translation 1 S.J.S.C. 332)	84, 95
Pacific Mediterranean Line, Panama v. Palestine Industries B.M. (C.A. 281/53, 9 P.D. 1779)	91
Peleg v. A.G. (C.A. 99/63, 17 P.D. 1122)	84, 130, 182, 186, 187
Peretz v. Peretz (C.A. 240/72, 26 P.D. (2) 793)	156
Perez v. Director of Estate Duty (C.A. 447/61, 16 P.D. 85)	205
Peru v. Qadi Madhhab (H.C.J. 349/65, 20 P.D. (2) 342)	163
Petach Tiqwa Municipality v. Tahan (C.A. 183/69, 23 P.D. (1) 398)	166
Plonit v. Plonit (C.A. 13/66, 20 P.D. (2) 512)	120
Pollak v. Pollak (H.C. 46/46, 13 P.L.R. 390)	195
Porter v. Sufrin (C.A. 79/52, 8 P.D. 1430)	195
Provalski v. Silber (C.A. 179/54, 11 P.D. 626)	92, 190
Rappaport v. Feldbrovski (C.A. 37/49, 4 P.D. 645)	90, 92
Rasabi v. Rasabi (C.A. 65/34, 2 P.L.R. 348)	93, 94
R.B. v. The Chief Rabbis of Israel (H.C.J. 235/68, 23 P.D. (1) 449)	86
Riesenfeld v. Jacobson (C.A. 337/62, 17 P.D. 1009)	176

TABLE OF CASES

Rinat v. Rinat (C.A. 426/65, 20 P.D. (2) 21)   198, 207
Rodnitzki v. The Rabbinical Court of Appeal (H.C.J. 51/69, 24 P.D. (1) 704)   107, 152, 160, 172, 173, 175, 186, 187, 203
Rogozinski v. State of Israel (C.A. 450/70, 26 P.D. (1) 129)   142, 157
Rosenberg v. Kremeraz (C.A. 88/57, 12 P.D. 1096)   86
Roshtash v. Roshtash (C.A. 247/64, 18 P.D. (4) 264)   94
Rufeisen v. Minister of Interior (H.C.J. 72/62, 16 P.D. 2428) (English translation S.J.S.C. Special volume, 1971, p. 1)   59, 61, 62

Segev, Reichert v. The Rabbinical Court and the Chief Rabbinate of Safed (H.C.J. 130–132/66, 21 P.D. (2) 505)   107, 112, 120, 149, 173, 174
Shalit v. Minister of Interior (H.C.J. 58/68, 23 P.D. (2) 477) (English translation S.J.S.C. Special volume, 1971, p. 35)   62, 147
Shauah v. Halabi (54/69, 73 P.M. 61)   87
Shomar v. Shomar (C.A. 139/38, 4 Ct. L.R. 91)   93
Sidis v. Rabbinical High Court, Jerusalem (H.C.J. 202/57, 12 P.D. 1528)   113, 154, 158, 206
Skindar v. Schwartz (C.A. 95/54, 9 P.D. 931)   204, 205
Skornik v. Skornik (C.A. 191/51 8 P.D. 141 (English translation 2 S.J.S.C. 327)   26, 43, 75, 179, 195, 196, 198, 201, 202
Staempfer v. A.G. (Cr.A. 174/54, 10 P.D. 5)   131
Streit v. The Chief Rabbi of Israel (H.C.J. 301/63, 18 P.D. (1) 598)   86, 106, 112, 113, 138, 149, 150, 151, 152, 157, 158, 162, 164

Tepper v. State of Israel (C.A. 373/72, 28 P.D. (2) 7)   142
The Southern Company "Marbek" B.M. v. Council of the Chief Rabbinate (H.C.J. 195/64, 18 P.D. (2) 324)   123
Trifman v. Victor (C.A. 346/63, 18 P.D. (1) 366)   133
Tzisis v. Barsel (C.A. 291/61, 15 P.D. 2087)   91, 92

Wandel-Hirshberg v. Yakobsfeld-Yakurska (C.A. 100/57, 12 P.D. 1896)   179
Wilner v. Barkat (C.A. 84/40, 7 P.L.R. 401)   126
Winter v. Beeri (S.T. 1/60, 15 P.D. 1457)   105, 115
Wolf v. Land Registrar (1181/51, 7 P.M. 327)   205

Yatom v. Yatom (799/59, 6 P.M. 473)   195
Yazdi v. Yazdi (C.A. 51/49, 4 P.D. 762)   92
Yeger v. Pelvitz (C.A. 563/65, 20 P.D. (3) 224)   175
Yosifof v. A.G. Cr. A. 112/50, 5 P.D. 481)   70, 76, 84, 178

Zaadeh v. C.E.O. Jerusalem (H.C. 24/41, 8 P.L.R. 175)   145
Zarfati v. Zarfati (1542/59, 23 P.M. 240)   195
Zemulun v. Minister of the Interior (H.C.J. 73/66, 18 P.D. (4) 645)   152
Zilcha v. Romili (C.A. 406/62, 17 P.D. 904)   84
Zukerman v. Zukerman (C.A. 72/62, 16 P.D. 1781)   198

2. Palestine and Israel Cases (according to File No. and Year)

Number	Year		Number	Year	
	a. *Palestine Cases*		839	67	87
69	25 (H.C.J.)	122	54	69	87
20	29 (C.A.)	92			
51	30 (C.A.)	93		c. *Israel Cases (Supreme Court)*	
8	32 (C.A.)	161	37	49 (C.A.)	90, 92
65	34 (C.A.)	93, 94	51	49 (C.A.)	92
36	37 (H.C.)	126	70	49 (C.A.)	190
63	37 (C.A.)	163	84	49 (C.A.)	197
85	38 (Cr.A.)	92, 94	91	49 (H.C.J.)	151
139	38 (C.A.)	93	112	50 (C.A.)	70, 76, 84, 178
11	40 (Cr.A.)	92			
84	40 (C.A.)	126	26	51 (C.A.)	26, 180, 181, 189
24	41 (H.C.)	145			
103	42 (H.C.)	126, 145	26	51 (H.C.J.)	167
11	43 (H.C.)	126	98	51 (Mo.)	83
38	44 (C.C.)	97	118	51 (C.A.)	84, 95
41	45 (C.C.)	91	191	51 (C.A.)	26, 43, 75, 179, 195, 196, 198, 201, 202
46	46 (H.C.)	195			
			79	52 (C.A.)	195
	b. *Israel Cases (District Court)*		110	53 (C.A.)	96
1181	51	205	238	53 (C.A.)	76, 123, 136, 137, 171, 177, 185, 195
115	54	89, 97, 98, 101, 102	281	53 (C.A.)	91
67	55	205	95	54 (C.A.)	204, 205
377	56	117	174	54 (Cr.A.)	131
779	59	117, 130	179	54 (C.A.)	92, 190
799	59	195	187	54 (H.C.J.)	154, 159
1542	59	195	109	56 (C.A.)	91
2542	62 (8)	98, 101	88	57 (C.A.)	86
60	64	98	100	57 (C.A.)	179
216	65	96, 98, 127	163	57 (H.C.J.)	82
315	65	193	202	57 (H.C.J.)	113, 154, 158, 206
77	66	95			
99	66	87, 99, 101, 104	280	57 (Mo.)	151
			160	58 (C.A.)	131

233

TABLE OF CASES

Number	Year		Number	Year	
447	58 (C.A.)	189	349	65 (H.C.J.)	163
10	59 (H.C.J.)	149, 162, 164	353	65 (C.A.)	114, 191
			426	65 (C.A.)	198, 207
313	59 (C.A.)	44, 158	485	65 (Cr.A.)	96
1	60 (S.T.)	105, 115	563	65 (C.A.)	175
13	60 (F.H.)	133	603	65 (C.A.)	194
141	60 (Cr.A.)	92	8	66 (C.A.)	191
151	60 (C.A.)	188	13	66 (C.A.)	120
186	60 (C.A.)	204, 205	14	66 (F.H.)	194
202	60 (C.A.)	198	73	66 (H.C.J.)	152
231	61 (C.A.)	189	130–132	66 (H.C.J.)	107, 112, 120, 149, 173
275	61 (C.A.)	189			
291	61 (C.A.)	91, 92	166	66 (C.A.)	120
447	61 (C.A.)	205	231	66 (C.A.)	120
634	61 (C.A.)	114, 191	359	66 (H.C.J.)	100, 112, 113, 119, 123, 194
47	62 (C.A.)	152			
72	62 (C.A.)	198	65	67 (C.A.)	27
72	62 (H.C.J.)	59, 61, 62	167, 220	67 (C.A.)	86
143	62 (H.C.J.)	86, 139, 142, 146, 157, 176	460	67 (C.A.)	191
			58	68 (H.C.J.)	62, 147
337	62 (C.A.)	176	171	68 (H.C.J.)	126
406	62 (C.A.)	84	181	68 (H.C.J.)	152
30	63 (H.C.J.)	113	235	68 (H.C.J.)	86
80	63 (H.C.J.)	107, 115, 160, 171, 174	10	69 (F.H.)	150, 155, 157, 158
86	63 (C.A.)	159	23	69 (F.H.)	114, 120, 155, 192, 206
99	63 (C.A.)	84, 130, 182, 186, 187	51	69 (H.C.J.)	107, 152, 160, 172, 173, 175, 186, 187, 203
111	63 (H.C.J.)	87			
301	63 (H.C.J.)	86, 106, 112, 113, 138, 149, 150, 151, 152, 157, 158, 162, 164	63	69 (C.A.)	99, 120
			173	69 (C.A.)	152
			183	69 (C.A.)	166
346	63 (C.A.)	133	571	69 (C.A.)	149, 170, 203
446	63 (C.A.)	133	450	70 (C.A.)	142, 157
194	64 (H.C.J.)	123	508	70 (C.A.)	156
214	64 (H.C.J.)	118, 194	29	71 (H.C.J.)	155, 173, 174
247	64 (C.A.)	94			
267	64 (C.A.)	98	61	71 (C.A.)	44, 120, 197, 207, 208
269	64 (C.A.)	128			
423	64 (C.A.)	185, 203	275, 330	71 (H.C.J.)	172
54	65 (C.A.)	114, 115	240	72 (C.A.)	156
174	65 (C.A.)	175	283	72 (H.C.J.)	189
256	65 (C.A.)	191	328	72 (C.A.)	198
290	65 (H.C.J.)	96	373	72 (C.A.)	142

3. English Cases

Bishop of Exeter v. Marshall, ([1868] L.R. 3 H.L. 17)	179
Bolton v. Bolton, ([1891] 65 L.T. 698)	151
Boys v. Chaplin, ([1971] A.C. 356)	196
Buerger v. N.Y. Life Assurance Co., ([1927] 96 L.J.K.B. 930)	109
Caudrey Case, ([1591] 5 Co. Rep La; 77 E.R. 1)	179
Chung Chi Cheung v. The King, ([1939] A.C. 160)	131
Cohn, *In re,* ([1945] 1 Ch. 5)	190
Guaranty Trust Co. of N.Y. v. Hannay & Co., ([1918] 2 K.B. 623)	109, 110
Lazard Bros. v. Midland Bank, ([1933] A.C. 289)	127
Mahadervan v. Mahadervan, ([1964] P. 233)	182
McHenry v. Lewis, ([1883] 47 L.T. 549)	151
Mirehouse v. Rennel, ([1833] 6 E.R. 1015)	134
Odessa, *The,* ([1915] P. 52)	131
Ottoman Bank of Nicosia v. Chakarian, ([1938] A.C. 260)	127
Teresa, *The,* ([1894] 71 L.T. 342)	151
Zemora, *The,* ([1916] 2 A.C. 77)	130

4. U.S. Cases

Erie R. Co. v. Tompkins, ([1938] 304 U.S. 64; 114 A. L. R. 1487)	110
Walton v. Arabian American Oil Company, (New York, 233 F. 2d 541 [2d Cir. 1956])	91

5. Rabbinical Courts Cases

Appeal 89/5720, 3, Law Reports of the Rabbinical Courts 369	106
Appeal 112/5725, 6, Law Reports of the Rabbinical Courts 54	188

INDEX

ADAPTATION
  in private international law, 199, 200, 202
  State law and religious law 201–208
    respective rights of wife and husband, 206–208
    rights of widow, 204, 205–206

AGUDAT ISRAEL
  121 n. 75

APPLICATION OF FOREIGN LAW
  judge's approach to foreign law, 85–86, 104
  question of law or fact, 83–84, 88, 89, 97 n. 36, 101, 129
  precedent of domestic Supreme Court, its binding force, 129, 130, 134 n. 132
  precedent of foreign court, its binding character, 109–111, 114 n. 42
  reviewing power of Supreme Court 126 n. 99
  See also PUBLIC POLICY

APPLICATION OF LAW
  81–82, 103–104, 113

APPLICATION OF RELIGIOUS LAW
  by choice of the parties, 90 n. 11a, 155
  difference between secular courts and religious courts, in, 76, 104–108, 136, 137, 138, 148, 174, 177, 187
  interpretation 83 n. 7, 93, 104, 105, 107–108, 109
  precedent of religious court, its binding character on secular courts, 109, 111, 113, 114, 115, 116, 120, 134
  precedent of secular Supreme Court, its binding character, 127–135
  on religious courts, 134
  reasons, of 180
  reviewing power of Supreme Court, 126
  secular judge's approach —
    to Jewish law 86, 96, 97, 98, 104, 128, 147, 160–161
    to other religious laws 86–87, 104
  See also PUBLIC POLICY, SUBSTANCE AND PROCEDURE

ARAB MINORITY
  problem of political identity, 46

BIGAMY
  interdiction, 155, 157
  permission by religious court, 70, 106, 150, 156–158
  previous religious marriage 27 n. 35, 96

BRITISH MANDATE OVER PALESTINE
  legal system, 53

CANON LAW
  aequitas canonica, 108
  aims of, 22–23
  and essence of Church, 21–22
  application, in Italy —
    proof of, 101 n. 53
    public policy, 147 n. 44, 148 n. 46
  enforcement, 31
  importance of faith in understanding, 107–108
  interpretation, 107–108, 124 n. 88

legal nature, 19, 21, 22, 31
marriage, 126, 147 n. 44
potestas fori externi, interni, 23 n. 21
precedent, 124 n. 88
proof of —
  in Italy, 101 n. 53
  in matters of personal status, *see* PROOF OF RELIGIOUS LAW
  in other matters, 96
public policy, 169
reception by state law 49 n. 2, 70–71, 125
relationship to state law, 19, 45, 49 n. 2, 50, 70–71, 205 n. 31
renvoi to secular law, 205 n. 31
salus animarum, 22, 169
sanction, 31 n. 47
sentire cum ecclesia, 107–108

CATHOLIC CHURCH
20, 21, 23, 31–32, 70, 72 n. 65, 125

CATHOLIC COMMUNITY
32

CATHOLIC COURTS
nature and function, 108 n. 22, 116 n. 49
Sacra Romana Rota, 125 n. 89
Signatura Apostolica, 125 n. 89
Vatican courts, recognition of decisions, 125–126

CATHOLIC SOCIETY
31

CHIEF RABBINATE
general, 30, 93
application of state law, 124
Chief Rabbinical Council, 118, 119, 121–124
Chief Rabbis, 118 n. 61, 112 n. 79, 157–158
status, 119
  in Jewish law, 117–119, 121
  in the state, 121–124, 157
supreme *halakhic* authority, 121–124

CHRISTIAN RELIGIOUS COURTS
163
composition, 60, 125
jurisdiction, 60

CIVIL SECULAR COURTS
application of religious law. See APPLICATION OF RELIGIOUS LAW
coexistence with Jewish religious courts as religious problem, 94, 120
conflict of laws, rules, 138
jurisdiction
  personal status, *See* PERSONAL STATUS
  holy places, 60 n. 11
supervision over religious courts, *see* HIGH COURT OF JUSTICE

CIVIL MARRIAGE
106, 150, 157
between Jews, celebrated abroad, 201–202
cohen and divorcee, 202
Jewish law, 106, 150
mixed marriage celebrated abroad, 176

COLLISION OF DUTIES
See CONFLICT OF NORMS

COLONIAL LAW
143 n. 27, 144, 145, 146

CONFLICT OF NORMS
39, 42, 44–46

CONFLICT OF LAWS
See PRIVATE INTERNATIONAL LAW

CUSTOM
131

DINA DE-MALKHUTA DINA
45

DIVORCE
against wife's will, 155, 165–166
see also PERSONAL STATUS

DYNAMIC REFERENCE
see RECEPTION by reference, static and dynamic

EDUCATION
religious education, 60 n. 11

EVIDENCE
181
see also SUBSTANCE AND PROCEDURE

EXCESS OF JURISDICTION
concept of, 112, 113

FACT REFERENCE
see RECEPTION by reference

INDEX

FREEDOM OF RELIGION
see STATE AND RELIGION

HALAKHA
see JEWISH LAW

HIGH COURT OF JUSTICE
functions, 113, 148, 162

HIGH COURT OF JUSTICE
supervision over religious courts, 13, 148, 151, 162, 163, 164
  error in religious law, 112
  excess of jurisdiction, 112, 154, 166
  non-application of state law, 154–155, 162
  violation of principles of natural justice, 112, 161, 162–163, 165–168

HUSBAND AND WIFE
See MATRIMONIAL PROPERTY, PERSONAL STATUS

HOLY PLACES
definition, 60 n. 11
protection, 60 n. 11

INTERNATIONAL LAW
20 n. 7, 36, 42, 61–62 n. 19, 64, 65, 110 n. 27, 130, 131

INTERPERSONAL LAW
maintenance, 68
see also INTERRELIGIOUS LAW

INTERPRETATION
61 n. 19, 103–104, 130

INTERRELIGIOUS LAW
137 n.8, 144 n. 31, 145 n. 34
relation to private international law, 144 n. 31
renvoi, 205 n. 31

ISRAEL LAW
legislation, 53
private international law, 138, 179
reception of English law, 53, 56, 57, 69, 95 n. 31
  in case of *lacuna* 91, 111, 131–132, 179
reception of Jewish law, 54–55, 59, 60, 61, 70, 78, 82 n. 7
  by reference 59, 60, 61, 68, 70, 73
  problems 54
  status of Jewish law 74–78, 84

relation to Jewish Law, 26–28, 54, 55

IURA NOVIT CURIA
91 n. 14, 93, 99 n. 44, 100 n. 47
See also JUDICIAL NOTICE, PROOF OF FOREIGN LAW, PROOF OF RELIGIOUS LAW

JEW
conversion to Christianity, 62 n. 20
conversion to Judaism, 73 n. 68, 100 n. 46
doubtful, 193
Falasha community, 119, 124
interpretation of term in secular legislation, 59, 61, 70, 73
Law of Return, 61–62, 73
Rabbinical Courts jurisdiction, 59–60, 73
statutory definition, 62 n. 21a

JEWISH LAW
aims of, 24, 169
actual validity, effectiveness, 29–31
appeal in, 118 n. 61a
application by secular courts, 96–97, 104–106, 108, see also APPLICATION OF RELIGIOUS LAW
child's custody, 105–106
civil marriage, 106, 150
codification of, 54, 105
conception of God in legal categories, 25
conflict of laws, rules, 137 nn. 7, 8
development of, 93 n. 24, 94, 96
divorce —
  in case of doubtful marriage, 193, 194
enforcement by the State, 30–31
error in, 121 n. 75
excommunication, 188
foreign law, recognition by, 137 nn. 7, 8
importance of faith in understanding, 108
legal nature, 24–25
  in Israel Law, 25–28
maintenance, 192, 202–203, 206–208
proof, 191–195
marriage —

238

between *cohen* and divorcee, 107 n. 16, 148 n. 46, 149, n. 49, 160–161, 170, 171, 172, 173, 174, 202
doubtful, 193–195
halitza, 172 n. 144, 176
impedimentum dirimens, 176
impedimentum impediens, 170, 171
Ketubah, 204
presumption of, 195
matrimonial property rights, 206–208
mixed marriage, 142, 148 n. 46, 176
national law of the Jews, 26–28, 54, 94, 96, 147
oath, 127–128, 188
paternity, 189
principles of natural justice, 163 nn. 104, 105
procedure —
competence of witnesses, 185, 186
modes of proof, 188
presumptions, 190, 191
proof of, *see* PROOF OF RELIGIOUS LAW
public policy, 169, 173
Rabbinical authority, 117–118, 121
reception by Israel law, 54–55
problems, 54, 61, 105
relationship to secular law of Israel, 45
relationship to state law, 45
res iudicata, 117
stare decisis, precedent, 116, 117–118, 120
universal (extraterritorial) character, 137
validity in the Israel legal system, 43, 44
widow, rights of, 204, 205
witnesses, 185–187
ad substantiam, 187

JUDAISM
organization of religious society, 29–31

JUDICIAL NOTICE
93, 94, 95 n. 31, 96, 97, 98, 99, 100, 101, 102, 127
and *stare decisis*, 129
see also PROOF OF FOREIGN LAW, PROOF OF RELIGIOUS LAW

JUDICIAL PROCESS
judge's ideology, 14, 105, 106, 107–108, 136, 139
nature of, 103–104

LACUNA
91

LAW OF RETURN
see JEW

LAW REFERENCE
see RECEPTION by reference

LEGAL CONCEPTS
13, 52

LEGAL NORM
conflict of norms, 39
structure, 57–58, 82 n. 6
fact situation, 58, 82 n. 6
legal result, 58, 82 n. 6
validity, 34, 38
see also APPLICATION OF LAW

LEGAL SYSTEM
basic norm, 34, 35, 36, 38, 43
dynamic character, 33
exclusiveness, 35–36, 37, 40, 42, 43, 44, 65
internal consistency, 33
relationships between different systems, 36–42, 43, 45–46, 63–67, 68, *see also* RECEPTION
relativity, 43, 44, 65, 165
rules of recognition, 35
unity, 33, 35, 37, 38, 39, 40, 42, 43, 44
validity, 33, 34, 35, 36, 38, 40, 41 n. 46

MARRIAGE
celebrated abroad according to Jewish Law, 26
concubinage, 175–176
doubtful marriage, 193–195
jurisdiction, 59
mixed marriage, 142, 176
private marriage in case of religious prohibition, 107 n. 16, 155 n. 71, 160–161, 170–175
private marriage, other cases, 173

promise of marriage, 175
See also CIVIL MARRIAGE
MATRIMONIAL PROPERTY RIGHTS
44, 158–159, 206–208
adaptation between state law and religious law, see ADAPTATION
MEJELLE
55
MILLET SYSTEM
13, 30, 122, 125
MONISM
38–39, 40
MORALITY
31, 36, 44
MOSLEM LAW
application in Israel, 55, 59
codification of, 55
legal nature, 24
reception of, by Ottoman law, 55

NATURAL CHILD
189
NATURAL JUSTICE
observance by religious courts, 112, 145, 161–168
principles, 161
NON LIQUET
Jewish law, 192, 193
NORMATIVE SCHOOL (Kelsen)
20, 21, 31 n. 47, 34, 35, 37, 38, 39, 40, 41, 58

OATH
127–128
OTTOMAN EMPIRE
13, 30, 53, 55, 122
legal system, 53, 55
Mejelle, 55
Jewish community, 30, 122

PATERNITY see PERSONAL STATUS
PERSONAL LAW
26, 27, 63, 68, 88, 90, 177, 178, 197
PERSONAL STATUS
child's custody—
Jewish law, 105–106
in State law, 159
conflict of laws, 138

definition, 63 n. 22
determination of, public interest, 92
jurisdiction, 59, 60, 155
maintenance, 63, 68, 156, 170 n. 130, 191, 192–195, 196, 197, 201, 202, 203, 206–208
quantum of, 195–198
marriage and divorce, 59, 68, 106, 107
see also CIVIL MARRIAGE
national law or law of domicile applicable to foreigners, 88 n. 3
paternity, 188–189
religious law applicable to questions of, 62, 63 n. 22, 68, 90, 91, 95, 152–153, 177, 180
replacement of religious law by state law, 152–153
succession, 204, 205
POLYGAMY see BIGAMY
POSITIVISM
19, 20, 21, 26, 28
PRECEDENT (Stare Decisis)
American law, 110 n. 27
and judicial notice, 129
binding force of Supreme Court decision on religious courts, 134, 155 n. 70
English Common law, 69 n. 47, 109 n. 26
Israel law, 127, 128, 131–135
Jewish Law, 116–117, 120
nature, 114
religious law decision of Supreme Court, binding force, 127–135
see also APPLICATION OF FOREIGN LAW, APPLICATION OF RELIGIOUS LAW
PRIEST, MEMBER OF RELIGIOUS ORDER
administration of oath to, 59, 69
status 56, 69
PRIVATE INTERNATIONAL LAW
as distinguished from reception of religious law, 50–51, 70, 89–90, 105, 141, 143, 144, 178, 201
foreign judgments enforcement, 67, 126, 139 n. 15, 141, 167

local law theory, 67 n. 41
nature of rules, 63-64, 65-67
relationship between state law and foreign law, 36, 41, 42, 50, 63-64, 65-67
see also ADAPTATION, APPLICATION OF FOREIGN LAW, PERSONAL STATUS, PROOF OF FOREIGN LAW, RELIGIOUS COURTS

PROOF OF FOREIGN LAW
comparative law, 89 n. 10, 90 n. 12, 91 n. 14, 91 n. 15, 92 n. 18, 100 n. 47, 100 n. 49
foreign religious law, 95, 96
in English law, 89, 91, 100 n. 48, 101 n. 50
in matters of personal status, 89, 92 n. 18, 19, 94 n. 28, 96
lack of evidence —
application of *lex fori* 90 nn. 12, 13, 91, 92 n. 18
possible solutions, 90 n. 13, 91 nn. 14, 15, 92 n. 18
presumption of identity of laws, 91, 92 n. 18

PROOF OF RELIGIOUS LAW
expert evidence, 92, 97-102, 132
judicial notice, 93, 94, 95, 96, 97, 98, 99, 100, 101, 102, 127, 128
lack of evidence —
possible solutions, 90 n. 13
question of fact, prior to 1945, 93, 127
question of law, after 1945, 93, 94, 97

PUBLIC POLICY
and ideological conflict on state and religion, 147, 161, 176
in application of colonial law, 144-146
in application of foreign law, 139, 140
negative function, 140, 141, 142, 143, 146, 148
positive function (direct application of State law), 140, 141
in application of foreign religious law, 140 n. 17
in application of religious law —

indirect influence, 150-152, 156-161
negative function (rejection of religious law), 142, 143, 146, 147-149, 150-152
positive function (direct application of State law), 153-154, 157
in enforcement of foreign judgments, 141
nature, 169, 175, 176
of foreign law, 168, 170 n. 131
of religious law, 168-177
in secular courts, 169-170, 171, 173, 174, 175, 176
nature, 169

RABBINICAL COURTS
attitude towards religiously prohibited marriages, 170, 171, 172
error in Jewish law, 112, 121
jurisdiction, 46 n. 67, 59-60, 88 n. 2, 152 n. 59, *see also* RELIGIOUS COURTS
nature and functions, 115-116
in the State, 118-119
precedent, binding character in Jewish Law, 116-118, 120
precedent of, binding character on secular courts, 113-114, 115, 116, 120
Rabbinical Court of Appeal, 117 n. 54, 118, 120, 121 n. 76, 122-123
problem under Jewish law, 118 n. 61a
Rabbinical district court, 118, 119
religious public policy, 172
status in the state, 111, 112, 118, 119

RABBIS
118, 121, *see also* CHIEF RABBINATE
RECEPTION
by reference, 56-70
conditional reference, 67-68
creative reference, 66-67, 72, 78
fact reference, 58, 59-62, 63, 71, 72, 73, 74, 81, 95, 96
formal reference, 60, 64, 65, 71-72, 75, 78
law reference, 58, 62, 63-67, 71, 72, 73, 74, 81, 95, 96, 194

241

static and dynamic references, 68–69, 115, 131 n. 120, 132 n. 121, 142
univalent and polyvalent references, 45, 88, 142
concepts of, 54 n. 9, 60–61
direct reception, 52, 53–55, 56, 82 n. 7
forms of, 52
general, 49–50
religious law, of, 54–55
See also STATE LAW AND RELIGIOUS LAW

RELIGIOUS COMMUNITIES
autonomy, 13, 143, 152
Jewish, 29
  organization, 29–31
  member of, 59, 73
jurisdiction, 13, 14
member of, 59, 73 n. 69

RELIGIOUS COURTS
application of State law, 113 n. 36, 153
  problems, 149, 153–154, 161 n. 96
  sanction of non-, 153–154, 164–168
attitude of religious judges regarding their status in the state, 46, 94, 111–112, 153
foreign law, non application, 137–138
judgment contrary to natural justice, 163–168
judgments, recognition by state law, 164–168
jurisdiction, 14, 59, 60, 75, 88 n. 2, 108
  restrictive interpretation by secular courts, 152
nature and functions, 115
outside Israel, recognition of decisions, 125–126
principles of natural justice, 112, 145, 161–168
private international law rules, non application of, 136, 138, 152
procedure, 162, 182
status in the state, 46, 75, 111, 118, 119, 148, 153
supervision, of, see HIGH COURT OF JUSTICE

revision of decisions by secular courts, see HIGH COURT OF JUSTICE
see also RABBINICAL COURTS, CATHOLIC COURTS, CHRISTIAN COURTS, SHARIA COURTS, APPLICATION OF RELIGIOUS LAW

RELIGIOUS INSTITUTIONS
autonomy in the state, 74, 111, 115, 121, 122, 123, 124
duty to apply state law, 153–154, 157–158

RELIGIOUS LAW
actual validity, effectiveness, 28–29
conflict of laws, rules, 137
enforcement by the State, 21 n. 9, 30, 184–185
foreign law, recognition, 137, 138
legal nature, 19–23, 28, 31
public policy, see PUBLIC POLICY
sanction, 21 n. 9, 23, 31 n. 47
transcendent purpose, 22, 23–24, 105, 169
universal character, 137, 138
validity in the law of the state
see STATE LAW AND RELIGIOUS LAW

RELIGIOUS LEGISLATION
115, 116, 123, 125

RELIGIOUS SOCIETY
general, 29
Jewish, 29–31

RENVOI
religious law to state law, 205 n. 31

RES IUDICATA
in Jewish law, 117
religious courts decision, 113, 114, 152

SABBATH
desecration of, in Holy Places, 60 n. 11

SACRED OBJECTS
injury to, under criminal law 60 n. 11

SANCTION
21 n. 9, 23, 31 n. 47

SANHEDRIN
115 n. 48, 116, 117

SCIENCE OF LAW
37, 39, 42

SECULAR COURTS *see* CIVIL COURTS
STARE DECISIS see PRECEDENT
STATE AND CHURCH
   19, 20, 70–71, 72
   see also STATE AND RELIGION
STATE AND RELIGION
   autonomy of religious institutions, legislative policy, 71–78
   enforcement of religious law by the state, 30, 54–55, *see also* STATE AND CHURCH
   ideological conflict, 13–14, 146, 147, 176
   freedom of religion, 13, 54, 60 n. 11, 142 n. 28, 160–161, 186–187
   pork, 82 n. 7
   religious education, 60 n. 11
   role of Supreme Court, 161
   "Who is a Jew," see *Jew*
   see also CANON LAW, CIVIL COURTS, CIVIL MARRIAGE, ISRAEL LAW, JEWISH LAW, MARRIAGE, STATE LAW AND RELIGIOUS LAW
STATE LAW
   relation to other normative orders, 28, 36, 43
   see also LEGAL SYSTEM
STATE LAW AND RELIGIOUS LAW
   abolition of religious norm by the State, 44
   collision of duties, 44–46
   enforcement of religious law by the State, 30

   reception of religious law by state law, 49, 50, 74–78, 124
      direct reception, 53–55, 82 n. 7
      by reference, 59, 60, 61, 62–63, 68, 69, 70–78
   relationships, 36, 43–46, 49–50, 124 n. 87
   replacement of religious law by state law, 152–153
   status of religious law, 72–78, 84–85, 94, 139, *See also* ADAPTATION
SUBSTANCE AND PROCEDURE
   distinction, 182, 183, 184, 190, 195, 196
   in private international law, 177, 179, 182, 183, 190, 195
   religious law in secular courts, 105, 137, 161–162, 177–182, 183, 184, 185–198, 203
      burden of proof, 192, 193, 194, 195
      excommunication, 188
      modes of proof, 185, 186, 188, 189, 190
      non liquet, 192–193
      presumptions, 184, 189, 190, 191, 192–195
      witnesses (competency), 185, 186, 187, 188

TALMUDIC LAW *see* JEWISH LAW

"WHO IS A JEW?" *see* JEW